Holy Spirit, Hover Over Me

The remarkable true story of the Holy Spirit miracles

Joshua Doshick Joe

Heavenly Publications
Audubon, PA. USA

Holy Spirit, Hover Over Me

Published by Heavenly Publications, Inc. on May 5, 2005

Scripture taken from the Holy Bible, the New King James Version ®. Copyright © 1982 by Thomas Nelson, Inc.

Used by permission. All rights reserved.

ISBN 0-9740677-1-7

Distributed by:

Heavenly Publications, Inc.

P. O. Box 7183

Audubon, PA 19407 U. S. A.

English: www.jesushp.com/english.html

Korean: www.jesushp.com

Email: info@jesushp.com, orders@jesushp.com

Tel: 610-650-4053

Fax: 610-650-4055

Holy Spirit,
Hover Over Me

Author: Joshua Doshick Joe, Pastor

The author, Rev. Joshua Doshick Joe, interpreted Dr. Belk's preaching from English into Korean while filled with the Holy Spirit. He is raising both hands to tens of thousands of church members at the Ju An Presbyterian Church, one of the ten largest churches in the world. The newly built two-story sanctuary was fully packed. At the same time, in the old sanctuary, they received this preaching through specially designed TV screens.

Rev. Joshua Doshick Joe interpreted Dr. Henderson Belk's preaching from English into Korean while filled with the Holy Spirit. He is raising one of his hands to tens of thousands of church members at the Ju An Presbyterian Church, one of the ten largest churches in the world. Dr. Belk is the founder and President of Henderson Christian University. The Belk family also owns Belk Department Stores, with about 400 stores in the southern USA. Through father and son, Dr. Belk's family built about 400 churches and offered them to the Almighty Heavenly Father. Dr. Belk is a very good Christian, filled in Holy Spirit, and turns all the glory to God.

The Senior Pastor of the Ju An Presbyterian Church, Rev. Na Gyum Il, exchanges greetings with the author. Rev. Na is holding the book, Holy Spirit, Hover Over Me, and behind him stands Dr. Paul Kim, the chairman of Henderson Christian University. In 1986 Rev. Na was hospitalized because of acute liver cancer and for some time was in a coma. The doctors at the hospital said, "He will die within thirty minutes. Please prepare his funeral service." However the Holy Spirit completely cured his acute liver cancer. Rev. Na is a witness who proves the Holy Spirit's miracles, testifying that the Holy Spirit can raise a dead person to life. The Holy Spirit said, "It was the Holy Spirit who prepared Rev. Na to introduce the book, Holy Spirit, Hover Over Me, to all the members of the Ju An Presbyterian Church, the largest Presbyterian church in the world."

The author, Rev. Joe, interpreted Dr. Belk's English preaching into Korean in a Holy Spirit-filled surrounding at Pyung Kang Je Il Church. This is one of the ten largest churches in the world. In response to the preaching, the sanctuary trembles at the sound of the congregation's amen. The main sanctuary cannot accommodate all the church members. Therefore those who could not enter the main church were watching the preaching on specially designed TV screens at over 40 different small churches built around the main sanctuary.

Recommendation Letter by Dr. Henderson Belk

February 17, 2005

Rev. Joshua Doshick Joe's book, *Holy Spirit, Hover Over* is very important to the whole Christian world. He is specially prepared for this task as a native Korean and the leader in America concerning what God is doing in our day.

Holy Spirit, Hover Over Me tells the story of God's calling Korea as His special, holy people to take His Message of love to Asia especially. It is no accident that six of the ten largest churches in the world today are located in South Korea. South Korea is the only country in Asia with a prominent Christian presence. They believe in God's Word and rise early in the morning seeking God's Will for themselves and the whole earth.

Rev. Joshua Doshick Joe correctly gives the Holy Spirit the glory for calling and blessing the Christians in Korea as "a chosen people, a royal priesthood, a holy nation, a people belonging to God" to declare the praises of God in the present day (1 Peter 2:9, NIV).

Dr. Henderson Belk
The founder and President of the Henderson Christian University.

The Founder & President of the World Evangelical Mission

Recommendation Letter by Rev. & Dr. Gyum Il Na

March 26, 2005

I congratulate Rev. Joshua Doshick Joe on the publication of *Holy Spirit, Hover Over Me* in English.

When I read *Holy Spirit, Hover Over Me* in Korean, I was so deeply moved by the Holy Spirit that I recommended that all the members of our congregation read it.

When you read this book, the Holy Spirit will minister powerfully through you.

It is a great pleasure for me to recommend that all Christians in the world read this book, which will set the Holy Spirit's fire in your heart.

Please use this book to work in the Holy Spirit's power, like the Apostles of Jesus in the first century. Then lead all the world's unbelievers, Christians who stopped going to church and idolaters deceived by Satan, to accept Jesus as their Savior Lord and become real Christians, for eternal life in heaven.

While praying to the Almighty Heavenly Father, please read this book and the Holy Spirit will solve your problems and heal your infirmities.

In the name of Jesus, I pray to Almighty God to use *Holy Spirit, Hover Over Me* as a major spiritual weapon to spread Jesus' gospel to the ends of the earth.

Rev. & Dr. Gyum Il Na
Senior Pastor of Ju An Presbyterian Church
Standing President of The World Evangelization Ass.
President of The Korean Christianity Revival Missions Association
Chairman of The Pastoral Research of Asia United Theological University

Recommendation Letter by Dr. & Rev. Su Hack Kim

March 7, 2005

I am very pleased to inform you that after praying and careful reading of this book for 40 days, the undersigned wrote this recommendation letter.

While reading the book, *Holy Spirit, Hover Over Me,* I was deeply moved by the Holy Spirit and I saw the following:

1. Miracles of God's Word were poured on a Christian who prays always.

2. The author has experienced numerous miracles of the Holy Spirit.

3. The life with faith working in action, developed from individual belief.

4. The enthusiasm to evangelize individuals, families, societies, nations and the world in the Holy Spirit's power.

5. I cannot deny that the author has experienced the Holy Spirit's innumerable, supernatural miracles through the years.

I pray to Almighty God, while recommending the book, *Holy Spirit, Hover Over Me*, together with the cross of Jesus' gospel to conquer all the people in the world.

Dr. & Rev. Su Hack Kim
Senior Pastor of Sae Byuk Church
Former Chairman of the General Assembly of Hapdong
Korean Presbyterian Church (GAHKPC)

Recommendation Letter by Dr. & Rev. Tae Hae Ye

March 8, 2005

I congratulate Rev. Joshua Doshick Joe on his book, *Holy Spirit, Hover Over Me*, to be published in English. I am very pleased to recommend *Holy Spirit, Hover Over Me* to be used as a weapon to chase away Satan and his soldiers, evil spirits and demons from innumerable Christians in the world.

The author of this book was specially trained by the Holy Spirit in discerning the spirits. He spreads Jesus' gospel all over the world while healing the sick with the Holy Spirit's power and delivering bread given by the Holy Spirit to poor homeless people.

I pray to the Most High and recommend that all Christians read this book because there is a strong enthusiasm in *Holy Spirit, Hover Over Me*, written in the Holy Spirit's power, to spread Jesus' gospel all over the world.

Dr. & Rev. Tae Hae Ye
Senior Pastor of Emmaus Mission Church
Main Speaker of The World Shepherd Mission
Evangelist delivering the gospel all over the world in the Holy Spirit's powerful anointing

Recommendation Letter by Dr. & Rev. Paul Kim
March 10, 2005

I express my greatest thanks and glory to the Trinity God who created the universe.

In the history of the Christian world, there are innumerable theologians claiming reforms in the Christian religion. I really congratulate the Missionary Joshua Doshick Joe on the publishing of his testimony, *Holy Spirit, Hover Over Me.*

Through this book, written according to the Holy Spirit's miracles which the author experienced, we wish that reformed theology which suffers from serious sickness, numerous churches and innumerable Christians in the world soaked in liberal thoughts, will be revived in the power of the Holy Spirit.

We recommend this book to be used as one of the main weapons in spreading Jesus' gospel to the ends of the earth.

Under the name of Jesus, we pray for the Almighty Heavenly Father to conquer the world with the Holy Spirit's miracle book, *Holy Spirit, Hover Over Me.*

Dr. & Rev. Paul Kim,
Chairman of the Henderson Christian University

Secretary of The General Assembly of Hapdong Korean Presbyterian Church (GAHKPC)
Administrator of The World Evangelical Mission

Introduction

Holy Spirit, Hover Over Me

The book *Holy Spirit, Hover Over Me* is a recorded testimony of how the Holy Spirit trained me spiritually and performed innumerable miracles through me since Jesus saved me from death on January 1, 1990. That was when I was born again in the Holy Spirit. All the incidents and miracles recorded in this book were really performed by the Holy Spirit, and this book's statements were given by the Holy Spirit in prayer.

The Holy Spirit tells us what we have to do, for all human beings to be saved eternally. God loves all of us and He wants to save all of us. I used to work and use all my effort to win money, business and honor in the world. I used to be a greedy businessman who knew only his own interests. I served three times as President of the Federation of Korean associations in the USA, representing all 2.5 million Korean-Americans in the

USA. I also served as chairman of the World Conference of Koreans Living Overseas, representing all seven million Koreans living overseas.

The Holy Spirit spiritually trained and changed me completely with His power. As a result of the Holy Spirit's spiritual training, I put aside all my works in the world and I became a man who does nothing but follow the words of the Holy Spirit.

In accordance with the Holy Spirit's leading, I have been delivering bread from the Holy Spirit to the poor churches, Christians, and pastors in the USA, and especially to shelters where poor homeless people are living. Regardless of whether it was cold, hot, raining or snowing, I gave bread, together with the Holy Spirit's message, to the shelters where poor, homeless people who are begging on the streets are living together.

The Holy Spirit spiritually trained and changed a sinful man like me who was very greedy, working only for his own interests, into a gentle missionary who preaches Jesus' gospel to all creations in the world and visits and prays for sick people. The Holy Spirit has healed innumerable sick people through my prayer. The Holy Spirit leads me to do only the works which glorify God.

During spiritual training, the Holy Spirit led me to only read the Bible from early morning to late at night for many years, and He taught me how to discern between the Holy Spirit and evil spirits on the basis of the Bible.

The Holy Spirit healed seven different chronic diseases I had, several of which I was suffering from for 30 to 40 years. God healed all of them with only prayer and the Holy Spirit's power, without any medicine. He healed three of my wife's infirmities, for which many medical doctors at modern hospitals couldn't find the cause. In addition to that, the Holy Spirit healed innumerable sick people through our prayer and the Holy Spirit's power.

Whenever demons tried to kill me, I cried, "Jesus, please help me, demons are trying to kill me." Then Jesus immediately appeared before me and saved me from the demon's attacks. Sometimes Jesus saved me from the evil spirits' attacks. Sometimes Jesus killed the evil spirits who tried to kill me, with His special light. Sometimes Jesus, embraced by the light, placed the demons which tried to kill me into transparent boiling oil tanks. Sometimes Jesus melted Satan, who appeared as a cobra bigger than an electric utility pole, with His special light.

The Holy Spirit, who always asks me to evangelize Jesus' gospel to anyone at any moment, sometimes guides unbelievers to believe in Jesus and leads them to heaven. Sometimes the Holy Spirit asks me to talk about heaven, which He showed me many times, to Christians who are dying of sickness. He wants to tell them that they will be sent to heaven, and He tells me to tell them not to worry about death. After telling them all about heaven through me, the Holy Spirit leads the dying person to heaven. Sometimes the Holy Spirit shows me the sulfur burning fire sea in hell where billions of spirits are crying and lamenting in torment, and He tells me to evangelize Jesus' gospel to all the unbelievers, as many as I can, in the world, in order to save all such people who were destined to be thrown into the fiery lake like them, because they do not believe in Jesus.

This is the way the Holy Spirit trained me how to evangelize. The Holy Spirit always says to me, "I am always with you, be bold in delivering the Holy Spirit's words to anyone in the world." The Holy Spirit showed me heaven and hell innumerable times and the holy angels always lead me and protect me from any evil.

Why should all human beings participate in the Worldwide Holy Spirit Revival Movement?

John 3: 3, 5
Jesus answered and said to him, "Most assuredly, I say to you, unless one is born again, he cannot see the kingdom of God."
Jesus answered, "Most assuredly, I say to you, unless one is born of water and the Spirit, he cannot enter the kingdom of God.

In order to be born again of water and the Spirit, man should participate in the Worldwide Holy Spirit Revival Movement. The Holy Spirit wants to set the Holy Spirit Revival Movement on fire all over the world.

Revelation: 2: 7 "He who has an ear, let him hear what the Spirit says to the churches. To him who overcomes I will give to eat from the tree of life, which is in the midst of the Paradise of God."

Here the church means human beings (refer to Corinthians 3:16-17). Only the people who obey the Holy Spirit's words will be allowed to eat from the tree of life which is in the paradise of God. That is, only the Christians who follow the Holy Spirit's words by their deeds will be sent to heaven.

Revelation: 2: 11 "He who has an ear, let him hear what the Spirit says to the churches. He who overcomes shall not be hurt by the second death."

It means anyone who doesn't follow the Holy Spirit's word will be cast into the fiery lake (refer to Revelation 20:14).

In order to hear and follow what the Holy Spirit says to us, we must participate in the Worldwide Holy Spirit Revival Movement and receive the Holy Spirit's baptism and experience the Holy Spirit's power. If you read this book, you will understand how the Holy Spirit ministers miracles. While you read this book, you will experience the Holy Spirit's ministry, you will receive the Holy Spirit's power and you will understand how much Jesus loves you individually. The Holy Spirit gives the heavenly blessing of feeding five thousand people with five loaves of bread and two fish to His children who really believe in God.

He raised the price of a $0.50 stock to over $130.00. He performed special miracles to feed over 400,000 to 450,000 people with two or three dozen donuts through us. Nothing is impossible with the Holy Spirit who cures incurable diseases. Whenever you see people who don't believe in God, you will have passion to save their spirits. You will not be able to pass them without boldly delivering Jesus' gospel. The Holy Spirit wants to give His power to all of us, in order that we will be able to courageously deliver Jesus' gospel as Jesus' apostles did boldly in the first century.

Mark 16: 15 And He said to them, "Go into all the world and preach the gospel to every creature."

Acts 1: 8 But you shall receive power when the Holy Spirit has come upon you; and you shall be witnesses to Me in Jerusalem, and in all Judea and Samaria, and to the end of the earth."

The Holy Spirit explained His words in detail on the basis of the Bible. All Christians and non-Christians should know the Bible in order to be saved and to know what kind of people are led by the Holy Spirit to heaven.

The Holy Spirit trained me spiritually for more than 12 and made me experience the Holy Spirit's powerful miracles innumerable times. The reason why the Holy Spirit wants to publish this book testifying to His miracles and experiences, is to show you how God loves each of us and wants all of us to participate in the Worldwide Holy Spirit Revival Movement and lead all of us to heaven for eternal life. All the materials recorded in this book are part of the miracles which really happened to me. We plan to continuously publish books like this, testifying to the Holy Spirit's miracles which happen through me.

I want to express my greatest thanks to all the people who helped me until this book was published.

First of all, I thank Dr. Su Hak Kim, a retired pastor who served as the first president and professor of Dae Shin Theological Seminary. He also served as acting president and chairman of Chong Shin Theological Seminary. He read the manuscript of this book, while praying for 40 days to write the recommendation for this book. He wrote the recommendation to revive the Holy Spirit's movement all over the world with the cross of Jesus Christ.

I want to express my greatest thanks to Dr. Henderson Belk, the founder and president of Henderson Christian University. His family owns the Belk Stores, with 400 stores in the southern USA. Through two generations, he and his father have established 400 churches for Almighty God. He is a good Christian, filled with the Holy Spirit's anointing, who goes to deliver Jesus' gospel to Koreans, Chinese, Japanese, and Muslims all over the world. He helped me so much in publishing this book, and introduced it to many churches and Christians all over the world.

I want to thank Dr. Gyum Il Na, the senior pastor of Ju An Presbyterian Church, the largest Presbyterian church in the world. On the first Sunday after the Korean edition of this book was published, he invited Dr. Belk to preach in English at his church, and the author of this book, Pastor Joshua Joe, filled with the Holy Spirit, delivered Dr. Belk's preaching in Korean. Dr. Na introduced this book to all his church members, saying that when you read it, the Holy Spirit will perform all kinds of supernatural miracles through you.

I want to thank Dr. Yun S. Park, the honorable pastor of Pyung Kang Jeil Church, one of the ten largest churches in the world. On the second Sunday after this book was published, he invited Dr. Belk to preach at his church, and the author of this book, filled with the Holy Spirit, delivered Dr. Belk's English preaching in Korean. Dr. Park also introduced this book to all the members of his church.

I want to express thanks to Dr. Paul Kim, Chairman of Henderson Christian University, who helped the author of this book in publishing it, and also did great job of introducing this book to big churches all over the world. He makes trips all over the world to deliver the gospel to Korea, China, Japan and Muslim countries.

I want to thank Dr. Tae Hae Ye, the senior pastor of Emmaus Mission Church, who is one of the greatest Holy Spirit-filled evangelists. He goes all over the world to deliver Jesus' gospel. He introduced this book to many churches all over the world.

I want to extend thanks to Pastor and Mrs. Jun Ho Lee, who helped a lot in publishing this book. Now they are retired from active ministry, but they are good Christians who spent their whole lives serving Almighty God.

I want to express thanks to Dr. Young Tae Lee and Dr. Soo Hee Oh who helped greatly in publishing this book. They are good Christians who serve the Methodist Church.

I want to express great thanks to my wife, who helped me with every part of publishing this book. Especially for the last 15 years, when the Holy Spirit was training me powerfully, my wife had to fully support our family. She did everything for our family without my help.

In addition to the people mentioned above, there are innumerable Christians who helped us in publishing this book and introducing it all over the world. I want to extend thanks to each of you through this letter.

There are many pastors, missionaries, elders, deacons, and Christians who have experienced the Holy Spirit's power through the author and by practicing the Holy Spirit's ministry in their churches. They helped us publish this book and introduced this book all over the world. I want to extend my greatest thanks to each of you.

To the Christians who help us serve the Holy Spirit's movement all over the world and to the kings, presidents, and world class business tycoons who will support us in spreading the Holy Spirit's movement, I want to extend my great thanks for your future support. Almighty God will reward you and your children a thousand times more than your financial support.

I want to extend my greatest thanks to the Almighty Heavenly Father, His Son Jesus Christ, and the Holy Spirit, who have spiritually trained the author of this book for the last 15 years and performed the Holy Spirit's innumerable miracles through him.

The Holy Spirit said, "This book will be translated into many languages, and it will used as a tool for spreading the Holy Spirit's movement and Jesus' gospel to all 6.3 billion people in the world, through the Internet and mass media."

People interested in evangelizing the gospel and participating in the Worldwide Holy Spirit Revival Movement and the people who are interested in distributing the book are welcome to contact the author.

I want to turn all the glory of publishing this book to the Almighty Heavenly Father who sent us His only Son to be crucified on the cross to save all the human beings in the world from their sins.

Under the name of Jesus, we pray for the Almighty Heavenly Father to give His unlimited blessings to all the readers of this book and change them into true and good sons and daughters of the Heavenly Father, who will spread Jesus' gospel to the ends of the earth.

Amen

By Rev. Joshua Doshick Joe, the Chairman of the Whole Race Gospel & Missionary Service on December 12, 2004.

CONTENTS

The following is the contents of *Holy Spirit, Hover Over Me*. These are the Holy Spirit's miracles which were performed through me.

Recommendation Letters

Introduction
Holy Spirit, Hover Over Me

Chapter 1: The Holy Spirit's word given to all human beings in the world

Chapter 5: The Holy Spirit's words and ministry about me and my family members

Chapter 6: The Holy Spirit's healing ministry about my flesh

Chapter 7: The Holy Spirit's healing of my wife

Chapter 8: The Holy Spirit's healing of others through my prayers

Chapter 9: God's love and blessing

Chapter 10: The Holy Spirit's words and training

about angels

Chapter 11: The Holy Spirit's words given to people who obstruct the Worldwide Holy Spirit Revival Movement

Chapter 12: The punishment given to Christians who disobey God's word

CHAPTER 1

The Holy Spirit's word given to all human beings ings in the world

1. The Holy Spirit's word given to all human beings in the world

I love all the human beings in this world, more than the universe. In order to save you all from sin, death and hell and to lead you all to heaven for your eternal life, Jesus Christ came to this world and was crucified for everyone.

All human beings were saved from sin by His valuable blood (refer Matthew 27:1-66).

It was the Jewish religious leaders who crucified Jesus on the cross, but this is nothing but a formality. Actually Jesus was crucified to save everyone from sin. He is the One, single Son of the heavenly Father who created the universe and all the creatures in the universe. If human beings had not had any sins, no man in the world could kill Him, nor could any creature in the universe touch Him.

Jesus fully fed five thousand adult men with five loaves of bread and two fish, not including women, children, and seniors who also ate fully. Twelve full baskets were left over (Matthew 14: 14-21).

He walked on water (Matthew 14: 22-34).

When He ordered the storms to be quiet, they stopped immediately (Matthew 8: 23-27).

When Jesus commanded a rotten, smelling, and spoiled corpse to rise (which had been dead for four days) the same corpse got up per His calling (John 11: 38-44).

Jesus cured lepers completely clean (Luke 5: 12-16), and cured a blind person so he could see (Matthew 9: 27-31).

Jesus controls everything in the world per His own mind.

Do you think that He was crucified because He lacked power and strength? It was because of the heavenly Father's love that Jesus should be crucified to save you from sin.

Mark 14: 36, Jesus said, "Abba, Father, all things are possible for You. Take this cup away from Me; nevertheless, not what I will, but what You will."

That is why Jesus did not complain of His being crucified on the cross. He was crucified to save you from sin, death and hell (refer Mark 15: 15-47).

There were many angel warriors around Jesus, and they could have completely destroyed not only the Jewish leaders but also the Roman soldiers, to save Jesus from the cross.

Matthew 26: 53-54 Jesus says, "Or do you think that I cannot now pray to My Father, and He will provide Me with more than twelve legions of angels? How then could the Scriptures be ful-

filled, that it must happen thus?"

**Refer to 2 Kings 6: 15-17: And when the servant of the man of
God arose early and went out, there was an army, surrounding
the city with horses and chariots. And his servant said to him,
"Alas, my master! What shall we do?"**
**So he answered, "Do not fear, for those who are with us are
more than those who are with them." And Elisha prayed, and said,
"Lord, I pray, open his eyes that he may see." Then the Lord
opened the eyes of the young man, and he saw. And behold, the
mountain was full of horses and chariots of fire all around Elisha.**

But in order to absolve you all from sin at once, Jesus, without any sin, became the scapegoat who was crucified on the
cross. You should always think of this universal truth, and you
must always be thankful to Jesus Christ for having saved you
from sin.

In addition to that, the Holy Spirit who came to earth after
Jesus went up to heaven is doing the same ministry as Jesus, all
over the world at this moment. That is, He gives life to dead
corpses and raises the dead, cures lepers clean, cures the blind
to see, heals patients with cancer, and He has been healing innumerable incurable diseases throughout the world since two
thousand years ago when Jesus went up to heaven.

(Refer to Matthew, Mark, Luke, John and Acts)

**Acts 5: 14-16 And believers were increasingly added to the
Lord, multitudes of both men and women, so that they brought
the sick out into the streets and laid them on beds and couches,**

that at least the shadow of Peter passing by might fall on some of them. Also a multitude gathered from the surrounding cities to Jerusalem, bringing sick people and those who were tormented by unclean spirits, and they were all healed.

However there are too many people in the world who do not understand this truth. Many believe in superstitious beliefs from their ancestors without knowing the truth. And many worship idols without any power by the fraud of Satan or demons which will finally drive them to the fearful fiery sea of hell.

There are too many sons and daughters who do not understand that they are being deceived by Satan and demons because of the circumstances of the world.

Exodus 20: 3-6 "You shall have no other gods before Me. "You shall not make for yourself a carved image--any likeness of anything that is in heaven above, or that is in the earth beneath, or that is in the water under the earth; you shall not bow down to them nor serve them. For I, the LORD your God, am a jealous God, visiting the iniquity of the fathers upon the children to the third and fourth generations of those who hate Me, but showing mercy to thousands, to those who love Me and keep My commandments."

I am telling you the truth. No one comes to the heavenly Father except through Jesus Christ.

John 14: 6 Jesus said to him, "I am the way, the truth, and the life. No one comes to the Father except through Me."

And no one can come to heaven without the Holy Spirit's guidance.

Revelation 2: 7 says, "He who has an ear, let him hear what the Spirit says to the churches. To him who overcomes I will give to eat from the tree of life, which is in the midst of the Paradise of God."

MY BELOVED SONS AND DAUGHTERS!

I want to save all of you who are wandering in the darkness without knowing the truth, and lead you to everlasting life. I entreat you with tears in My eyes to come to the truth, and the way leading you to heaven. This is the truth and the way. Believe Jesus Christ and follow Him. This is the only truthful way along which you can follow.

Of all the religions of the world, of all the spirits claiming to be gods, no spirits which you believe in now can lead you to the truth and the way to heaven. They are only deceiving and luring you.

Only the triune God, Almighty heavenly Father, Jesus Christ and the Holy Spirit can lead your spirit to eternal life in heaven.

MY SONS AND DAUGHTERS!

Regardless of what religions you have been believing, I want to forgive all your sins with Jesus' love, and lead you to the true way to heaven where the heavenly Father, Jesus Christ, and the Holy Spirit, that is, the triune God, are enjoying their lives permanently. Do not doubt this even a little bit. Follow the way. Whatever sins you have committed in your past, if you confess them and repent for your sins before God, I will absolve you from your sins which are red like blood, and change you to white like snow.

Isaiah 1: 18-20 says: "Come now, and let us reason together," Says the Lord, "Though your sins are like scarlet, They shall be as white as snow; Though they are red like crimson, They shall be as wool. If you are willing and obedient, You shall eat the good of the land; But if you refuse and rebel, You shall be devoured by the sword"; For the mouth of the Lord has spoken.

Do not be deceived by Satan and demons any more. Follow the words of truth. This is the only way which leads you and your family members to everlasting life in heaven. (Refer to John 14:6)

I want all 6.3 billion people in the world to receive God's important message, to understand their wrongdoings of the past and follow the truth and way leading to heaven.

1 Timothy 2: 3-4 For this is good and acceptable in the sight of God our Savior, who desires all men to be saved and to come to the knowledge of the truth.

I do not want even one person to fail on the way to heaven. Satan and demons are always making all kinds of plots and frauds to lure you to the ever-burning fire sea of hell.

Revelation 21: 8 But the cowardly, unbelieving, abominable, murderers, sexually immoral, sorcerers, idolaters, and all liars shall have their part in the lake which burns with fire and brimstone, which is the second death.

MY BELOVED SONS AND DAUGHTERS!

Never be deceived by Satan's lie and demons' fraud. Right at this moment, Holy Spirit restoration movements are rising all over the world.

A great many of My servants, fully inspired by the Holy Spirit, who have the Holy Spirit's experiences, are curing all kinds of incurable diseases under the name of Jesus Christ, Almighty Heavenly Father's words, and the Holy Spirit's power and grace. And they are doing impossible works with the Holy Spirit's help.

All the miracles which happened two thousand years ago, when Jesus was living in the world, are happening right now. Do not doubt this even a little bit. Visit Holy Spirit-inspired congregations and watch with your own eyes and experience them yourself. And receive the Holy Spirit's baptism and follow the truth and way to secure your eternal life.

Acts 3: 1-10 Now Peter and John went up together to the temple at the hour of prayer, the ninth hour. And a certain man lame from his mother's womb was carried, whom they laid daily at the gate of the temple which is called Beautiful, to ask alms from those who entered the temple; who, seeing Peter and John about to go into the temple, asked for alms.

And fixing his eyes on him, with John, Peter said, "Look at us." So he gave them his attention, expecting to receive something from them. Then Peter said, "Silver and gold I do not have, but what I do have I give you: In the name of Jesus Christ of Nazareth, rise up and walk."

And he took him by the right hand and lifted him up, and immediately his feet and ankle bones received strength. So he, leaping up, stood and walked and entered the temple with them-- walking, leaping, and praising God. And all the people saw him walking and praising God. Then they knew that it was he who sat begging alms at the Beautiful Gate of the temple; and they were filled with wonder and amazement at what had happened to him.

I want to lead all of you to eternal life in heaven. I don't want even one of you to be deceived by Satan, who is luring you to the fiery lake of burning sulfur in hell. Your ancestors, forefathers, friends and relatives who were deceived by the frauds and lies of Satan and demons are crying, lamenting and suffering from all kinds of hardship in the ever burning sulfur fire sea of hell. They will be in the permanent fire sea everlastingly crying and lamenting, regretful for not having believed in Jesus Christ when they were living in the world.

I do not want any one of the 6.3 billion people to fall into the fire sea. Do not be deceived by Satan and demons. Believe in Jesus Christ immediately, and follow Him. That is the only way to lead you and your family to heaven.

This is the Holy Spirit's message for all the human beings living in the world today.

The Holy Spirit's message was received at 7:45 PM on July 13, 1997 in prayer.

2. The love of money is the root of all kinds of evil

The Holy Spirit gave His words to all the Christians in this world who love money.

On May 27, 1997 at 5:55 in the early morning when I was praying, the Holy Spirit said the following.

1 Timothy 6: 9-12: But those who desire to be rich fall into temptation and a snare, and into many foolish and harmful lusts which drown men in destruction and perdition. For the love of money is a root of all kinds of evil, for which some have strayed from the faith in their greediness, and pierced themselves through with many sorrows.

But you, O man of God, flee these things and pursue righteousness, godliness, faith, love, patience, gentleness. Fight the good fight of faith, lay hold on eternal life, to which you were also called and have confessed the good confession in the presence of many witnesses.

When I finished reading the above statements, the Holy Spirit told me the following.

Money is the root of all kinds of evil. I love you more than anyone else does. Do not be too greedy for money. Do you know how many people have been cast into the darkness because of money? If you have a lot of money, you will be more greedy for money. If you are greedy, you will be controlled by the flesh. If a human being is controlled by the flesh, the spirit which the Holy Spirit planted in your heart will be blown out and extinguished. If that happens, the Holy Spirit will leave you and you will be the enemy of God. If you become the enemy of God, after you are dead, you will be far away from heaven, and you must spend your eternal life in darkness.

That is why the Holy Spirit gave you all kinds of hardships for the past seven years, to save you from the root of all kinds of evil. But you are trying to be trapped again by temptation for money. Do you think the Holy Spirit will let you be trapped again into greed for money? This is the truth.

I know that you have to do business to make a living. Therefore the Holy Spirit who knows everything is giving you just enough money for your needs. The Holy Spirit doesn't want to give you extra money, as He did in the past. A great many rich people around you are lying and doing all kinds of wrong doings in order to earn more money. Do you think they will be led to heaven after death? It is easier for a camel to go through the eye of a needle than for a rich man to enter the kingdom of God.

Read Mark: 10:17-27. It means that rich people cannot enter the kingdom of God, heaven.

You have been trained spiritually by the Holy Spirit for the last seven years, but now are you trying to return to your past? No, you must not go that way. A great many of My servants are spending their eternal life in darkness because of money. Do you think that all the pastors of big churches will enter heaven? They will not. They commit more sins than the pastors of small churches. Therefore the Holy Spirit is always telling them, "Do not expand your sect's power, by your greed, to gain more property for your churches. But save the poor dying people without any food to eat, and lead them to God.

"However My foolish servants who cannot understand the truth, they have ears, but they cannot hear and they have eyes but they cannot see. They are doing all kinds of fighting with all their power to expand their own church sect's power and for their own personal power expansion. I want you to go and take a look inside the big churches. They are too miserable and sorrowful.

"My big servants who believe in God, with the responsibility of leading My innumerable sons and daughters to heaven, My servants and My big servants are using all their efforts and energy only to expand their own churches' assets and their own personal power, while doing nothing to save the poor dying people with no food to eat in Africa and other areas in the world and lead them to God, which God likes most.

"The purpose of Jesus Christ's having come to the world and His having been crucified on the cross is not only for His servants to expand their own church sect's power and their own personal power. My big servants, they ignore the pastors of small churches, they are doing their best to please the rich people who are coming to their churches, but they don't pay any attention to the poor old people coming to their churches.

And if any beggars come to their churches, they do not even look at them. Jesus was not beaten by the whip with blood all over His body, nor was His living body crucified on the cross, to help His big servants who only fight for their own churches' power expansion and their own personal interests. They are committing big sins.

"Their main responsibility is to give food, clothes and shelter to the poor, dying people without any food to eat and lead them to God, even if they do not have money to spend. That is one of the main reasons for Jesus' having been crucified on the cross. But they are only doing the works which are very far from Jesus' main purpose of having been crucified. They are doing nothing but expanding their own church's power and their own personal interests and power.

"How can I send such servants to heaven? This is the biggest
problem."

**Matthew 25: 31-46 "When the Son of Man comes in His glory,
and all the holy angels with Him, then He will sit on the throne of
His glory. All the nations will be gathered before Him, and He will
separate them one from another, as a shepherd divides his sheep
from the goats. And He will set the sheep on His right hand, but
the goats on the left.**

**Then the King will say to those on His right hand, 'Come, you
blessed of My Father, inherit the kingdom prepared for you from
the foundation of the world: for I was hungry and you gave Me
food; I was thirsty and you gave Me drink; I was a stranger and
you took Me in; I was naked and you clothed Me; I was sick and
you visited Me; I was in prison and you came to Me.'**

**"Then the righteous will answer Him, saying, 'Lord, when did
we see You hungry and feed You, or thirsty and give You drink?
When did we see You a stranger and take You in, or naked and
clothe You? Or when did we see You sick, or in prison, and come
to You?' And the King will answer and say to them, 'Assuredly, I
say to you, inasmuch as you did it to one of the least of these My
brethren, you did it to Me.'**

**"Then He will also say to those on the left hand, 'Depart from
Me, you cursed, into the everlasting fire prepared for the devil
and his angels: for I was hungry and you gave Me no food; I was
thirsty and you gave Me no drink; I was a stranger and you did
not take Me in, naked and you did not clothe Me, sick and in
prison and you did not visit Me.'**

**"Then they also will answer Him, saying, 'Lord, when did we
see You hungry or thirsty or a stranger or naked or sick or in
prison, and did not minister to You?' Then He will answer them,
saying, 'Assuredly, I say to you, inasmuch as you did not do it to**

one of the least of these, you did not do it to Me.' And these will go away into everlasting punishment, but the righteous into eternal life."

All My servants will understand the meaning of the Bible passage shown above.

The Holy Spirit always insists for His servants to read Romans chapter 8, Galatians chapter 5, and Revelation chapter 2 and 3. The ones following the flesh are dead, and they will be cast into the fire sea in hell but the ones following the Spirit will receive eternal life and will spend their eternal life in heaven.

Of course, the Holy Spirit knows everything very well. If a person has a great deal of money, he can donate more money to the church, and he can do more good business. However the Holy Spirit loves much more the ones who are poor and not greedy, who conscientiously help the poor. He prefers these to big donations and good business.

Luke 16: 19-31 "There was a certain rich man who was clothed in purple and fine linen and fared sumptuously every day. But there was a certain beggar named Lazarus, full of sores, who was laid at his gate, desiring to be fed with the crumbs which fell from the rich man's table. Moreover the dogs came and licked his sores. So it was that the beggar died, and was carried by the angels to Abraham's bosom. The rich man also died and was buried. And being in torments in Hades, he lifted up his eyes and saw Abraham afar off, and Lazarus in his bosom.

"Then he cried and said, 'Father Abraham, have mercy on me, and send Lazarus that he may dip the tip of his finger in water

**and cool my tongue; for I am tormented in this flame.' But Abra-
ham said, 'Son, remember that in your lifetime you received your
good things, and likewise Lazarus evil things; but now he is comforted and you are tormented. And besides all this, between us
and you there is a great gulf fixed, so that those who want to pass
from here to you cannot, nor can those from there pass to us.'**

**"Then he said, 'I beg you therefore, father, that you would send
him to my father's house, for I have five brothers, that he may
testify to them, lest they also come to this place of torment.'
Abraham said to him, 'They have Moses and the prophets; let
them hear them.' And he said, 'No, father Abraham; but if one
goes to them from the dead, they will repent.' But he said to him,
'If they do not hear Moses and the prophets, neither will they be
persuaded though one rise from the dead.'"**

Now I think you understand why the Holy Spirit prevents
you from having a lot of money. The Holy Spirit will give you
any great amount of money you need to do God's business.
However He will not give you the money to satisfy your personal greed. This is a basic truth of God. Right here is the reason why a great many of God's servants, sons, and daughters
who used to do big business with a lot of money fail in business.

God gave a great deal of wealth to the pastors of big
churches, however they did not use the money for the God's
purpose. Therefore most of the big churches can do nothing but
face God's final angry judgment.

I do not want you to be such a foolish and idiotic servant of
God but think about the real purpose of Jesus' having been cru-

cified on the cross once again. And follow that way. That is the only way the Holy Spirit leads you, step-by-step carrying the cross on your back to heaven.

And I want you to send the Holy Spirit's words to many pastors of big churches in the world. And spread these truthful words all over the world. Many of My servants will repent with tears in their eyes.

The Holy Spirit's words were given at 5:55 AM on May 27, 1997 in early morning prayer.

3. The act of adultery causes God's anger

7/15/97 1:00 PM in prayer, the Holy Spirit gave the following words about the adultery to all the people in the world.

Matthew 5: 27-28 "You have heard that it was said to those of old, 'You shall not commit adultery.' But I say to you that whoever looks at a woman to lust for her has already committed adultery with her in his heart."

When I finished reading this, the Holy Spirit told me the following:

Human beings commit a lot of adultery. Especially in this age, men and women are committing adultery, whenever they meet by chance, as if committing adultery is no sin at all. Such deeds are like animals, and are great sins against God.

You must not share love with any other woman or man except your own wife or husband, whom God gave you. Such dirty deeds are not permitted at all for any reasons. People in this age, especially, are sharing love between men and women without any worries. But God treats adultery as one of the biggest sins.

In the law, Moses commanded to stone such women (John 8: 3-5).

And Jesus said, "Anyone who looks at a woman lustfully has already committed adultery with her in his heart."

Adultery is such a fearful sin to mankind. The people in the current age are committing a lot of great and serious sins against God by committing adultery with boyfriends and girlfriends, even if they have their own husbands or wives. Such deeds are sins against God beyond expression. There are great numbers of shepherds worshiping God who are committing such sins. As a result of that sin, there are innumerable numbers of My servants who have to spend their eternal lives in darkness. The numbers of such sinners among believers are uncountable, beyond expression.

Therefore, whenever you meet anyone, tell them to never

think of adultery, even in their dreams. Such sins are momen-
tarily forgotten deeds that destroy one's eternal life completely.
God treats them as big sins, after murder. Adultery is such a big
sin.

**Numbers 25: 1-13 Now Israel remained in Acacia Grove, and
the people began to commit harlotry with the women of Moab.
They invited the people to the sacrifices of their gods, and the
people ate and bowed down to their gods. So Israel was joined to
Baal of Peor, and the anger of the Lord was aroused against Israel.**

**Then the Lord said to Moses, "Take all the leaders of the people
and hang the offenders before the Lord, out in the sun, that the
fierce anger of the Lord may turn away from Israel."**

**So Moses said to the judges of Israel, "Every one of you kill his
men who were joined to Baal of Peor."**

**And indeed, one of the children of Israel came and presented to
his brethren a Midianite woman in the sight of Moses and in the
sight of all the congregation of the children of Israel, who were
weeping at the door of the tabernacle of meeting.**

**Now when Phinehas the son of Eleazar, the son of Aaron the
priest, saw it, he rose from among the congregation and took a
javelin in his hand; and he went after the man of Israel into the
tent and thrust both of them through, the man of Israel, and the
woman through her body. So the plague was stopped among the
children of Israel. And those who died in the plague were twenty-
four thousand.**

**Then the Lord spoke to Moses, saying: "Phinehas the son of
Eleazar, the son of Aaron the priest, has turned back My wrath
from the children of Israel, because he was zealous with My zeal
among them, so that I did not consume the children of Israel in
My zeal. Therefore say, 'Behold, I give to him My covenant of
peace; and it shall be to him and his descendants after him a**

covenant of an everlasting priesthood, because he was zealous for his God, and made atonement for the children of Israel.'"

The above shown Bible words clearly tell you how fearful adultery is. Because of adultery, a plague occurred and 24,000 Israelites lost their lives. Now you understand how adultery is a huge sin committed against the Almighty God. If any of you have committed adultery in the past, confess and repent with tears before God, and never repeat the same sin again.

Adultery is one of the biggest sins which causes human beings to be dropped into the fiery sea of hell. It is similar to how cancer kills human beings in the world. Therefore whenever you deliver Holy Spirit's words to any churches in the world, especially emphasize the sin of adultery. Avoid animal-like deeds, but keep your body clean and Holy as a child of God.   -

1 Corinthians 3: 16 Do you not know that you are the temple of God and that the Spirit of God dwells in you? If anyone defiles the temple of God, God will destroy him. For the temple of God is holy, which temple you are.

This Bible passage says you have to keep your body clean and sacred. This is the only way to lead you to heaven step-by-step, carrying the cross on your back, following the Holy Spirit's guidance. Deliver this Holy Spirit message about adultery to all the people in the world so as that none of My sons and daughters may commit sins against God by adultery.

The Holy Spirit's words were given at 1:00 PM on July 15, 1997 in prayer.

4. Watch your mouth and refrain from speaking

April 26, 1997 at 5:00 PM in prayer, the Holy Spirit gave the following message to all His sons and daughters in the world.

James 3: 1-18 My brethren, let not many of you become teachers, knowing that we shall receive a stricter judgment. For we all stumble in many things. If anyone does not stumble in word, he is a perfect man, able also to bridle the whole body. Indeed, we put bits in horses' mouths that they may obey us, and we turn their whole body. Look also at ships: although they are so large and are driven by fierce winds, they are turned by a very small rudder wherever the pilot desires. Even so the tongue is a little member and boasts great things.

See how great a forest a little fire kindles! And the tongue is a fire, a world of iniquity. The tongue is so set among our members that it defiles the whole body, and sets on fire the course of nature; and it is set on fire by hell. For every kind of beast and bird, of reptile and creature of the sea, is tamed and has been tamed by mankind.

But no man can tame the tongue. It is an unruly evil, full of deadly poison. With it we bless our God and Father, and with it we curse men, who have been made in the similitude of God. Out of the same mouth proceed blessing and cursing. My brethren, these things ought not to be so. Does a spring send forth fresh

water and bitter from the same opening? Can a fig tree, my
brethren, bear olives, or a grapevine bear figs? Thus no spring
yields both salt water and fresh.

Who is wise and understanding among you? Let him show by
good conduct that his works are done in the meekness of wisdom.
But if you have bitter envy and self-seeking in your hearts, do not
boast and lie against the truth. This wisdom does not descend
from above, but is earthly, sensual, demonic. For where envy and
self-seeking exist, confusion and every evil thing are there.

But the wisdom that is from above is first pure, then peaceable,
gentle, willing to yield, full of mercy and good fruits, without par-
tiality and without hypocrisy. Now the fruit of righteousness is
sown in peace by those who make peace.

When I finished reading the above statements, the Holy
Spirit told me the following:

Watch your mouth and refrain from speaking. All evil comes
from the tongue. Human beings cannot live without moving
their tongues. All people who are living, speak. The words spoken once from your mouths cannot be collected again. And the
words are the root of all kinds of evil. Your mouth makes your
life shorter, or your life longer, or sends you to heaven or
throws you into hell.

Matthew 12: 36-37 But I say to you that for every idle word men
men may speak, they will give account of it in the day of judgment.
For by your words you will be justified, and by your words you
will be condemned.

The words from your mouth are so important. You will be

judged by the words from your own mouth, whether you will go to heaven or be thrown into hell. All the words spoken by your mouth from birth to the day you die are recorded in the record book of your life, in heaven. Therefore I ask you to watch your mouth.

And if you convict, judge or curse others by your mouth, tongue, or in your heart, you should immediately kneel down and confess all that you did, to God, and repent for all you did, in front of Him.

If you did not confess and repent immediately all that you did wrong, you should do it later. Otherwise the words you spoke unintentionally will be a big obstacle to you. In order to clean up all such things, you should confess and repent in front of God at least once a day. If you committed too many sins when you were young, and cannot remember them clearly, the Holy Spirit will remind you of your sins and sometimes He will show you visions of your sins.

Then you should confess them by speaking human language or in heavenly tongues. By any form you should confess and repent all your sins to God and you should be forgiven for your sins. The words you are speaking are so important. Innumerable servants and My people, the Israelites, were saved from Egypt but they did not watch their mouths and reproached the heavenly Father. Therefore they died in the wilderness.

Refer to Numbers chapter 13 and 14. Moses sent twelve men, one from each ancestral tribe, to explore Canaan, the land God

was giving to the Israelites.

Now they departed and came back to Moses and Aaron and all
the congregation of the children of Israel in the Wilderness of
Paran, at Kadesh; they brought back word to them and to all the
congregation, and showed them the fruit of the land. Then they
told him, and said: "We went to the land where you sent us.

It truly flows with milk and honey, and this is its fruit. Nevertheless the people who dwell in the land are strong; the cities are
fortified and very large; moreover we saw the descendants of
Anak there. The Amalekites dwell in the land of the South; the
Hittites, the Jebusites, and the Amorites dwell in the mountains;
and the Canaanites dwell by the sea and along the banks of the
Jordan."

Then Caleb quieted the people before Moses, and said, "Let us
go up at once and take possession, for we are well able to overcome it."

But the men who had gone up with him said, "We are not able
to go up against the people, for they are stronger than we." And
they gave the children of Israel a bad report of the land which
they had spied out, saying, "The land through which we have gone
as spies is a land that devours its inhabitants, and all the people
whom we saw in it are men of great stature. There we saw the
giants (the descendants of Anak came from the giants); and we
were like grasshoppers in our own sight, and so we were in their
sight."

Numbers 14: 1-19 So all the congregation lifted up their voices
and cried, and the people wept that night. And all the children of
Israel complained against Moses and Aaron, and the whole congregation said to them, "If only we had died in the land of Egypt!
Or if only we had died in this wilderness! Why has the Lord
brought us to this land to fall by the sword, that our wives and

children should become victims? Would it not be better for us to return to Egypt?" So they said to one another, "Let us select a leader and return to Egypt." Then Moses and Aaron fell on their faces before all the assembly of the congregation of the children of Israel.

But Joshua the son of Nun and Caleb the son of Jephunneh, who were among those who had spied out the land, tore their clothes; and they spoke to all the congregation of the children of Israel, saying: "The land we passed through to spy out is an exceedingly good land. If the Lord delights in us, then He will bring us into this land and give it to us, 'a land which flows with milk and honey.' Only do not rebel against the Lord, nor fear the people of the land, for they are our bread; their protection has departed from them, and the Lord is with us. Do not fear them."

And all the congregation said to stone them with stones. Now the glory of the Lord appeared in the tabernacle of meeting before all the children of Israel.

Then the Lord said to Moses: "How long will these people reject Me? And how long will they not believe Me, with all the signs which I have performed among them? I will strike them with the pestilence and disinherit them, and I will make of you a nation greater and mightier than they."

And Moses said to the Lord: "Then the Egyptians will hear it, for by Your might You brought these people up from among them, and they will tell it to the inhabitants of this land. They have heard that You, Lord, are among these people; that You, Lord, are seen face to face and Your cloud stands above them, and You go before them in a pillar of cloud by day and in a pillar of fire by night.

Now if You kill these people as one man, then the nations which have heard of Your fame will speak, saying, 'Because the Lord was not able to bring this people to the land which He swore to give them, therefore He killed them in the wilderness.' And now, I pray, let the power of my Lord be great, just as You have spoken,

saying, 'The Lord is longsuffering and abundant in mercy, forgiving iniquity and transgression; but He by no means clears the
guilty, visiting the iniquity of the fathers on the children to the
third and fourth generation.' Pardon the iniquity of this people, I
pray, according to the greatness of Your mercy, just as You have
forgiven this people, from Egypt even until now.''

Numbers 14: 26-38 And the Lord spoke to Moses and Aaron,
saying, "How long shall I bear with this evil congregation who
complain against Me? I have heard the complaints which the
children of Israel make against Me. Say to them, 'As I live,' says
the Lord, 'just as you have spoken in My hearing, so I will do to
you: The carcasses of you who have complained against Me shall
fall in this wilderness, all of you who were numbered, according to
your entire number, from twenty years old and above.

Except for Caleb the son of Jephunneh and Joshua the son of
Nun, you shall by no means enter the land which I swore I would
make you dwell in. But your little ones, whom you said would be
victims, I will bring in, and they shall know the land which you
have despised. But as for you, your carcasses shall fall in this wilderness. And your sons shall be shepherds in the wilderness forty
years, and bear the brunt of your infidelity, until your carcasses
are consumed in the wilderness.

According to the number of the days in which you spied out the
land, forty days, for each day you shall bear your guilt one year,
namely forty years, and you shall know My rejection. I the Lord
have spoken this. I will surely do so to all this evil congregation
who are gathered together against Me.

In this wilderness they shall be consumed, and there they shall
die.'"

Now the men whom Moses sent to spy out the land, who returned and made all the congregation complain against him by
bringing a bad report of the land, those very men who brought the

evil report about the land, died by the plague before the Lord. But Joshua the son of Nun and Caleb the son of Jephunneh remained alive, of the men who went to spy out the land.

By reading the above Bible passages, you can understand that all the Israelites who grumbled against the Lord were struck down and died of a plague before God. No one in the world can say anything against Almighty God. He is the creator of all the human beings in the world. Therefore we have to obey the Lord. Whatever He says is the truth in the world.

Therefore wherever you go, tell as follows:
1. Whoever they are, never say anything about other people.
2. Whoever they are, never convict other people.
3. Whoever they are, never decide or judge other people.
4. About God, never even think of negative things at all.
5. About God, never say unfair or unjust things at all.
6. About God, it is better for you not to tell jokes.
7. If you have to talk about another person, think that he is Jesus. Then you will watch your mouth.
8. If you spoke wrong of others by mistake, immediately confess and repent to them in front of God. This is the true way to heaven step-by-step, carrying the cross on your back, following the Holy Spirit's guidance.

The Holy Spirit's words were given at 5:00 PM on April 26, 1997 in prayer.

5. Self fighting, throw away your greedy mind

‣ **Romans 8: 12-14 Therefore, brethren, we are debtors--not to
the flesh, to live according to the flesh. For if you live according to
the flesh you will die; but if by the Spirit you put to death the
deeds of the body, you will live. For as many as are led by the
Spirit of God, these are sons of God.**

When I finished reading Romans chapter 8, the Holy Spirit
told me the following:

My son!
These words mean that you are being led by the Holy Spirit,
after abandoning the flesh's greed. All human-beings' spirits
cannot be saved from death because of the flesh's greed. That is
to fight and to struggle against yourself.

Many of My servants cannot win the fight against themselves. They are deceived by Satan's temptation and lost by the
flesh's greed and finally are thrown into eternal death. How
horrible is this fighting? That is, the decision to send you to
eternal life or throw you to hell forever depends on your self-
fighting.

Think about these words deeply. They are not simple matters
to pass away. Whatever hardship you are facing, you should
abandon the flesh's greed and you should follow the real way,

being led by the Holy Spirit.

Galatians 5: 16-26 I say then: Walk in the Spirit, and you shall not fulfill the lust of the flesh. For the flesh lusts against the Spirit, and the Spirit against the flesh; and these are contrary to one another, so that you do not do the things that you wish. But if you are led by the Spirit, you are not under the law.

Now the works of the flesh are evident, which are: adultery, fornication, uncleanness, lewdness, idolatry, sorcery, hatred, contentions, jealousies, outbursts of wrath, selfish ambitions, dissensions, heresies, envy, murders, drunkenness, revelries, and the like; of which I tell you beforehand, just as I also told you in time past, that those who practice such things will not inherit the kingdom of God.

But the fruit of the Spirit is love, joy, peace, longsuffering, kindness, goodness, faithfulness, gentleness, self-control. Against such there is no law. And those who are Christ's have crucified the flesh with its passions and desires. If we live in the Spirit, let us also walk in the Spirit. Let us not become conceited, provoking one another, envying one another.

The above shown Bible passages clearly say, "In your body the Holy Spirit and flesh's greed are in conflict with each other." Sinful nature desires all the dirty things, such as sexual immorality, impurity, debauchery, idolatry, witchcraft, and such things. Those who desire the sinful nature cannot inherit the kingdom of God. That means they cannot go to heaven but they will be thrown into the fire of hell. However those who are led by the Holy Spirit will bear the fruits of the Holy Spirit such as love, joy, peace, patience, kindness, goodness, faithfulness and such things.

Against such thing there is no law. That means there is no law that can stop them from going to heaven. That is, they will go to heaven without any problems. Therefore, however hard it is, I want you to abandon all your greed by the leading of the Holy Spirit to receive eternal life in heaven.

That is the way through which you can reach eternal life, carrying a cross on your back, being led by the Holy Spirit step-by-step. Never envy your old friends who are wealthy and sharing power with other powerful people. That is not the way to heaven. I know that there are many people who are doing business with the help of powerful politicians. Never envy whatever big business they are doing. All the wealth they own is like dew on the grass. That means all their wealth will disappear into the sky, when the sun begins to shine.

My son, you should follow the real way the Holy Spirit is leading you. That is the only the way which is leading you to eternal life. Therefore on Friday afternoon the Holy Spirit inside of your heart asks you with a strong fire to go to Reverend Y's church. Singing, dancing with the Holy Spirit, speaking in the tongue of God, prophesying, falling and enjoying the Holy Spirit is the real way the Holy Spirit leads to eternal life. Without such experiences with the Holy Spirit, it is very difficult to abandon the flesh's greed to follow the Holy Spirit's way to heaven.

Matthew 7: 13-14 "Enter by the narrow gate; for wide is the gate and broad is the way that leads to destruction, and there are many who go in by it. Because narrow is the gate and difficult is

the way which leads to life, and there are few who find it."

Wherever you go, I want you to worship in such a church. This is the reason why the Holy Spirit asks you to tell all the pastors you meet, to invite the pastors through whom the Holy Spirit performs powerful miracles, to get the Holy Spirit's baptism and experience the Holy Spirit's ministry.

John 3: 3 Jesus answered and said to him, "Most assuredly, I say to you, unless one is born again, he cannot see the kingdom of God."

Jesus said clearly, unless one is born of water and the spirit, one cannot enter the kingdom of God.

Revelation 2: 11 "He who has an ear, let him hear what the Spirit says to the churches. He who overcomes shall not be hurt by the second death."

It means that the ones who obey the Holy Spirit's words and follow God's word in deed shall not be thrown into the fire sea in hell. Namely it means that the spirits of the people who don't obey and follow the Holy Spirit's word shall be cast into the lake of fire in hell. The second death means to throw the spirits into the lake of fire.

Revelation 20: 14 Then Death and Hades were cast into the lake of fire. This is the second death.

Whenever you have the chance to talk with pastors, tell all My servants the truthful words.

Be bold, and courageous, whenever you deliver the Holy
Spirit's message. You don't need to fear anyone. I am always
with you and angels around you are protecting you all the time.

**The Holy Spirit's words given at 4:04 AM April
21, 1997, in prayer.**

CHAPTER 2

The Holy Spirit's words about the Worldwide Holy Spirit Revival Movement

1. Why is the Worldwide Holy Spirit Revival Movement necessary?
2. How to discern between the Holy Spirit and evil spirits, which the Holy Spirit taught me on the basis of the Bible
3. How to cast out demons, the Holy Spirit taught me
4. Phenomena which appear when the Holy Spirit is present with you
5. Be careful about false prophets
6. The Holy Spirit helps poor churches and pastors in difficulty
7. The Holy Spirit encourages the pastors who are leading the Holy Spirit Movement

8. The Holy Spirit protects the pastors in the Holy
   Spirit Movement

1. Why is the Worldwide Holy Spirit Revival Movement necessary?

The Holy Spirit says the following according to the Holy Bible.

February 18, 1998 at 4:45 AM in early morning prayer, the Holy Spirit gave the following words about the worldwide Holy Spirit's Revival Movement to all the Christians in the world.

The Holy Bible is God's word, therefore you cannot add or deduct anything from the Bible.

Revelation 22: 18-19 For I testify to everyone who hears the words of the prophecy of this book: If anyone adds to these things, God will add to him the plagues that are written in this book; and if anyone takes away from the words of the book of this prophecy, God shall take away his part from the Book of Life, from the holy city, and from the things which are written in this book.

As said in the Holy Bible, you should believe the words as they were written in the Bible. You should not explain or preach the Bible according to your own mind.

All of you should believe in God and worship Him in accordance with the Holy Bible. You should keep your savior, Jesus' words as your fundamental principle, and follow His words to be saved. I want you to find out what Jesus said about the Holy Spirit.

John 3: 3-7 Jesus answered and said to him, "Most assuredly, I say to you, unless one is born again, he cannot see the kingdom of God." Nicodemus said to Him, "How can a man be born when he is old? Can he enter a second time into his mother's womb and be born?"

Jesus answered, "Most assuredly, I say to you, unless one is born of water and the Spirit, he cannot enter the kingdom of God. That which is born of the flesh is flesh, and that which is born of the Spirit is spirit. Do not marvel that I said to you, "You must be born again."

As in the above words, you must believe in Jesus and be again of water and the Spirit to enter the kingdom of God. It is the basic principle to experience the Holy Spirit's ministry and be baptized by the Holy Spirit for you to be born again in water and the Holy Spirit.

There are some cases for the people who read the Bible a lot to be born again of the Holy Spirit for the purpose of being used specially by God. Such people are yearning for the Holy Spirit's ministries. They go anywhere Holy Spirit Services are open, following the Holy Spirit's leadings.

But most Christians who have not experienced the Holy Spirit's ministry do not believe the Bible 100% as it is written. They believe the Bible while thinking, deciding and judging with human reason, knowledge, and intelligence. For such people who believe in God with human intelligence, reason and knowledge, God does not answer their prayers, however long the prayers may be. For such believers to be born again, they must attend the Holy Spirit's services.

Even though you have been going to church for many decades, if you are not born again of water and the Holy Spirit, you did not experience the Holy Spirit. If you cannot go to heaven, what will you do? Therefore it is the Holy Spirit's plan to lead all of you to the Holy Spirit's ministry services, for the purpose of all of you to be born again of water and the Holy Spirit, and finally all of you to be led to heaven.

John 14: 6 Jesus said to him, "I am the way, the truth, and the life. No one comes to the Father except through Me."

As in the above statement, no one comes to the Father except through Jesus. It is the truth to follow Jesus' words, if you want to go to heaven. That is the only way.

John 14: 16-17 And I will pray the Father, and He will give you another Helper, that He may abide with you forever--the Spirit of truth, whom the world cannot receive, because it neither sees Him nor knows Him; but you know Him, for He dwells with you and

will be in you.

John 14: 20-21 At that day you will know that I am in My Father, and you in Me, and I in you. He who has My commandments and keeps them, it is he who loves Me. And he who loves Me will be loved by My Father, and I will love him and manifest Myself to him.

As told in the above, Jesus sent the Holy Spirit to us. And He said to us, "The Holy Spirit - the Spirit of truth will live in you and you will know Him." He will lead you to the right way. If you obey Him, the heavenly Father will love you and Jesus will show Himself to you.

The Holy Spirit lives in you and you must follow His words of truth. It is difficult for you to realize what Jesus said without being baptized by the Holy Spirit. The people who cannot receive the Holy Spirit's answer directly, how can they receive guidance from the Holy Spirit directly?

You have to experience the Holy Spirit's ministry and be baptized by the Holy Spirit to understand the Holy Spirit's instructions.

John 15: 11, 26-27 "These things I have spoken to you, that My joy may remain in you, and that your joy may be full."
"But when the Helper comes, whom I shall send to you from the Father, the Spirit of truth who proceeds from the Father, He will testify of Me. And you also will bear witness, because you have been with Me from the beginning."

The Holy Spirit testifies with truth only for Jesus and He delivers the Gospel all over the world. And if the Holy Spirit lives in you, you will always be fully inspired by the Holy Spirit. And you will understand that the Holy Spirit lives with you.

John 16: 12-14 "I still have many things to say to you, but you cannot bear them now. However, when He, the Spirit of truth, has come, He will guide you into all truth; for He will not speak on His own authority, but whatever He hears He will speak; and He will tell you things to come. He will glorify Me, for He will take of what is Mine and declare it to you."

Jesus said to His disciples, "I have much more to say to you, more than you can now bear." But when the Holy Spirit comes, He speaks only truth and He will lead you to the truth about going to heaven. However if you cannot understand truth, are not baptized by the Holy Spirit, and are not attending the Holy Spirit's services, how can He lead you to heaven under the guidance of the Holy Spirit?

You must be baptized by the Holy Spirit to be led by the Holy Spirit to heaven. You have to participate in Holy Spirit Services often to receive the Holy Spirit's guidance, read the Bible and pray to God always. The more often you attend Holy Spirit ministries, the more of the Holy Spirit's power you will get.

Acts 1: 4-5, 8 And being assembled together with them, He commanded them not to depart from Jerusalem, but to wait for the Promise of the Father, "which," He said, "you have heard from Me; for John truly baptized with water, but you shall be

baptized with the Holy Spirit not many days from now."

But you shall receive power when the Holy Spirit has come upon you; and you shall be witnesses to Me in Jerusalem, and in all Judea and Samaria, and to the end of the earth."

After Jesus was resurrected from death, He commanded His apostles to wait in Jerusalem to receive the Holy Spirit's baptism in a few days. Until then innumerable people followed Him, but no one was baptized by the Holy Spirit. Not all who go to church once a week for many years are baptized by the Holy Spirit.

Christian believers baptized by the Holy Spirit are doing works which glorify the heavenly Father, to please Jesus and the Holy Spirit, more than anything else. They attend the Holy Spirit's services which are held very far away, driving for several hours, following the Holy Spirit.

Holy Spirit-filled Christians are dancing, singing, clapping hands, falling on the floor, speaking in heavenly tongues, prophesying, shaking their bodies or hands and seeing visions of heaven and hell, in the Holy Spirit's services. They are enjoying a heavenly party at the invitation of the Holy Spirit. Many people show different reactions according to the Holy Spirit's will, in the presence of the Holy Spirit. Without the Holy Spirit's baptism you cannot be born again by the Holy Spirit, and you cannot receive the Holy Spirit's guidance leading to truth.

Acts 2: 1-4 When the Day of Pentecost had fully come, they were all with one accord in one place. And suddenly there came a sound from heaven, as of a rushing mighty wind, and it filled the whole house where they were sitting. Then there appeared to them divided tongues, as of fire, and one sat upon each of them. And they were all filled with the Holy Spirit and began to speak with other tongues, as the Spirit gave them utterance.

This is the Holy Spirit's baptism and this is how Christians are born again by the Holy Spirit. And this is what Christian believers receive by the Holy Spirit's full inspiration. The more often you receive such Holy Spirit baptism, the more power He will give you. According to the Holy Spirit's power you receive, the Holy Spirit's ministry you lead will be different.

Some pastors lead the Holy Spirit's ministry very powerfully, and some lead the Holy Spirit's services very weakly. That is the difference. Before receiving this baptism, they also prayed very hard for many days (Acts 1:12-14). Without the Holy Spirit's baptism, it is difficult for you to be born again by the Holy Spirit, and you cannot receive the Holy Spirit's guidance.

If you receive such a powerful Holy Spirit baptism and experience strong Holy Spirit ministries, you will be fully inspired by His power, you will receive His guidance, and you will not follow your human reason, knowledge, intelligence and learning in believing the Bible and glorifying the heavenly Father, pleasing Jesus and the Holy Spirit.

The apostle Peter witnessed all of Jesus' ministries from the beginning until Jesus was caught by a large crowd armed with swords and clubs, sent by the chief priests and elders of the people. Still, Peter betrayed Jesus three times in one night, by saying that he did not know Jesus at all. Refer to Matthew 26: 69-75.

After he was baptized by the Holy Spirit, such a coward as Peter preached very boldly in front of a large crowd of Jewish people. As a result of that he led 3,000 Israelites to Jesus in one day. These were the same people who were so stubborn and crucified Jesus on the cross. It was not Peter's preaching method, but the Holy Spirit who moved all the people to Jesus, when He gave His power to Peter. Refer to Acts 2: 5-47.

Most of the apostles, who were fully inspired by the Holy Spirit's power, healed many incurable diseases and showed all kinds of miracles by the Holy Spirit's guidance. Refer to Acts chapters 3, 4, and 5. Without the Holy Spirit's power, it is very difficult for a man to lead so many people to Jesus.

Today, right at this moment, the Holy Spirit ministries which happened in the apostle Peter's day are happening all over the world. You do not believe the Bible 100% as it is written and you explain the Bible by your own human reason, knowledge, intelligence and learning in school.
Therefore the Holy Spirit does not perform any miracles through you. The Holy Spirit wants to give His power to anyone who wants to receive it. If you want to be born again by the Holy Spirit, and to be led to heaven, you have to attend the Holy Spirit ministry services often and you must be baptized by the Holy Spirit.

Acts 3: 1-8 Now Peter and John went up together to the temple at the hour of prayer, the ninth hour. And a certain man lame from his mother's womb was carried, whom they laid daily at the gate of the temple which is called Beautiful, to ask alms from those who entered the temple; who, seeing Peter and John about to go into the temple, asked for alms. And fixing his eyes on him, with John, Peter said, "Look at us." So he gave them his attention, expecting to receive something from them.

Then Peter said, "Silver and gold I do not have, but what I do have I give you: In the name of Jesus Christ of Nazareth, rise up and walk." And he took him by the right hand and lifted him up, and immediately his feet and ankle bones received strength. So he, leaping up, stood and walked and entered the temple with them-- walking, leaping, and praising God.

This is the Holy Spirit's miracle. The Holy Spirit will per- form such miracles through you also, if you receive the Holy Spirit's power. Even today the Holy Spirit gives His power to Christian believers who believe in Jesus 100% as written in the Bible.

Acts 5: 1-11 But a certain man named Ananias, with Sapphira his wife, sold a possession. And he kept back part of the proceeds, his wife also being aware of it, and brought a certain part and laid it at the apostles' feet. But Peter said, "Ananias, why has Satan filled your heart to lie to the Holy Spirit and keep back part of the price of the land for yourself? While it remained, was it not your own? And after it was sold, was it not in your own control? Why have you conceived this thing in your heart? You have not lied to men but to God."

Then Ananias, hearing these words, fell down and breathed his

last. So great fear came upon all those who heard these things. And the young men arose and wrapped him up, carried him out, and buried him. Now it was about three hours later when his wife came in, not knowing what had happened. And Peter answered her, "Tell me whether you sold the land for so much?"

She said, "Yes, for so much." Then Peter said to her, "How is it that you have agreed together to test the Spirit of the Lord? Look, the feet of those who have buried your husband are at the door, and they will carry you out." Then immediately she fell down at his feet and breathed her last. And the young men came in and found her dead, and carrying her out, buried her by her husband. So great fear came upon all the church and upon all who heard these things.

Never try to deceive the Holy Spirit. In your heart, by your mouth, or by your acts, never tell lies to the Holy Spirit, who knows everything about you, more than you know. Whoever tries to deceive the Holy Spirit will be punished fearfully, as above. Always be careful about your actions and your mouth. Even today many believers and non-believers who do not obey the Holy Spirit's commands, who libel the Holy Spirit's ministries or who groundlessly slander the pastors filled with the Holy Spirit's power leading the Holy Spirit's miracles, are punished to death by the Holy Spirit all over the world.

Acts 9: 1-9,17-18 Then Saul, still breathing threats and murder against the disciples of the Lord, went to the high priest and asked letters from him to the synagogues of Damascus, so that if he found any who were of the Way, whether men or women, he might bring them bound to Jerusalem. As he journeyed he came near Damascus, and suddenly a light shone around him from heaven. Then he fell to the ground, and heard a voice saying to him,

"Saul, Saul, why are you persecuting Me?" And he said, "Who are You, Lord?" Then the Lord said, "I am Jesus, whom you are persecuting. It is hard for you to kick against the goads." So he, trembling and astonished, said, "Lord, what do You want me to do?"

Then the Lord said to him, "Arise and go into the city, and you will be told what you must do." And the men who journeyed with him stood speechless, hearing a voice but seeing no one. Then Saul arose from the ground, and when his eyes were opened he saw no one. But they led him by the hand and brought him into Damascus. And he was three days without sight, and neither ate nor drank.

And Ananias went his way and entered the house; and laying his hands on him he said, "Brother Saul, the Lord Jesus, who appeared to you on the road as you came, has sent me that you may receive your sight and be filled with the Holy Spirit." Immediately there fell from his eyes something like scales, and he received his sight at once; and he arose and was baptized.

It was all the Holy Spirit's ministry which made Saul, who was on the way to Damascus to arrest the followers of Jesus Christ, fall to the ground and make him blind and change him to be the great apostle, Paul. When the Holy Spirit's presence appears to your body, your body can do nothing against His presence.

All your physical power goes away and you automatically fall on the ground. Many of My servants who have no experience with the Holy Spirit's miracles at all explain the Holy Spirit's ministry by their own will. They make all kinds of groundless stories, like hypnotism, heresy, or craziness. Slandering the Holy Spirit's ministry is same as slandering the Holy

Spirit.

Matthew 12: 31-32 "Therefore I say to you, every sin and blasphemy will be forgiven men, but the blasphemy against the Spirit will not be forgiven men. Anyone who speaks a word against the Son of Man, it will be forgiven him; but whoever speaks against the Holy Spirit, it will not be forgiven him, either in this age or in the age to come.

Right now, all different kinds of Holy Spirit Miracles are happening all over the world. If you try to find the churches being led by the Holy Spirit, there are countless small and large churches where you can experience the Holy Spirit Ministry.

Romans 8: 5-14 For those who live according to the flesh set their minds on the things of the flesh, but those who live according to the Spirit, the things of the Spirit. For to be carnally minded is death, but to be spiritually minded is life and peace. Because the carnal mind is enmity against God; for it is not subject to the law of God, nor indeed can be. So then, those who are in the flesh cannot please God.

But you are not in the flesh but in the Spirit, if indeed the Spirit of God dwells in you. Now if anyone does not have the Spirit of Christ, he is not His. And if Christ is in you, the body is dead because of sin, but the Spirit is life because of righteousness. But if the Spirit of Him who raised Jesus from the dead dwells in you, He who raised Christ from the dead will also give life to your mortal bodies through His Spirit who dwells in you.

Therefore, brethren, we are debtors--not to the flesh, to live according to the flesh. For if you live according to the flesh you will die; but if by the Spirit you put to death the deeds of the body, you will live. For as many as are led by the Spirit of God, these are

sons of God.

God's words above are very clear and precise. The mind controlled by the flesh is dead, but the mind controlled by the Holy Spirit is life and peace. That is, if you live according to your flesh, you will die. That means you cannot go to heaven. It does not matter how many years you have been going to church. If you do not follow the Holy Spirit's guidance, but follow your own flesh's mind, reason, knowledge, intelligence and learning in school, and do not believe the Holy Bible 100% as it was written, you can never go to heaven. But you will be thrown into the sulfur fire sea of hell. However, to be born again of water and the Holy Spirit and to receive the Holy Spirit's guidance to heaven, you must go to the Holy Spirit's ministry services often and be baptized by the Holy Spirit.

Galatians 5: 16-26 I say then: Walk in the Spirit, and you shall not fulfill the lust of the flesh. For the flesh lusts against the Spirit, and the Spirit against the flesh; and these are contrary to one another, so that you do not do the things that you wish. But if you are led by the Spirit, you are not under the law.

Now the works of the flesh are evident, which are: adultery, fornication, uncleanness, lewdness, idolatry, sorcery, hatred, contentions, jealousies, outbursts of wrath, selfish ambitions, dissensions, heresies, envy, murders, drunkenness, revelries, and the like; of which I tell you beforehand, just as I also told you in time past, that those who practice such things will not inherit the kingdom of God.

But the fruit of the Spirit is love, joy, peace, longsuffering, kindness, goodness, faithfulness, gentleness, self-control. Against such there is no law. And those who are Christ's have crucified

the flesh with its passions and desires. If we live in the Spirit, let us also walk in the Spirit. Let us not become conceited, provoking one another, envying one another.

As told in the above Bible passage, you must follow the Holy Spirit's guidance. If you follow the Holy Spirit's leading, you will throw away the flesh's greed. Because of your greed, you cannot communicate with the Holy Spirit directly. Whoever strongly shows these acts of the flesh, such as sexual immorality, impurity, idolatry and debauchery, are against the Holy Spirit and are controlled by Satan.

Such people controlled by Satan cannot go to heaven. However if you follow the Holy Spirit's leading, you will lose all your flesh's greed and you will have the fruits of the Holy Spirit such as love, joy, peace, patience and others. Such people led by the Holy Spirit will be led to heaven. If you attend the Holy Spirit's services often, experience the Holy Spirit's ministry yourself, believe the Bible 100% as it was written, and follow the Holy Spirit's leading, you will get the fruit of the Holy Spirit.

You have to abandon all your flesh's greed, follow the Holy Spirit's guidance, receive the fruit of the Holy Spirit, and live by the Holy Spirit's leading. In order to abandon flesh's greed, you must experience the Holy Spirit's ministry and you must be baptized by the Holy Spirit. You cannot bear the fruit of the Holy Spirit without His help. That is the spiritual war in your body.

Without the Holy Spirit's experience and baptism, you cannot abandon flesh's greed controlled by Satan. The Holy Spirit

will arrest Satan and demons and chase them away from your
body. And He will arm you with God's words and bear the fruit
of the Holy Spirit in you. If you have the fruit of the Holy Spirit
in your heart, you will have the kingdom of God in your heart.
Such people controlled by the Holy Spirit are called sons of
God.

**Revelation 2: 7 "He who has an ear, let him hear what the Spirit
Spirit says to the churches. To him who overcomes I will give to
eat from the tree of life, which is in the midst of the Paradise of
God."**

The above mentioned Bible passage means that only the people who obey the Holy Spirit's words and follow them in their
deeds will be able to go to the paradise of God. On the contrary, the people who don't obey the Holy Spirit and not follow
the Holy Spirit's words will not be able to go to heaven.

The word "churches" in the above shown statement means
Christians.

**1 Corinthians 3: 16-17 Do you not know that you are the temple
of God and that the Spirit of God dwells in you? If anyone defiles
the temple of God, God will destroy him. For the temple of God is
holy, which temple you are.**

**Revelation 2: 11 "He who has an ear, let him hear what the
Spirit says to the churches. He who overcomes shall not be hurt by
the second death."**

All human beings must listen to the Holy Spirit and obey

Him and follow Him in deed. It means that the people who obey the Holy Spirit and follow Him in deed to the end will not be thrown into the fiery lake.

Whatever handicaps obstruct you, you must listen to what the Holy Spirit says to the churches and must follow the Holy Spirit's guidance. In order to hear what the Holy Spirit says to you, you must experience the Holy Spirit's ministry and you have to be baptized by the Holy Spirit.

Such people controlled by the Holy Spirit can eat the fruit from the tree of life in heaven. Only such people will go to heaven. And such people will not be hurt by the second death. Therefore we all must participate actively in the worldwide Holy Spirit revival movement.

Revelation 20: 12-15 And I saw the dead, small and great, standing before God, and books were opened. And another book was opened, which is the Book of Life. And the dead were judged according to their works, by the things which were written in the books.

The sea gave up the dead who were in it, and Death and Hades delivered up the dead who were in them. And they were judged, each one according to his works. Then Death and Hades were cast into the lake of fire. This is the second death. And anyone not found written in the Book of Life was cast into the lake of fire.

All human beings will be judged according to what they have done at God's judgment. Those who do not believe in Jesus Christ who was crucified on the cross for our sins, do not confess all their sins before God, do not forgive others' wrong doings, do not obey the Holy Spirit's guidance, but follow only the flesh's greed given by Satan will be thrown into the fiery lake at God's judgment.

God is love and the heavenly Father wants to save our spirits from the fiery lake. Therefore He sent the Holy Spirit to us. And the Holy Spirit came to save all the souls who believe in Jesus, our Lord, the Son of God. God tells you to obey the Holy Spirit and follow His guidance and participate actively in the worldwide Holy Spirit revival movement. This is not for others. The Holy Spirit does the most important ministry to save your spirit and send your soul to heaven.

Revelation 21: 6-8 And He said to me, "It is done! I am the Al-Alpha and the Omega, the Beginning and the End. I will give of the fountain of the water of life freely to him who thirsts. He who overcomes shall inherit all things, and I will be his God and he shall be My son. But the cowardly, unbelieving, abominable, murderers, sexually immoral, sorcerers, idolaters, and all liars shall have their part in the lake which burns with fire and brim-stone, which is the second death."

Here the water of life means the Holy Spirit's water of life. Those who cannot accept the Holy Spirit's water of life, because they are too cowardly and unbelieving of God's words and do not follow God's words, and those who practice magic arts, the idolaters and all liars following Satan's directions, will be thrown into the lake of fire. This is the second death. How fearful these words are! It means that whoever does not receive the Holy Spirit's water of life, because he is too cowardly and does not believe God's words, will be thrown into the lake of fire.

The Holy Spirit will always accept you with love. The Holy Spirit settles everything with Jesus' love but those who deny the Holy Spirit's words, those who do not follow the Holy Spirit's leading to the end will be thrown into the lake of fire. This is the truth of the universe.

Revelation 3: 15-16 "I know your works, that you are neither cold nor hot. I could wish you were cold or hot. So then, because you are lukewarm, and neither cold nor hot, I will vomit you out of My mouth."

I think you understand the above Bible passage. Those who do not follow ardently the Holy Spirit's leading and those who are lukewarm in believing God will be thrown into the lake of fire. Receive the Holy Spirit's baptism to be born again of water and the Holy Spirit, and be led by the Holy Spirit.

Mark 16: 17-18 "And these signs will follow those who believe: In My name they will cast out demons; they will speak with new tongues; they will take up serpents; and if they drink anything deadly, it will by no means hurt them; they will lay hands on the sick, and they will recover."

The Holy Spirit also performs such miracles today all over the world, through Christians who really believe in God from their heart and follow the Holy Spirit's words in deed. We must all believe in God from our heart so that the Holy Spirit may perform miracles through us all. This was what Jesus Christ said to His eleven disciples after He was resurrected from death.

Why must all human beings participate in the worldwide Holy Spirit revival movement?

The Holy Spirit testified to us why all human beings should participate in the worldwide Holy Spirit revival movement by showing many Bible passages telling us that we have to partici- pate. Participating in the Holy Spirit movement is not for the benefit of others. It is for your own eternal life in heaven after you are dead.

John 3: 5 Jesus answered, "Most assuredly, I say to you, unless one is born of water and the Spirit, he cannot enter the kingdom of God."

In order to be born again of water and the Spirit, we must participate in the worldwide Holy Spirit revival movement. Also the Holy Spirit will always be with you and He will lead you to the truth and teach you everything. He will also tell you the things to come in the future.

John 14: 16-17 And I will pray the Father, and He will give you another Helper, that He may abide with you forever--the Spirit of truth, whom the world cannot receive, because it neither sees Him nor knows Him; but you know Him, for He dwells with you and will be in you.

Exactly as Jesus said, the Holy Spirit came to us from heaven on the day of Pentecost in Acts chapter 2. The Holy Spirit came powerfully down to 120 Christians who were heart-fully praying after Jesus ascended to heaven.

Acts 2: 1-4 When the Day of Pentecost had fully come, they were all with one accord in one place. And suddenly there came a sound from heaven, as of a rushing mighty wind, and it filled the whole house where they were sitting. Then there appeared to them divided tongues, as of fire, and one sat upon each of them. And they were all filled with the Holy Spirit and began to speak with other tongues, as the Spirit gave them utterance.

The Holy Spirit performed all kinds of miracles through the Christians who really believed in God and followed the Holy Spirit's words in deed and received the Holy Spirit's powers, exactly as when Jesus was ministering in the world. Right at this moment, also, the Holy Spirit performs all kinds of miracles which are impossible for scientists and medical doctors to perform, all over the world through innumerable Christians who have received the Holy Spirit's power and grace. The Holy Spirit performs innumerable miracles even through the writer of this book at this moment.

In accordance with Jesus' saying in advance, the Holy Spirit is showing all kinds of miracles which no human beings can perform, to testify that all the words recorded in the Bible, the words of almighty God, are true and fact.

John 11: 38-44 Then Jesus, again groaning in Himself, came to the tomb. It was a cave, and a stone lay against it. Jesus said, "Take away the stone."
Martha, the sister of him who was dead, said to Him, "Lord, by this time there is a stench, for he has been dead four days."

**Jesus said to her, "Did I not say to you that if you would believe
you would see the glory of God?" Then they took away the stone
from the place where the dead man was lying.**

**And Jesus lifted up His eyes and said, "Father, I thank You that
that You have heard Me. And I know that You always hear Me,
but because of the people who are standing by I said this, that they
may believe that You sent Me." Now when He had said these
things, He cried with a loud voice, "Lazarus, come forth!" And he
who had died came out bound hand and foot with grave-clothes,
and his face was wrapped with a cloth. Jesus said to them, "Loose
him, and let him go."**

Some people say, "How can a virgin conceive a baby without
a man?" And they assert that the stories in the Bible are the
statements which cannot be proved by science and only foolish
people who do not know the world believe and little children
who know nothing believe the Bible.

The Holy Spirit said the following. The Holy Spirit ministers
through the prayers of Holy Spirit-filled pastors or Christians
all over the world. The tumors of cancer are melting, arthritis
patients who were suffering for many decades are healed, patients with paralysis are healed and walking, blind people read
Bibles and deaf persons are healed and enjoy hearing through
the Holy Spirit's miraculous power all over the world. Patients
who were suffering from incurable diseases couldn't tolerate the
pain, so they were crying.

But when the hands of the Holy Spirit-filled Christians touch
them, the pain stops immediately and the patients dance joyfully and the demons go crying out of the patents. All these are
the Holy Spirit's miracles. Through the writer of this books, the

Holy Spirit also performed innumerable such miracles.

If you want to prove what I say, I invite you to any prayer house or church where the Holy Spirit ministers powerfully. There are countless such prayer houses and churches all over the world. You will be able to see and experience the Holy Spirit's miracles which you haven't experienced, even if you attended church for many decades.

If you can't find such prayer houses or churches, please contact the author of this book, he will gladly guide you to the places where the Holy Spirit ministers powerfully. The Holy Spirit ministers all over the world. No one can prove the Holy Spirit's miracles with science or medical science. The way we can experience the Holy Spirit's ministry is to believe the words of Jesus and follow the Holy Spirit's guidance while obeying the Almighty God's words and praying. That is the only way we can meet and experience the Holy Spirit.

If the Holy Spirit had not ministered so powerfully in the last 2000 years since Jesus was crucified, there would not be so many Christians in the world, today. The Holy Spirit proves and testifies that all that was spoken by Jesus was true. The Holy Spirit proved all that was spoken by Jesus with the Holy Spirit's power, which cannot be testified by science or medical science. Therefore there are innumerable Christians who believe and obey Almighty God in the world.

Whether you believe the words of Jesus or not, heaven, hell, God's judgment, angels and all the spiritual things will stay forever as they have been so far. If there are people who do not believe the words of Jesus but act according to human greed and their own mind, not following the leading of the Holy Spirit, those same people will be lamenting and weeping forever in ever-burning fire of hell.

How can you spend eternity in the fearful ever-burning fiery sea? Whenever I was confronted with the moment of death, Jesus saved me from death and showed me heaven and hell. I saw innumerable spirits wailing and weeping forever in the fiery sulfur burning sea in hell. Jesus said to me, "They did not believe Jesus, almighty God the heavenly Father, and did not obey the Holy Spirit when they were living in the world, therefore they were cast into the fiery lake in hell."

They were so miserable and fearful that I could not see them clearly with human eyes. Therefore I put aside all the things in the world, but instead of them I am now working as a missionary, delivering Jesus' gospel to all the people in the world and following the words of the Holy Spirit in deed, while testifying of the miracles which the Holy Spirit performed through me.

Revelation 2: 11 "He who has an ear, let him hear what the Spirit says to the churches. He who overcomes shall not be hurt by the second death."

This Bible passage means that only the people who obey the Holy Spirit and follow the words of the Holy Spirit in deed to the end will be saved and led to heaven, but those who do not obey the Holy Spirit and not follow the words of the Holy

Spirit will be cast into the sulfur burning fiery lake. We all have to remember the meaning of the message above, which Jesus gave to the apostle John.

I wish all the people in the world would accept Jesus Christ as their Savior Lord and obey the words of the Holy Spirit and participate actively in the worldwide Holy Spirit's revival movement. Participating in the worldwide Holy Spirit's revival movement is not an optional issue which we may select or not. In order to be led to heaven by the Holy Spirit, we all must obey the Holy Spirit.

This is the message given by Jesus, our Savior Lord, to the apostle John for all human beings in the world to follow.

In the name of Jesus we pray that God may change all the readers of this book to obey the Holy Spirit to the end, and that the Holy Spirit may save all of them and lead them to heaven.

The Holy Spirit's words were given at 4:48 am on February 17, 1998 in morning prayer.

2. How to discern between the Holy Spirit and evil spirits, which the Holy Spirit taught me on the basis of the Bible

In early morning prayer on February 20, 1998, the Holy Spirit told me how to discern between the Holy Spirit and evil spirits. Today innumerable pastors and Christians who do not know how to discern between the Holy Spirit and evil spirits believe the words of evil spirits to be the words of the Holy Spirit and sometimes they claim the words of the Holy Spirit to be the words of demons. All these accidents happen because they do not know how to discern between the Holy Spirit and evil spirits.

In order to prevent such accidents from happening again, the Holy Spirit taught the writer of this book how to discern between the Holy Spirit and evil spirits on the basis of the Bible. The following are the words of the Holy Spirit about how to discern between the Holy Spirit and evil spirits.

Galatians 5: 16-26 I say then: Walk in the Spirit, and you shall not fulfill the lust of the flesh. For the flesh lusts against the Spirit, and the Spirit against the flesh; and these are contrary to one another, so that you do not do the things that you wish. But if you are led by the Spirit, you are not under the law. Now the works of the flesh are evident, which are: adultery, fornication, uncleanness, lewdness, idolatry, sorcery, hatred, contentions, jealousies, outbursts of wrath, selfish ambitions, dissensions, heresies, envy, murders, drunkenness, revelries, and the like; of which I tell you beforehand, just as I also told you in time past, that those who practice such things will not inherit the kingdom of God. But the fruit of the Spirit is love, joy, peace, longsuffering, kindness, goodness, faithfulness, gentleness, self-control. Against such there is no law. And those who are Christ's have crucified the

flesh with its passions and desires. If we live in the Spirit, let us also walk in the Spirit. Let us not become conceited, provoking one another, envying one another.

Romans 8: 5-14 For those who live according to the flesh set their minds on the things of the flesh, but those who live according to the Spirit, the things of the Spirit. For to be carnally minded is death, but to be spiritually minded is life and peace. Because the carnal mind is enmity against God; for it is not subject to the law of God, nor indeed can be. So then, those who are in the flesh cannot please God. But you are not in the flesh but in the Spirit, if indeed the Spirit of God dwells in you. Now if anyone does not have the Spirit of Christ, he is not His. And if Christ is in you, the body is dead because of sin, but the Spirit is life because of right-eousness.

But if the Spirit of Him who raised Jesus from the dead dwells in you, He who raised Christ from the dead will also give life to your mortal bodies through His Spirit who dwells in you.

Therefore, brethren, we are debtors--not to the flesh, to live according to the flesh. For if you live according to the flesh you will die; but if by the Spirit you put to death the deeds of the body, you will live. For as many as are led by the Spirit of God, these are sons of God.

As shown in the Bible passages above, the sinful nature and the Holy Spirit are always in conflict each other in our body. If we follow the Holy Spirit's guidance, we will be led to heaven, while bearing the fruits of our works.

However if someone only follows his own selfish mind, human intelligence and dirty temptations which Satan lures him with, the Holy Spirit will leave him. Then when such a person finally dies, he will be cast into the ever burning fire in hell.

Therefore we must all follow only the way of truth which the
Holy Spirit leads. In order to do such things, we must know
how to discern the works done by the Holy Spirit from those
done by Satan or evil spirits. There are innumerable souls who
were thrown into hell, while following the temptation of Satan,
because they were not able to discern the spirits.

To prevent such tragedy, the Holy Spirit taught me how to
tell the difference between the Holy Spirit and Satan, on the
basis of the Bible. He trained me spiritually for many years.
The Holy Spirit asked me to spread how to distinguish between
the spirits, to all Christians. Therefore I testify it to everyone,
all over the world.

gift of discernment

The Holy Spirit wants all the readers of this book to study
and learn how to discern the spirits on the basis of the Bible.
And He wants all of you to pray to God to receive the ability to
differentiate between the spirits for yourself. If you really pray
to God to receive this skill, the Holy Spirit will gladly give it to
you.

It is impossible to tell the spirits apart without the help of the
Holy Spirit, because Satan and evil spirits are always telling
lies in order to lure Christians into permanent destruction. The
Holy Spirit always tells the truth, in accordance with the Bible.

I will describe what the Holy Spirit does and what Satan
for you to learn.

1) The Holy Spirit does the following:

(1) He does only works which can glorify God, and He testifies that Jesus Christ is the only Savior Lord who can save all human beings from their sin.

(2) He does only works which are beneficial to churches.

(3) He does all His efforts in raising "The Worldwide Holy Spirit Revival Movement" to save all the human beings in the world and to deliver the gospel all over the world. And He performs many different miracles to inform all the people in the world that nowadays the Holy Spirit still does His ministries.

(4) He asks you to deliver the gospel to all the people in the world and lead them to God.

(5) He asks you to visit patients in hospitals and lead them to believe Jesus Christ.

(6) He says everything according to the Holy Bible.

(7) He always makes you happy, glad, peaceful, and He gives you love. He makes you love others, even if someone wants to fight against you. He makes your heart want to give something to others, even if you have nothing with you.

(8) He always speaks with a soft, clear voice having love, kindness, gentleness and tenderness beyond expression.

(9) He never speaks any vulgar or bad words to anyone.

(10) Even though I am very upset and mad with someone, my anger melts like snow when I hear His voice.

(11) Sometimes His voice shakes the world. But I find love, tenderness and gentleness in His voice.

(12) He never says anything about others, but He tells me to do only the works which will glorify God.

(13) He never tells you how to make big money just for yourself. However He prepares for you the funds to be used for

the glory of God. He gives His unlimited blessings to the Christians who really believe in God and financially support His ministry in deed. Sometimes He performs financial miracles for His children who financially support His ministry.

(14) He asks you to live your life according to the Holy Bible.

(15) He does not want you to have a great deal of money.

(16) He asks you to help starving, poor people. But He wants you to help first the people whom you can lead to Jesus Christ.

(17) He wants big churches to give money to save the poor, starving people and lead them to God instead of spending the same money for expanding the churches' assets.

(18) He wants you to be satisfied with what you have, and compare yourself with the people who are poorer than you.

(19) When you are depressed by seeing rich people, He reminds you of the things made of solid gold and diamonds in heaven, and leads you to think that the riches in the world cannot be compared with the ones in heaven.

(20) He never wants you to decide, judge and convict others.

(21) He asks all human beings to throw away greed. If you are continuously baptized by the Holy Spirit's powerful anointing, your greedy mind will vanish from you.

(22) He never wants you to talk wrongly of others, and He wants you to be very careful in speaking.

(23) He wants everybody to be led by the Holy Spirit.

(24) He never lets you commit adultery.

(25) He never wants you to drink any alcoholic drinks. If you are drunk, you cannot communicate with the Holy Spirit.

(26) He wants us to praise and worship God in Holy Spirit-filled churches. In such churches, Christians are dancing, singing, clapping hands, falling on the floor, speaking in heavenly

tongues, prophesying, and seeing visions. They are enjoying God's party at the Holy Spirit's invitation. In such way they are baptized in Holy Spirit's power.

(27) He asks us to confess our sins and forgive others everyday.

(28) He asks us to praise and worship God, pray and confess before God, and read the Bible everyday.

(29) He wants to talk with us directly.

(30) He cannot talk with us directly because our spirit is completely surrounded by our flesh's greed and sin.

(31) If we really believe 100% in God and all the words of the Bible as they are written, and if we change our life per the Bible and confess all our sins everyday, He will open a channel for us to talk with Him directly, whenever we want.

(32) When Satan or devils tell us groundless lies, the Holy Spirit will show us a special sign by making our heart uneasy, shaking, or pounding to inform us that devils are telling us lies.

(33) If you have spiritual sight, He will immediately show you a vision that Satan or devils are lying. But such things will be given to you when you experience a lot of the Holy Spirit's ministries.

(34) He wants us to check all messages from spirits with the Holy Bible as our standard mirror. The Holy Bible is the word from God, who tells only the truth, that will lead us to understand the truth.

(35) If you receive the words from the Holy Spirit in prayer, those words will be realized into fruit.

If you cannot discern between the Holy Spirit and evil spirits, please keep record all the words given by the Holy Spirit and wait for some time. If the words were given by the Holy Spirit, they will bear the fruit. If the words were given by devils, they will be finished into nothing. If you have many words from the Holy Spirit, some will be realized early and others will be realized later.

To experience the fruit of the Holy Spirit, we have to follow the words of the Holy Spirit in deed.

(36) The Holy Spirit speaks only the truth, He never lets you tell lies.

(37) If you receive the method of how to identify the Holy Spirit from devils directly, your heart will be changed to show thc fruits of the Holy Spirit.

Galatians 5: 22-26 But the fruit of the Spirit is love, joy, peace, longsuffering, kindness, goodness, faithfulness, gentleness, self-control. Against such there is no law. And those who are Christ's have crucified the flesh with its passions and desires. If we live in the Spirit, let us also walk in the Spirit. Let us not become conceited, provoking one another, envying one another.

When you will have the Spirit's fruit as above, then the Holy Spirit will open a channel for you to talk with the Holy Spirit any time you want. This is the way the Holy Spirit leads you step-by-step to heaven, carrying a cross on your back. In addition to these methods to identify the Holy Spirit, there are innumerable other ways. I cannot record everything now.

2) Satan does the following:

(1) Satan always works against God.

(2) If any spirit tries to lead you away from the direction

which the Holy Spirit tries to lead you to, please think that spirit must be Satan, a devil, or a demon. You are 99% correct.

(3) If any spirit approaches you by speaking in soft words, ask him to tell you everything according to the Holy Bible. If the spirit is the Holy Spirit, He will explain everything according to the Bible for you to understand easily, while looking in the Bible. However if the spirit is an evil spirit, he will try to lure you with other deceits, because he was found to be evil in the light of the Holy Spirit's presence.

(4) If that spirit is found to be Satan, a devil, or a demon, do not be embarrassed at all. Arrest them boldly with the name of Jesus and chase them out of your flesh with the name of Jesus Christ, the Holy Spirit's power, and the almighty heavenly Father's words.

Evil spirits will tell all kinds of lies to us. However we should not be deceived by their deceitful lure. We have to chase them out of our flesh. If we fully understand how to discern between the Holy Spirit and evil spirits, as taught by the Holy Spirit in this book, evil spirits will go crying out of your flesh, because their presence was revealed by the Holy Spirit's anointing.

However we have to always be careful. We have to compare what the Holy Spirit told in prayer with the Bible and we have to wait to see the fruits of the words of the Holy Spirit. The Holy Spirit always moves us with His unlimited love, peace and joy. If you pray for the Lord to show you how to discern the spirits, He will give it to you without fail. If you apply what the Holy Spirit teaches you in this chapter, you will easily be able to discern the spirits' deceits.

We pray under the name of Jesus Christ for the almighty heavenly Father to give the Holy Spirit's power to discern the spirits to all the readers of this book.

The Holy Spirit's words were given in early morning prayer on February 20, 1998.

3. How to cast out demons, the Holy Spirit taught me

1) The method of chasing away Satan and evil demons

My innumerable servants, pastors who have not experienced the Holy Spirit's ministries, do not know how to chase Satan or devils from Christians who are attending their churches.

If any Christian going to their church speaks any strange words, such pastors are embarrassed and have an incorrect view, thinking this person is caught by an evil spirit, demon, heretic, mystic or is out of their mind. All these kinds of pastors' judgments come from their having no spiritual experience of the Holy Spirit's ministries.

The pastors who were educated and trained in accordance

with human reason, knowledge, information and learning in theological schools, yet do not have any experience of the Holy Spirit's ministry cannot settle this kind of spiritual problem.

However the pastors or Christians who have experienced the Holy Spirit's ministries many times can easily chase Satan or demons out of Christians with spiritual problems. But the devils which were chased out of your body may enter you again, therefore the best way is to chase them out of your body for yourself.

Matthew 12: 43-45 "When an unclean spirit goes out of a man, he goes through dry places, seeking rest, and finds none. Then he says, "I will return to my house from which I came.' And when he comes, he finds it empty, swept, and put in order. Then he goes and takes with him seven other spirits more wicked than himself, and they enter and dwell there; and the last state of that man is worse than the first. So shall it also be with this wicked generation."

In Seoul, Korea, sometimes you see people wearing worn out and ripped clothes, in bare feet without any shoes, carrying the name Jesus Christ all over their clothes, hat, and everywhere else, and yelling all over the street. These are people who were good believers of God.

Once the Holy Spirit is present with them, the evil spirits that have been with him for a long time will be revealed by the Holy Spirit's power. Then these evil spirits start lying and speaking as if they are the Holy Spirit.

In this way, the evil spirits command him to do such things which do not glorify Jesus Christ. Such persons do not know how to discern between the Holy Spirit and evil spirits. Therefore these poor people are deceived by evil spirits. Such persons are abandoned by their families and churches and are wandering in the streets, begging and yelling.

From now on if you find such persons, do not run away from them. Do not take them to mental hospitals. They cannot be cured by the medical doctors working in hospitals. Only the Holy Spirit can cure such people suffering from mental diseases caused by the evil spirits in the world.

Instead, please approach them and teach them how to discern between the Holy Spirit and evil spirits, which you will learn in this book. Please arrest the evil spirits deceiving such persons in the name of Jesus, and cast the evil spirits out of such people forever in the name of Jesus, with the Holy Spirit's power and the words of the Almighty heavenly Father.

Please give them the book *Holy Spirit, Hover Over Me* to read carefully and please lead such mental patients to the churches or prayer houses where the Holy Spirit ministers powerfully. Ask them to read *Holy Spirit, Hover Over Me* and the Bible (from the beginning of Matthew to the end of Acts) continuously, and they will be changed into really good Christians.

As explained above, please teach such mental patients how to discern between the Holy Spirit and evil spirits. When mental patients begin to understand how to discern the spirits, the evil spirits will begin to leave them. When such mental patients understand fully how to discern between the Holy Spirit and evil spirits, and if those patients continue to cast out the evil spirits in the name of Jesus, the evil spirits will leave them crying, because they cannot deceive this person any more, in the presence of the Holy Spirit.

There are no spirits that are stronger than the Holy Spirit. The Holy Spirit is present in the bodies of all Christians who really believe in Jesus and Almighty God. We want to ask you to command to courageously arrest all the evil spirits in the name of Jesus and cast them away into the ever burning fiery lake of hell under the name of Jesus, the Holy Spirit's power, and the words of the Almighty heavenly Father. If the evil spirits do not leave them, please ask the mental patients to carefully read this book, *Holy Spirit, Hover Over Me*, a few more times, while praying. While they are reading this book, the Holy Spirit will pour more anointing on the patients and the evil spirits will leave them crying.

2) The Holy Spirit and fleshly lusts are fighting one another in your body

A) Spirit
Your spirit was planted in your heart by the Holy Spirit when you accepted Jesus Christ as your savior. That spirit always stays in your heart. If you are born again by the Holy Spirit's power or if you attend the Holy Spirit-inspired services often, your spirit will grow steadily.

Your spirit knows only God's works. He does only the works which will glorify God. Therefore the Holy Spirit always stays with your spirit and He talks only with your spirit. He never talks with your flesh or mind. Therefore it is very difficult for you to receive the answer directly from the Holy Spirit.

B) The Flesh's Lusts

The flesh's thoughts control all human knowledge, reason, learning, and information in the brain. Satan controls the flesh's lust. The flesh's lust is completely controlled by Satan, therefore it works in accordance with Satan's instructions. Murder, greed, adultery, idolatry and witchcraft; all such bad things are produced by Satan and they are directed by the flesh's lusts, controlled by Satan. The flesh follows its lust's instructions directed by Satan. As a result of this chain, the flesh works for Satan.

C) The Flesh

The flesh does all the bad works instructed by the flesh's lusts controlled by Satan. Satan does the following. *Talking about keeping old low*

Matthew 15: 19-20 For out of the heart proceed evil thoughts, murders, adulteries, fornications, thefts, false witness, blasphemies. These are the things which defile a man, but to eat with unwashed hands does not defile a man.

If you read Romans 1: 28-32, Galatians 5: 19-21, and 2 Timothy 3: 1-8 in the Bible, you will understand what Satan does.

Therefore in your body there is a spiritual war between your spirit and flesh's lusts. That war is between the Holy Spirit and Satan. That is the war between good and evil.

Galatians 5: 16-26 I say then: Walk in the Spirit, and you shall not fulfill the lust of the flesh. For the flesh lusts against the Spirit, and the Spirit against the flesh; and these are contrary to one another, so that you do not do the things that you wish. But if you

are led by the Spirit, you are not under the law. Now the works of the flesh are evident, which are: adultery, fornication, uncleanness, lewdness, idolatry, sorcery, hatred, contentions, jealousies, outbursts of wrath, selfish ambitions, dissensions, heresies, envy, murders, drunkenness, revelries, and the like; of which I tell you beforehand, just as I also told you in time past, that those who practice such things will not inherit the kingdom of God.

But the fruit of the Spirit is love, joy, peace, longsuffering, kindness, goodness, faithfulness, gentleness, self-control. Against such there is no law. And those who are Christ's have crucified the flesh with its passions and desires. If we live in the Spirit, let us also walk in the Spirit. Let us not become conceited, provoking one another, envying one another.

In this war, if the Holy Spirit wins the victory, you will be led to heaven under His guidance. On the contrary, if you are stubborn and greedy, following only the flesh's lusts controlled by Satan, when you die you will be thrown eternally into the fiery sulfur sea of hell.

In order to win the victory for Jesus Christ, you must be fully inspired by the Holy Spirit by experiencing the Holy Spirit's ministries. You must have a strong determination to win the victory for Jesus by following the Holy Spirit's guidance, continuously reading *Holy Spirit, Hover Over Me* and the Holy Bible from the beginning of Matthew to the end of Acts in turn, following the instructions and advice of the pastors and Christians who have a lot of spiritual experience in the Holy Spirit's ministry.

Never be afraid of such spiritual warfare in your body. There are wars between the Holy Spirit and Satan in the pastors,

Christians, or any human beings who do not have Holy Spirit experiences and are not fully inspired by the Holy Spirit. The spiritual wars in your heart which are so important will lead you to heaven or hell after you die.

1 John 4: 4 You are of God, little children, and have overcome them, because He who is in you is greater than he who is in the world.

3) The evil spirits are chased away from your body by the Holy Spirit

The evil spirits, such as Satan, devils, or demons, obstruct and confuse Holy Spirit-inspired Christians and pastors. Christians and pastors who have not experienced the Holy Spirit's ministries know nothing about Satan's obstructions and simply follow the flesh's lusts, doing works controlled by Satan. Therefore it is not necessary for Satan to bother such pastors and Christians who are following the flesh's instructions.

However when the Holy Spirit enters your body with strong, fully-inspired Holy Spirit power, shining with Jesus' powerful light, all the evil spirits which have been hidden in your body for a long time, are revealed clearly in the bright light of the Holy Spirit's power. Therefore such evil spirits are scared to death and are at a loss of what to do.

They know that they cannot fight against the Holy Spirit's power, but will be chased out of your body by the Holy Spirit's power. They begin to confuse you with lies, frauds, threats, and groundless rumors.

Luke 11: 20-22 But if I cast out demons with the finger of God, surely the kingdom of God has come upon you. When a strong man, fully armed, guards his own palace, his goods are in peace. But when a stronger than he comes upon him and overcomes him, he takes from him all his armor in which he trusted, and divides his spoils.

As in the Bible statement above, if you drive out demons by the finger of God, then the kingdom of God has come to you. You do not need to be embarrassed at such evil spirits' acts, groundless lies, frauds, or threats. But be calm and ask pastors or Christians who have a lot of experience with the Holy Spirit's ministries and follow their advice.

Any human being, whether he or she is Christian or non-Christian, if any Holy Spirit empowered pastor or Christian prays spiritually and gives them the Holy Spirit's power with Jesus' love and light to the person who receives the prayer, immediately innumerable evil spirits, Satan, or demons in the darkness which have been controlling his or her soul for a long time will be at a loss. And they will try to get out of him or her.

Matthew 8: 28-34 When He had come to the other side, to the country of the Gergesenes, there met Him two demon-possessed men, coming out of the tombs, exceedingly fierce, so that no one could pass that way. And suddenly they cried out, saying, "What have we to do with You, Jesus, You Son of God? Have You come here to torment us before the time?" Now a good way off from them there was a herd of many swine feeding. So the demons begged Him, saying, "If You cast us out, permit us to go away into

the herd of swine." And He said to them, "Go." So when they had come out, they went into the herd of swine. And suddenly the whole herd of swine ran violently down the steep place into the sea, and perished in the water.

Then those who kept them fled; and they went away into the city and told everything, including what had happened to the demon-possessed men. And behold, the whole city came out to meet Jesus. And when they saw Him, they begged Him to depart from their region.

Luke 8: 30 Jesus asked him, saying, "What is your name?" And he said, "Legion," because many demons had entered him.

You know that such a great number of demons entered into two people. Such evil spirits can be chased away only by the name of Jesus Christ, The Holy Spirit's power and the words of the Almighty heavenly Father. No other names can chase them out of your body.

These evil spirits are the ones which have been controlling your soul and flesh and leading you in Satan's direction for long time. If you do not chase them out of your body and if you believe their lies, frauds, threats or groundless rumors, you will be heretics and false prophets.

Never try to settle such spiritual problems by yourselves, but consult with a pastor or a Christian who has a lot of experience in the Holy Spirit's ministries, and follow their advice.

In order to lead you in the direction which the Holy Spirit

leads, the Holy Spirit directly told you how to discern between the Holy Spirit and Satan in the previous chapters. Never be embarrassed or scared or afraid. Whoever he is, the person who does not have much Holy Spirit ministries, if a Holy Spirit-inspired pastor or Christian prays spiritually, you will see that a great number of evil spirits in darkness are embarrassed and try to get out of him.

Sometimes we may see some pastors or elders who were really good believers of God and who performed a lot of the Holy Spirit's miracles through them, suddenly deny the Holy Spirit's ministry and Jesus to be the Son of God, but declare himself or herself to be the resurrected Jesus Christ or God in the world.

Such people who have been leading a great multitude of church members do not believe the words of the Bible but make special doctrines for themselves against the Holy Bible and finally became chief of the heretic sects. Such people who did not know how to discern between the Holy Spirit and evil spirits or demons were deceived by evil spirits and finally became heretical. Most of these people do not read the Bible a lot and do not know how to discern the spirits, therefore they became heretics.

You are able to cast the evil spirits that deceive such heretic leaders from them, in the name of Jesus and by the Holy Spirit's power. However such heretic leaders do not know that they are being deceived by evil spirits telling lies, that they are the resurrected Jesus or God. In addition to that, a great multitude of people who do not know how to discern the spirits follow such heretical leaders. They are so deeply indulged in the deceit of demons and evil spirits that they do not even try to learn how to discern the spirits.

We have to be filled with the Holy Spirit's anointing in accordance with the words of the Bible. And we have to go to church and read the Bible continuously. The Holy Spirit leads us to read the Bible continuously. The Holy Spirit leads us in the right direction towards eternal life, while educating us with the words of the Bible. If any spirit lures you to follow it without any words of the Bible, it is not the Holy Spirit. If it is found to be an evil spirit that tells you lies, you must chase it out of your body.

But if you do not confess your sin continuously, it may come into your body again. Therefore the Holy Spirit asks you to confess every day and read *Holy Spirit, Hover Over Me* and the Bible continuously, and when you read them, the Holy Spirit will give you more Holy Spirit's power and will chase them away. And you have to attend the Holy Spirit's services and experience Him yourself and try to chase out the evil spirits in darkness for yourself. Therefore I will teach you how to chase out evil spirits.

4) Spiritual war

Even the strongest and most powerful demons are like mice in front of the Holy Spirit. It means that evil spirits are powerless before the Holy Spirit. And you must chase them out of your body completely by the name of Jesus Christ, the Holy Spirit's power, and the Almighty heavenly Father's words.

It is not that chasing the demons out of your body is performed only by certain pastors. If any Christian who believes the Bible 100%, received a lot of the Holy Spirit's power, and experienced a lot of the Holy Spirit's ministries, prays to God under the name of Jesus while reading the Bible, the Holy Spirit performs His ministry to chase the demons out of your body.

Mark 16: 17-18 And these signs will follow those who believe: In My name they will cast out demons; they will speak with new tongues; they will take up serpents; and if they drink anything deadly, it will by no means hurt them; they will lay hands on the sick, and they will recover.

As we can see from the statement above, after prayer to God under the name of Jesus, commanding the demons to be arrested by the name of Jesus, and chasing them away from your body by the name of Jesus, the Holy Spirit's power, and Almighty God's words, you will immediately feel that the demons are chased away from your body. The above shown Bible passage is greatly used in casting out the evil spirits from human bodies by many Holy Spirit filled pastors and Christians.

Do not be disappointed at all, when you find that they are not completely arrested and chased out of your body. They come into your body and go out as they want. Please read this book *Holy Spirit, Hover Over Me* a couple of times more carefully while praying to God. When you read this book, the Holy Spirit will pour more anointing on your body. After reading this book, please arrest the evil spirits and cast them away from your body, and they will leave your body crying.

Whenever you need to chase out demons, do it by yourself, in the same way that you learned from a pastor or Christian who has experienced the Holy Spirit's ministries a lot. Continue to read this book and the Bible in turn. About reading the Bible to chase away evil spirits, I want you to read only the following: from the beginning of Matthew to the end of Acts in the New Testament and confess your sin before God everyday, while attending the Holy Spirit's ministry services.

The more you read this book and the Bible, the more you confess your sins before God, the more often you attend the Holy Spirit's services, and the more Jesus' light enters into your body, the weaker the evil spirits in your body will be and finally they will go out completely, crying and looking for a new place. And the Holy Spirit will control your soul 100%.

This is the spiritual war in your body. This is the way to heaven, carrying a cross on your back, step-by-step, under the guidance of the Holy Spirit. All human beings have such spiritual problems in their bodies, therefore Jesus said the following:

John 3: 3 Jesus answered and said to him, "Most assuredly, I say to you, unless one is born again, he cannot see the kingdom of God."

Now you understand why you must participate in the Holy Spirit's services and must be baptized by the Holy Spirit. I want all of you to follow the way which leads to heaven under the guidance of the Holy Spirit. The Holy Spirit wants to lead all of us to eternal life in heaven where the Almighty heavenly Father and His Son, our Savior Lord Jesus Christ, are staying forever.

The Holy Spirit's words were given at 4:45 AM on February 23, 1998 in morning prayer.

4. Phenomena which appear when the Holy Spirit is present with you

On January 22, 2000 a pastor asked me, "What kind of phenomenon appears, when the Holy Spirit is present with us?" The Holy Spirit replied as follows.

1) The phenomenon happens when people are clapping hands, dancing and singing

2 Timothy 3: 16 All Scripture is given by inspiration of God, and is profitable for doctrine, for reproof, for correction, for instruction in righteousness,

The Bible is the word of God and nothing is wrong in God's

word, and it is all the truth. Therefore we have to find the words in the Bible and make sure of what is written in the Bible. In the Bible there are many paragraphs and sentences asking us to sing and praise God joyfully.

Psalm 149: 1-3 Praise the Lord! Sing to the Lord a new song, And His praise in the assembly of saints. Let Israel rejoice in their Maker; Let the children of Zion be joyful in their King.
Let them praise His name with the dance; Let them sing praises to Him with the timbrel and harp.

Psalm 47: 1 Oh, clap your hands, all you peoples! Shout to God with the voice of triumph!

Psalm 63: 2-4 So I have looked for You in the sanctuary, To see Your power and Your glory. Because Your loving-kindness is better than life, My lips shall praise You. Thus I will bless You while I live; I will lift up my hands in Your name.

Psalm 100: 1 Make a joyful shout to the Lord, all you lands!

As in the Bible passages above, God asks His children, His sons and daughters to raise their hands up, clap hands, sing praises and dance in His presence. When unbelievers see such phenomenon, it looks like Christians are crazy and out of their minds. However we are the sons and daughters of Almighty God, it is natural that we should sing praises and dance in the presence of the Holy Spirit like little children do.

Mark 10: 15 Assuredly, I say to you, whoever does not receive the kingdom of God as a little child will by no means enter it.

Romans 14: 16-17 Therefore do not let your good be spoken of as evil; for the kingdom of God is not eating and drinking, but righteousness and peace and joy in the Holy Spirit.

As the Bible shows above, Jesus said, "Whoever does not receive the kingdom of God as a little child will by no means enter it." Therefore we do not need to be shameful of singing praises and dancing joyfully before God. Please sing praises joyfully and dance merrily, as much as you can, in the presence of the Holy Spirit. And the Holy Spirit will anoint you to enjoy peace, love, and joy in the Holy Spirit, who will lead you to heaven.

Psalm 16: 11 You will show me the path of life; In Your presence is fullness of joy; At Your right hand are pleasures forevermore.

2) Falling on the floor and trembling

When the Holy Spirit is present, human beings cannot endure His power, so they fall down and tremble.

Acts 9: 3-6 As he journeyed he came near Damascus, and suddenly a light shone around him from heaven. Then he fell to the ground, and heard a voice saying to him, "Saul, Saul, why are you persecuting Me?" And he said, "Who are You, Lord?" Then the Lord said, "I am Jesus, whom you are persecuting. It is hard for you to kick against the goads." So he, trembling and astonished, said, "Lord, what do You want me to do?" Then the Lord said to

him, "Arise and go into the city, and you will be told what you
must do."

Revelation 1: 17-19 And when I saw Him, I fell at His feet as
dead. But He laid His right hand on me, saying to me, "Do not be
afraid; I am the First and the Last. I am He who lives, and was
dead, and behold, I am alive forevermore. Amen. And I have the
keys of Hades and of Death. Write the things which you have seen,
and the things which are, and the things which will take place
after this."

Ezekiel 1: 28, 2:1-3 Like the appearance of a rainbow in a cloud
on a rainy day, so was the appearance of the brightness all around
it. This was the appearance of the likeness of the glory of the
LORD. So when I saw it, I fell on my face, and I heard a voice of
One speaking.

And He said to me, "Son of man, stand on your feet, and I
will speak to you." Then the Spirit entered me when He spoke
to me, and set me on my feet; and I heard Him who spoke to
me. And He said to me: "Son of man, I am sending you to the
children of Israel, to a rebellious nation that has rebelled
against Me; they and their fathers have transgressed against Me
to this very day."

Ezekiel 3: 22-24 Then the hand of the LORD was upon me there,
there, and He said to me, "Arise, go out into the plain, and there I
shall talk with you." So I arose and went out into the plain, and
behold, the glory of the LORD stood there, like the glory which I
saw by the River Chebar; and I fell on my face. Then the Spirit
entered me and set me on my feet, and spoke with me and said to
me: "Go, shut yourself inside your house."

Matthew 28: 1-4 Now after the Sabbath, as the first day of the week began to dawn, Mary Magdalene and the other Mary came to see the tomb. And behold, there was a great earthquake; for an angel of the Lord descended from heaven, and came and rolled back the stone from the door, and sat on it. His countenance was like lightning, and his clothing as white as snow. And the guards shook for fear of him, and became like dead men.

Daniel 5: 5-6 In the same hour the fingers of a man's hand appeared and wrote opposite the lamp-stand on the plaster of the wall of the king's palace; and the king saw the part of the hand that wrote. 6 Then the king's countenance changed, and his thoughts troubled him, so that the joints of his hips were loosened and his knees knocked against each other.

Daniel 10: 5-11 I lifted my eyes and looked, and behold, a certain man clothed in linen, whose waist was girded with gold of Uphaz! His body was like beryl, his face like the appearance of lightning, his eyes like torches of fire, his arms and feet like burnished bronze in color, and the sound of his words like the voice of a multitude.

And I, Daniel, alone saw the vision, for the men who were with me did not see the vision; but a great terror fell upon them, so that they fled to hide themselves. Therefore I was left alone when I saw this great vision, and no strength remained in me; for my vigor was turned to frailty in me, and I retained no strength. Yet I heard the sound of his words; and while I heard the sound of his words I was in a deep sleep on my face, with my face to the ground.

Suddenly, a hand touched me, which made me tremble on my knees and on the palms of my hands. And he said to me, "O Daniel, man greatly beloved, understand the words that I speak to you,

and stand upright, for I have now been sent to you." While he was
speaking this word to me, I stood trembling.

As in the Bible passages above, when the Holy Spirit's powerful anointing falls upon men, they fall down to the ground.
Some people are trembling, some are laughing, some are speaking in heavenly tongues and some are seeing visions of the
Holy Spirit and heaven.

Apostles like Paul and John, and prophets like Ezekiel and
Daniel, they all fell down to the ground and trembled when
they met God. This is a normal phenomenon when you meet
the Holy Spirit. Through this kind of process, you are baptized
in the Holy Spirit's power. People who experience such Holy
Spirit's ministry are changed greatly in their hearts.

3) Holy laughing

Job 8:20-22 Behold, God will not cast away the blameless, Nor
will He uphold the evildoers. He will yet fill your mouth with
laughing, And your lips with rejoicing. Those who hate you will be
clothed with shame, And the dwelling place of the wicked will
come to nothing.

Psalm 126: 1-3 When the Lord brought back the captivity of
Zion, We were like those who dream. Then our mouth was filled
with laughter, And our tongue with singing. Then they said
among the nations, "The Lord has done great things for them."
The Lord has done great things for us, And we are glad.

Matthew 5: 11 Blessed are you when they revile and persecute
you, and say all kinds of evil against you falsely for My sake.

Luke 6: 21-23 Blessed are you who hunger now, For you shall be filled. Blessed are you who weep now, For you shall laugh. Blessed are you when men hate you, And when they exclude you, And revile you, and cast out your name as evil, For the Son of Man's sake. Rejoice in that day and leap for joy! For indeed your reward is great in heaven, For in like manner their fathers did to the prophets.

As shown in the above mentioned Bible passages, when the Holy Spirit is present with us, holy laughter sometimes continues without stopping for two or three hours. This is the Holy Spirit's ministry. When the holy laughter stops, the difficult problems we had are solved by themselves and our hearts become peaceful and we rejoice in love from God. This is the Holy Spirit's baptism.

4) Speaking in heavenly tongues, translating tongues, prophecy, healing the sick, performing miracles and seeing visions

1 Corinthians 12: 4-11 There are diversities of gifts, but the same Spirit. There are differences of ministries, but the same Lord. And there are diversities of activities, but it is the same God who works all in all.
But the manifestation of the Spirit is given to each one for the profit of all: for to one is given the word of wisdom through the Spirit, to another the word of knowledge through the same Spirit, to another faith by the same Spirit, to another the gift of healing by the same Spirit, to another the working of miracles, to another prophecy, to another discerning of spirits, to another different

kinds of tongues, to another the interpretation of tongues. But one
and the same Spirit works all these things, distributing to each one
individually as He wills.

As in this Bible passage, the Holy Spirit distributes many
kinds of power to each one individually, as He wills.

**1 Corinthians 12: 30-31 Do all have gifts of healings? Do all
speak with tongues? Do all interpret? But earnestly desire the best
gifts. And yet I show you a more excellent way.**

**Acts 2: 1-18 When the Day of Pentecost had fully come, they
were all with one accord in one place. And suddenly there came a
sound from heaven, as of a rushing mighty wind, and it filled the
whole house where they were sitting. Then there appeared to them
divided tongues, as of fire, and one sat upon each of them. And
they were all filled with the Holy Spirit and began to speak with
other tongues, as the Spirit gave them utterance.**
**And there were dwelling in Jerusalem Jews, devout men, from
every nation under heaven. And when this sound occurred, the
multitude came together, and were confused, because everyone
heard them speak in his own language. Then they were all amazed
and marveled, saying to one another, "Look, are not all these who
speak Galileans? And how is it that we hear, each in our own language in which we were born?**
**Parthians and Medes and Elamites, those dwelling in Mesopo-
tamia, Judea and Cappadocia, Pontus and Asia, Phrygia and
Pamphylia, Egypt and the parts of Libya adjoining Cyrene, visitors from Rome, both Jews and proselytes, Cretans and Arabs--
we hear them speaking in our own tongues the wonderful works
of God." So they were all amazed and perplexed, saying to one
another, "Whatever could this mean?" Others mocking said,**

"They are full of new wine." But Peter, standing up with the eleven, raised his voice and said to them, "Men of Judea and all who dwell in Jerusalem, let this be known to you, and heed my words.

For these are not drunk, as you suppose, since it is only the third hour of the day. But this is what was spoken by the prophet Joel: "And it shall come to pass in the last days, says God, That I will pour out of My Spirit on all flesh; Your sons and your daughters shall prophesy, Your young men shall see visions, Your old men shall dream dreams. And on My menservants and on My maidservants I will pour out My Spirit in those days; And they shall prophesy."

In these Bible passages, when all the disciples of Jesus Christ spoke in the Galilean tongue, all the other Jews who came from different countries heard them speak in their own languages where they were born. This is why the Holy Spirit gave the gift of interpretation of tongues to each Jew.

Acts 10: 44-45 While Peter was still speaking these words, the Holy Spirit fell upon all those who heard the word. And those of the circumcision who believed were astonished, as many as came with Peter, because the gift of the Holy Spirit had been poured out on the Gentiles also.

As in the Bible passages above, when the powerful Holy Spirit is present with you, the Holy Spirit performs His ministry through you today, exactly same as He did through the disciples of Jesus in the first century.

When the Holy Spirit is present with us, sometimes the Holy

Spirit's tongue comes automatically from our mouth, and we can't stop speaking in tongues. When Christians who received the gift of interpretation of tongues speak in heavenly tongues, saying tatata dododo, at the same time the Holy Spirit tells them the exact meaning in a low soft voice in their brain. Sometimes the Holy Spirit informs the Christians who received the gift of interpretation of the meaning of other Christians who speak in tongues.

It is difficult for Christians who haven't experienced the Holy Spirit's ministries to understand such miracles performed by the Holy Spirit. Only Christians who have experienced such ministries will understand that it is the Holy Spirit's ministries through which Christians are being baptized and filled with the Holy Spirit who leads us to heaven.

John 3: 3-7 Jesus answered and said to him, "Most assuredly, I say to you, unless one is born again, he cannot see the kingdom of God." Nicodemus said to Him, "How can a man be born when he is old? Can he enter a second time into his mother's womb and be born?" Jesus answered, "Most assuredly, I say to you, unless one is born of water and the Spirit, he cannot enter the kingdom of God. That which is born of the flesh is flesh, and that which is born of the Spirit is spirit. Do not marvel that I said to you, 'You must be born again.'"

John 14: 6 Jesus said to him, "I am the way, the truth, and the life. No one comes to the Father except through Me."

Our Savior Jesus Christ, the King of Kings in the universe said this. Who can dare challenge Jesus Christ? We all must follow what Jesus said and the way which the Holy Spirit leads. We don't have to judge anything by seeing the appearance of the Holy Spirit's ministry. All such things such as anxiety, un-easiness, jealousy, greed and the heart which didn't like to read the Bible are disappearing by the Holy Spirit's baptism.

As a result of that, peace, joy, and love are overflowing in our hearts. All who have experienced such a Holy Spirit bap-tism will have hearts to believe the Bible 100% as it is written. And such people will be changed into the people who only want to read the Bible. Such people cannot pass unbelievers without delivering Jesus' gospel to them. In addition to that, the heart which was full of the flesh's greed and selfishness are changed to bear the fruit of the Holy Spirit.

Galatians 5: 22-23 But the fruit of the Spirit is love, joy, peace, longsuffering, kindness, goodness, faithfulness, gentleness, self-control. Against such there is no law.

This means that ones who bear such fruit of the Holy Spirit will be automatically led to heaven. That is, there is no law which prevents such people from going to heaven. The Holy Spirit leads such people to heaven.

Romans 8: 12-14 Therefore, brethren, we are debtors--not to the flesh, to live according to the flesh. For if you live according to the flesh you will die; but if by the Spirit you put to death the deeds of the body, you will live. For as many as are led by the Spirit of God, these are sons of God.

All the infirmities of your flesh will be cured. This is the process of being baptized and being born again in the Holy

Spirit.

It is the Holy Spirit's worldwide movement which teaches and leads you to the Holy Spirit's powerful ministry and baptism to be born again in the Holy Spirit.

The Holy Spirit's words were given in early morning prayer on January 22, 2000.

5. Be careful about false prophets

At 9:08 am on May 17, 1997 in morning prayer, the Holy Spirit said the following about false prophets.

Matthew 7: 15-20 "Beware of false prophets, who come to you in sheep's clothing, but inwardly they are ravenous wolves. You will know them by their fruits. Do men gather grapes from thornbushes or figs from thistles? Even so, every good tree bears good fruit, but a bad tree bears bad fruit. A good tree cannot bear bad fruit, nor can a bad tree bear good fruit. Every tree that does not bear good fruit is cut down and thrown into the fire. Therefore by their fruits you will know them."

When I finished reading the above statements, the Holy Spirit told me the following:

The false prophets pretend to believe in God, but they really do not believe in God. Instead they are founders of heretical religious groups and they insist and pretend that they are the sons of God in place of Jesus, or they are gods who lure and tempt people to the wrong direction. In the world, there are innumerable people who have made their own religions and insist that they are gods.

Such heretical religious sects do not recognize the God of the trinity. Some of them recognize God but do not recognize Jesus Christ and the Holy Spirit, and insist that Jesus is one of the prophets. In addition to that they ignore the Holy Spirit and His ministry.

These heretics assert that their founders are gods, instead of Jesus, and they lure people into believing that works were done by their founders instead of the Holy Spirit. There are innumerable heretical religious groups like this which decoy, tempt, and lure people to believe their own founders, instead of God. The founders or leaders of such religious sects are called false prophets.

The spirits which do such things against Jesus Christ, not only obstructing God's ministry but calling themselves gods, are called the spirits of the Antichrist. I want you to find such evil spirits and chase them out of your body completely.

1 John 4: 1-6 Beloved, do not believe every spirit, but test the spirits, whether they are of God; because many false prophets have gone out into the world. By this you know the Spirit of God: Every spirit that confesses that Jesus Christ has come in the flesh

**is of God, and every spirit that does not confess that Jesus Christ
has come in the flesh is not of God. And this is the spirit of the
Antichrist, which you have heard was coming, and is now already
in the world.**

**You are of God, little children, and have overcome them, be-
cause He who is in you is greater than he who is in the world. They
are of the world. Therefore they speak as of the world, and the
world hears them. We are of God. He who knows God hears us; he
who is not of God does not hear us. By this we know the spirit of
truth and the spirit of error.**

The spirits of the Antichrist, the soldiers of Satan, always try
to decoy the sons and daughters of Almighty God to destroy
them in hell. They make all kinds of deceitful intrigue to lure
Christians to destruction. If any spirit approaches you, ask him
who he is. If he says, "I am the Holy Spirit," ask him to tell you
everything on the basis of the Bible. If he is the Holy Spirit, He
will tell you everything biblically for you to understand easily.
But if he is an evil spirit, he will say all kinds of dirty words
against Jesus and will ask you why the Bible is necessary to
talk with you. Then the evil spirit's natural character is revealed
to you.

The Holy Spirit is always glorifying God. Pray and ask the
Holy Spirit to give you the power to discern between the Holy
Spirit and evil spirits. The Holy Spirit will show you how to
discern between the spirits.

When such false prophets as stated above are preaching to
people, if you pray to God while hiding yourself among the
people, such preachers will fall on the floor and finally die.

This is exactly the same as the exorcists or Buddhist monks who fall on the floor and die, if you continuously pray to the Holy Spirit. You have to evangelize to such people boldly and tell them that they are lost, and are not on the way leading to the Kingdom of God, heaven.

There are uncountable idols in the world. The Holy Spirit's ministry and evangelism are very necessary for all the people in the world. In the future you should boldly witness for the Holy Spirit's ministry and evangelize everyone not to be deceived by idols and false prophets any more. Right now there are many Christian missionary groups who are evangelizing God's word in the world.

However some parts of the world are not as active as expected, because the people are immersed very deeply in idols. There are many countries where Christian missionaries cannot minister actively because of the governments' Antichrist policies, whose leaders are deceived by Satan to believe idols.

I want you to boldly deliver the Holy Spirit's messages to the kings and presidents of such countries and tell them not to be deceived by Satan any more. God loves even such kings and presidents and He wants to save such souls. And God wants you to lead such people to Jesus' salvation. I want you to declare boldly that they should come to Jesus. The Holy Spirit and His angels are always with you. Don't be afraid of anything but boldly declare Jesus' gospel to them also.

Galatians 5: 16-17 I say then: Walk in the Spirit, and you shall not fulfill the lust of the flesh. For the flesh lusts against the Spirit,

and the Spirit against the flesh; and these are contrary to one another, so that you do not do the things that you wish.

As shown in the Bible passage above, the Holy Spirit and the lust of the flesh are always against one another. Through your greedy mind, Satan, the Devil, and evil spirits always attempt to lure you into destruction, while pretending to be angels of light.

Therefore you have to follow the Holy Spirit's leading all the time, while discerning the spirits. When the Holy Spirit's powerful presence is shown through your body, all the evil spirits which were bothering you for many years will cry and leave you. The Holy Spirit will also search out all the evil spirits which were giving you trouble for many decades and chase them away from your flesh by force.

This is the way through which the Holy Spirit leads you to heaven for your eternal life. How the Holy Spirit teaches you to discern the spirits was written in detail in this book. I want you to study about how to discern the spirits and follow the Holy Spirit's guidance step by step. I want you to deliver Jesus' gospel boldly even to the leaders of heretical sects, and the Holy Spirit and His angels will be with you forever and will protect you from any circumstance in the world.

The Holy Spirit's words were given at 9:08 AM on May 17, 1997 in early morning prayer.

6. The Holy Spirit helps poor churches and pastors in difficulty

Acts 12: 1-11 Now about that time Herod the king stretched out his hand to harass some from the church. Then he killed James the brother of John with the sword. And because he saw that it pleased the Jews, he proceeded further to seize Peter also. Now it was during the Days of Unleavened Bread. So when he had arrested him, he put him in prison, and delivered him to four squads of soldiers to keep him, intending to bring him before the people after Passover. Peter was therefore kept in prison, but constant prayer was offered to God for him by the church.

And when Herod was about to bring him out, that night Peter was sleeping, bound with two chains between two soldiers; and the guards before the door were keeping the prison. Now behold, an angel of the Lord stood by him, and a light shone in the prison; and he struck Peter on the side and raised him up, saying, "Arise quickly!" And his chains fell off his hands.

Then the angel said to him, "Gird yourself and tie on your sandals"; and so he did. And he said to him, "Put on your garment and follow me." So he went out and followed him, and did not know that what was done by the angel was real, but thought he was seeing a vision. When they were past the first and the second guard posts, they came to the iron gate that leads to the city, which opened to them of its own accord; and they went out and went down one street, and immediately the angel departed from him.

And when Peter had come to himself, he said, "Now I know for certain that the Lord has sent His angel, and has delivered me

from the hand of Herod and from all the expectation of the Jewish
people."

1) When Pastor C. was having difficulties

In early morning prayer on March 8, 1997, Pastor C. was
crying in front of me, asking me to come to his church and help
him. Then I saw another Pastor, Pastor K., for a few seconds.
The Holy Spirit asked me to call him and go to his church and
help him. I went to Pastor C.'s church per the Holy Spirit's instructions, and I found about five or six Christians serving the
Sunday service.

The Holy Spirit told me, "He is the pastor selected by the
Holy Spirit to revitalize the Holy Spirit movement in Philadelphia." That church was so poor. However I told him all that the
Holy Spirit told me about him, "You are the pastor selected by
the Holy Spirit to revitalize the Holy Spirit movement in Philadelphia," and he was crying in front of me about that.

He was very pleased to hear what I said, but he didn't try to
believe what I said. He told me that he could not continue his
church service any more, because if a new family came to his
church for a few of weeks, some pastors would secretly tell the
newcomers that Pastor C. is heretical. Then the newcomers
would not come any more.

And he told me that the main figure libeling him was Pastor
K., whom I saw for a few seconds in my prayer when Pastor C.
was crying before me. I was very surprised to hear that the pastor slandering him as heretic was the same pastor who was seen

for a few seconds when Pastor C. was crying before me.

At midnight prayer at my home, the Holy Spirit told me that He sent me to Pastor C.'s church to inform me about what was happening there. And He gave me the Holy Spirit's message to be delivered to Pastor K., as follows:

"My loving Pastor K. I love you so much, because you do your best to serve God in your poor conditions.

Pastor K.! I want you to be careful of the following. Forgive all the wrongdoings done by your old, close friend, with Jesus' love. Do not slander him with groundless rumors. Your actions are shading the light of the Almighty God's glory.

I want you to confess everything to God and repent with all your heart, and God will let you realize what you are doing. Attend Reverend Y.'s Holy Spirit service and learn God's ministry and power, and I will use you a lot later."

I called Pastor K. and informed him of the Holy Spirit's message, and later I gave him the confirmation of the phone call, in writing. He obeyed the Holy Spirit's message. Later I found that Pastor K. went to Pastor Y.'s church to attend the Holy Spirit's ministry per the Holy Spirit's instructions. And later I found out that Pastor K. was no longer slandering Pastor C.

At the same time the Holy Spirit gave similar orders to Pastor C. also not to fight any more. So I delivered the Holy Spirit's message in writing and verbally to Pastor C. separately.

The Holy Spirit knows the cause of troubles between the churches, in detail. The Holy Spirit informs the cause of troubles to both of the churches and gives them God's messages not to fight any more. Both of them agreed 100% with the Holy Spirit's orders and they told me that they would do exactly what the Holy Spirit asked them to do.

If the Holy Spirit had not helped to solve the problem between two pastors, the Holy Spirit-filled pastor might have been continuously slandered as a heretic. Slandering Holy Spirit-filled pastors as heretics is the Antichrist's action against Almighty God. Pastor K., who was slandering Pastor C. as heretic, did not know that he was obstructing the Holy Spirit. He did such acts for his own interests and benefits.

Matthew 12: 31-32 "Therefore I say to you, every sin and blasphemy will be forgiven men, but the blasphemy against the Spirit will not be forgiven men. Anyone who speaks a word against the Son of Man, it will be forgiven him; but whoever speaks against the Holy Spirit, it will not be forgiven him, either in this age or in the age to come."

We always have to be careful about our words and our actions. We have to know how to discern the spirits and we have to follow the Holy Spirit's words glorifying Almighty God.

2) When Pastor C was libeled as a heretic by ten pas-pastors

After several months, Pastor C. appeared before me again when I was praying early in the morning. The Holy Spirit asked me to visit his church and help him, so I went to his church. Pastor C. told me that about ten different pastors slandered him and his church with groundless rumors. The Holy Spirit asked me to send the Holy Spirit's warning message to all ten different pastors, not to slander Pastor C. as a heretic.

So I sent the Holy Spirit's warning messages to everyone who slandered Pastor C. with groundless rumors. Later we found that the slandering stopped. The Holy Spirit knows our individual thoughts in detail, and our plans in advance.

In addition to that, the Holy Spirit knows that human beings decide everything for their own interests and profits and work for their own benefits. Therefore the Holy Spirit gives His warning messages to the pastors who slander other pastors as heretics for their own interests with groundless rumors. And the Holy Spirit asks them to obey the Holy Spirit's message, leading the right way to eternal life in heaven.

When the pastors who receive the Holy Spirit's warning messages do not obey the Holy Spirit's message but keep doing actions which shade the glory of God or hurt the Holy Spirit's movement, the Holy Spirit hits these pastors with fearful punishments which are impossible for the human beings to solve. I am a living witness who delivers the Holy Spirit's messages.

Under the name of Jesus we pray all the people who receive the Holy Spirit's messages will obey the Holy Spirit's words. If they obey the Holy Spirit's words, He will give them God's unlimited blessings for generations.

3) When Pastor C.'s church was confiscated by the landlord, after finishing six months of work

After several months, Pastor C. appeared again while crying before me in my morning prayer and asked me to come to him and help him. And the Holy Spirit asked me to call him.

When I called him, he told me that he would move to another place. They found a place, but they had to make a whole new room there to use for the church. After spending about six months to make the new church (all the walls, ceilings, and floor) the owner of the building asked him to vacate the place.

When Pastor C. said that he spent much time and money to renovate the church, the owner told him, "You spent your time and money for God's house, how can you ask to get the money from God?" The owner of the building refused to pay back anything for Pastor C.'s money and time. Already Pastor C. gave up the whole thing and he planned to start the church somewhere else, and his wife was sick in bed.

The Holy Spirit gave a strong warning message for me to deliver to the owner of the building. So I delivered the Holy Spirit's message to the owner of the building per the Holy Spirit's instructions. The owner was moved greatly by the Holy Spirit's message and he repented of everything that he did wrong to God, and gave back the four year lease at half price, while giving credit for all the time and money Pastor C. spent repairing the church for the last six months.

Several pastors filled with much Holy Spirit power have already performed the Holy Spirit's ministry at this same church. In addition to that, at the end of April 1999 a famous and well-known Pastor who leads a Holy Spirit service in Korea where tens of thousands of people come, is scheduled to lead the Holy Spirit service at a school auditorium prepared solely by Pastor C.

This is the Holy Spirit's miracle. Pastor C. who was crying before me with five to six people at his church is able to prepare the Holy Spirit's ministry with the famous Pastor. That is the Holy Spirit's ministry, without which he cannot perform the Holy Spirit's service.

All that the Holy Spirit said to me one year and eleven months ago when he was crying with five to six people without any money is being realized. "He is the pastor who was selected by the Holy Spirit to revitalize the Holy Spirit movement in Philadelphia" . Now his church has grown very much compared to the time when I first visited him. The Holy Spirit helps the poor churches like Pastor C.'s.

7. The Holy Spirit encourages the pastors who are leading the Holy Spirit Movement

**Matthew 12: 22-29 Then one was brought to Him who was de-
mon-possessed, blind and mute; and He healed him, so that the
blind and mute man both spoke and saw. And all the multitudes
were amazed and said, "Could this be the Son of David?" Now
when the Pharisees heard it they said, "This fellow does not cast
out demons except by Beelzebub, the ruler of the demons."**

**But Jesus knew their thoughts, and said to them: "Every king-
dom divided against itself is brought to desolation, and every city
or house divided against itself will not stand. If Satan casts out
Satan, he is divided against himself. How then will his kingdom
stand? And if I cast out demons by Beelzebub, by whom do your
sons cast them out?**

**Therefore they shall be your judges. But if I cast out demons by
the Spirit of God, surely the kingdom of God has come upon you.
Or how can one enter a strong man's house and plunder his goods,
unless he first binds the strong man? And then he will plunder his
house.**

There are many pastors who have received the Holy Spirit's
powerful influence and lead large congregations of the Holy
Spirit's ministry. There are also many denominations and pastors in the world who slander and libel such Holy Spirit influenced pastors as heretics. The pastors slandering the Holy
Spirit-inspired pastors do not even have the Holy Spirit's power
to discern between the Holy Spirit and Satan. They slander the
most powerful Holy Spirit-inspired pastors who lead many tens
of thousands of Christians in their congregations or churches
without any specific reasons.

There are many powerful Holy Spirit-filled pastors who are
slandered as heretics in the world. The Holy Spirit asked me to

watch video tapes showing the Holy Spirit's ministry being led by such powerful Holy Spirit-inspired pastors who are being slandered as heretics. When I watch such video tapes per the Holy Spirit's instructions, He shows and confirms to me that all the miracles performed through them were done by the Holy Spirit.

The Holy Spirit has trained and taught me how to discern between the Holy Spirit and demons, through the Bible, for many years. Therefore I know right away which miracles were done by Satan to deceive Christians and which ones were done by the Holy Spirit.

The Holy Spirit confirms through me that such powerful Holy Spirit-inspired pastors are not heretics, but they are real pastors who received the Holy Spirit's powerful influence. And the Holy Spirit encourages them and tells them that they are the pastors the heavenly Father loves.

In addition to that, the Holy Spirit asked me to deliver many warning messages to the leading pastors of the associations of churches or associations of the pastors who slandered the Holy Spirit-inspired pastors in Korea and the USA. There are many pastors who received the Holy Spirit's warning messages from me in Korea and the USA. The Holy Spirit wants to help all the Holy Spirit-inspired pastors wherever they are in the world.

8. The Holy Spirit protects the pastors in the Holy Spirit Movement

Sometimes the Holy Spirit asks me to visit the churches or congregations led by such missionaries or pastors who were trained under powerful Holy Spirit-inspired pastors who were slandered as heretics.

The Holy Spirit asks me to deliver the message to such missionaries or pastors, that all the miraculous ministries performed through the powerful Holy Spirit-filled pastors who were slandered as heretics was done by the Holy Spirit. The Holy Spirit asks me to give the same messages to the pastors or Christians who slandered the Holy Spirit-filled pastors as heretics.

In addition to that, He asks me to teach them how to discern between the Holy Spirit and demons. There are many missionaries and pastors who are slandered as heretics because they were trained and taught under the powerful Holy Spirit-inspired pastors who are slandered as heretics in the world.

The Holy Spirit wants to help and encourage such missionaries and pastors wherever they are in the world. I am the Holy Spirit's servant, the witness who delivers the Holy Spirit's messages directly to the pastors or missionaries involved, according to the Holy Spirit's instructions. Some pastors who were slandered as heretics gave up serving as pastors, because they were afraid of being libeled as heretics. When they received the Holy Spirit's messages saying, "They are not heretics but that was the

Holy Spirit's ministry." They were so pleased that some of them were crying loudly.

We should not slander the pastors filled in the Holy Spirit's power, by calling them heretics. People slander the Holy Spirit-filled pastors because of their ignorance about the Holy Spirit. The Holy Spirit punishes the people who slander the Holy Spirit-inspired pastors or Christians, with punishments which are impossible for human beings to solve.

There are many people who were punished severely because they did not obey the Holy Spirit. This kind of deed against the Holy Spirit Movement is a foolish acts of killing oneself and throwing oneself forever into the fiery lake in hell. No one in the world can win a victory against the Holy Spirit. Such persons will fall without knowing the reason.

Matthew 12: 31-32 "Therefore I say to you, every sin and blasphemy will be forgiven men, but the blasphemy against Spirit will not be forgiven men. Anyone who speaks a word against the Son of Man, it will be forgiven him; but whoever speaks against the Holy Spirit, it will not be forgiven him, either in this age or in the age to come.

Hebrews 6: 4-6 For it is impossible for those who were enlightened, and have tasted the heavenly gift, have become partakers of the Holy Spirit, and have tasted the good word of God and the powers of the age to come, if they fall away, to renew them again to repentance, they crucify again for themselves the Son of God, and put Him to an open shame.

The writer of this book is a living witness who saw many

Christians and pastors who were punished by the Holy Spirit's
angels because they did not obey the Holy Spirit's messages. If
any of you obstructed or slandered the Holy Spirit's movement,
confess and repent with tears in your eyes for your sins before
God. The Holy Spirit who loves all of us may forgive all our
sins.

CHAPTER 3

Jesus whom I saw

1. Jesus saved me from the slaughterhouse of men
2. Jesus' light, which destroyed a demon which tried to kill me
3. Jesus put the evil spirits which tried to kill me into a boiling oil tank
4. Jesus' light melted a cobra bigger than an electric utility pole which tried to kill me

Jesus whom I saw

Since January 1, 1990, I have met Jesus Christ and have seen heaven, hell and God's judgment innumerable times in the Holy Spirit's power. Whenever evil spirits tried to kill me, I called in a loud voice, "Jesus, demons are trying to kill me, please save me." I was crying for help to Jesus, and then Jesus immediately appeared and saved me from the demons' plots to kill me. Here I will testify to how He saved me from the hands of Satan, the devil, demons and evil spirits.

Right now, in order to obstruct the worldwide Holy Spirit revival movement, evil spirits are making all kinds of plans to kill me. However the Holy Spirit is present with me 24 hours a day and His angels always protect me from Satanic attacks. Therefore the evil spirits cannot attack me. When they tried to kill me, how did the Holy Spirit protect me? I will testify to how the Holy Spirit did it.

The Holy Spirit said to me, "Announce the truth that the Holy Spirit and His angels protect all His sons and daughters who actively participate in the worldwide Holy Spirit revival movement, from any Satanic attacks all over the world 24 hours a day."

Matthew 1: 18-21 Now the birth of Jesus Christ was as follows: After His mother Mary was betrothed to Joseph, before they came together, she was found with child of the Holy Spirit. Then Joseph her husband, being a just man, and not wanting to make her a public example, was minded to put her away secretly. But while he thought about these things, behold, an angel of the Lord appeared to him in a dream, saying, "Joseph, son of David, do not be afraid to take to you Mary your wife, for that which is conceived in her is of the Holy Spirit. And she will bring forth a Son, and you shall call His name JESUS, for He will save His people from their sins." *Lord, thank you! I love you!*

In the Bible, the Old and New Testaments, the Almighty Heavenly Father showed His revelations to His prophets and servants in dreams. At first, God also showed His presence with me and taught me His words in dreams. The following stories cover the incidents which happened in my dreams, but they influenced me to change my life more powerfully than the incidents which occurred in my real life. These incidents completely changed my life and are more clearly recorded in my brain than daily life today, even though 12 years have passed since the incidents happened.

1. Jesus saved me from the slaughterhouse of men

On January 1, 1990 I was kidnapped by two strong young men and was taken to a mountainous place by force in a station wagon. There were two white painted houses on the mountain and between them there was a small brook, by which a couple of small willow trees were standing.

It was dark but outside of the house was bright with light. When I was taken into the house, I was shocked. I found several people who were dead, and several other people standing were being killed one by one. That is, it was a human slaughterhouse. The way they killed the people was as follows:

First they laid a person on a white sheet-covered bed, then they covered him with tree bark, one foot high. The bark looked like cork scraps from wine bottles. Then they covered this with another white sheet, to suffocate him to death. When the person on the bed was dead, they rolled the bed to the next room and they laid the next person on the new bed and killed him in exactly the same way as the first one.

When I first entered that house, there were four people in front of me. But when I saw the people being killed one by one, I could not express the feeling of terror for the unfair treatment and the feeling of sorrow in my heart. My turn to be killed on the bed was coming closer to me, but there was nothing I could do to save my life. It was exactly same the feeling as when prisoners sentenced to capital punishment watch other prisoners being hanged, while waiting for their turn to be executed.

I looked around the room to see if there were any doors

through which I could sneak out of the slaughter room, but there was only the door through which I came in. In front of the door were two giant persons dressed in white, standing guard. Therefore there was no way I could sneak out and I could not even dream of running out.

I already gave up on saving my life, and I had to wait for my turn to be executed. People who have not experienced death cannot understand what I felt at that time. I was too mortified. What kinds of big sins did I commit, which were enough to receive this capital punishment without notice even to my family members? My assets and money in the world could not save me from death. There was nothing that could save me from being executed. *(His dream)*

Right at that moment I felt strongly that I have to cling to the Almighty Heavenly Father as the last way to save my life from death. Sometime in the past when I read the Bible, I read that nothing was impossible with God. God raises the dead to life, He cures completely the incurable sick patients, and He fully fed five thousand people with five loaves of bread and two fish and the leftover food filled twelve baskets full.

I made up my mind to pray to Jesus Christ who stopped the fearful stormy winds at sea by commanding the wind to cease and tranquilized the sea immediately. I began to cry, asking God to save me from death. I didn't know how to pray to God. "O my God, please save me from death! Please save me from death! If God saves me, I will do whatever God asks me to do." I repeated these prayers continuously. My prayer, "Please save me from death," was a real prayer coming from the deepest part of my heart, after I gave up on saving my life. I already gave up all the things in the world. At the same time, I couldn't control my mind because of my sorrow about being killed in a few minutes.

All the people who were in front of me were already slaughtered, one by one. It was my turn to be killed! I already gave up my life, and I was caught in depression and fear. At the same time I worried, "If the scraps of cork enter my nostrils, what can I do? Or what can I do, if I am not accepted into heaven for eternal life? My whole life, I did nothing for Almighty God, so I couldn't expect to go to heaven."

Trembling with the fear of death, at the moment when my right foot stepped on the killing bed, Jesus Christ appeared before me, with brown, long wavy hair, short side burns, dressed in a white gown. Jesus said to the people dressed in white long gowns, "When this man dies, he will not be laid over here but he will be buried in a tomb behind you."

All the people in the room turned behind to see where Jesus was pointing, in front of us, there was a big lake with crystal clear water and at the edge of the lake there was a steep rock mountain about 50-70 meters high, like a wall. On the top of the mountain, there was a wide flat ground which was very bright under the sunlight. And right in the center of the flat ground there was a big swimming pool made of cement concrete without water, and right in the center of the pool there was a coffin made of cement, about 2m x 3m x 1.2 m high.

Jesus was pointing with the finger of His right hand to the coffin where I would be buried. At that time, trembling in fear of death, I kneeled down by Jesus who was standing, pointing to my tomb. Then one of the men dressed in white who was killing the people in the room said to me, "This is what Jesus is doing, watch it carefully." Immediately from the high in the sky a bright beam of light was shining right into the water in the lake.

The diameter of the beam was about 70 cm - 1 m. The light was bright as an automobile headlight shining at midnight when there is no moon. It was daytime but everyone could clearly see the bright beam of light. And the light was shining on the middle of the water between Jesus and the tomb I would be buried in. As soon as the light was shining on the water, all the fish in the lake started rushing toward the light. All the big fish were going high in the air, embraced by the light. When they went about 100-200m, they all fell into my coffin which was in the grave made like a cement concrete pool.

At the same time water also went up high in the air dropped into my coffin. So my coffin was filled about 90% with fish and water, and the fish were swimming in the crowded coffin. I began to worry about what to do if the fish and water get into my nostrils. So I asked Jesus, "If the fish and water get into my nostrils, what can I do?"

Jesus replied, "Do not worry anything about them, I will make sure nothing goes into your nostrils."

At the same time I woke from the dream. It was a dream which I had 12 years ago, but it is still clearly recorded in my brain. From that day my life changed 100%. That is, the purpose of my life changed from money and business to Jesus and heaven. Whatever large amount of money I may earn, what can I do with it? When my life is finished, I can take nothing with me. While I follow money and business, if I die and am thrown into the fiery lake of hell, what good are they to me?

From that day, I desperately wanted to go to church. On Sundays I couldn't stay home without going to church. Whether I was in Korea, Japan, or in the USA, wherever I was in the world, I went to church on Sundays. In church I sat in the very front, right before the preacher and listened to the preaching without even blinking my eyes. The words were sweet like honey to me. I couldn't afford to miss even one word of the preaching.

At home I listened to the hymns and blessing hymns all day long. And I used to wear earphones to listen to hymns at work or home all day long. And I wanted to read the Bible all the time. So from early in the morning until late in the night, I only read the Bible for many years. Before the dream I didn't believe the stories in the Bible but after this incident I came to believe all the words in the Bible 100% as written.

In addition to that, "I thought that Jesus Christ who caught so many fish with His light and put them into my coffin can do anything in the world. And nothing is impossible with Him." Amen! Therefore all the words in the Bible were as sweet as honey to me. And I came to believe all the words in the Bible word by word. From that time, wherever I went, I carried the Bible in my hand.

Even in the bathroom I read the Bible and while eating meals also, I read the Bible. I couldn't let go of the Bible from my hands.

In addition to that, whoever met, whoever they were, I told them about the dream I had. And I asked them to believe Jesus. And I printed a small booklet called, "Jesus whom I saw," telling about my dreams in which whenever evil spirits tried to kill me, Jesus saved me from their attacks. And I gave them out to whomever I met.

I found that only Jesus could save me from death in the world. Meanwhile I realized that the Trinity God: Almighty God, His Son Jesus Christ, and the Holy Spirit is only God who can save human beings from death and lead men to eternal life in heaven. And I made up my mind to realize the words of Jesus in deeds.

Mark 16: 15 And He said to them, "Go into all the world and preach the gospel to every creature. 16 He who believes and is baptized will be saved; but he who does not believe will be condemned."

I was born again in the Holy Spirit January 1, 1990.

2. Jesus' light, which destroyed a demon which tried to kill me

On January 27, 1991, I was staying at the River Park Hotel by the man made falls on the way to Kimpo International Airport in Seoul, Korea. When I was sleeping, I suddenly felt a strong electric current running through my whole body, then my body was shrunk and I couldn't breathe at all. I felt as if I was dying.

It was dark all around me and I was in a coma. My whole body was paralyzed, so I couldn't move at all. I felt as if someone pressed down on me with many tons of steel plates. I was at the moment of death. Whenever the demons tried to kill me, I always called Jesus to save me from death.

I called "Jesus, I am dying, please save me from death."

Immediately a beam of light like a flashlight at night with about a 15 cm diameter shone from the right side of my bed to the left side of my bed. The light was shining about 1 m high on the wooden cabinet standing against the wall, on which was standing a Japanese Samurai ceramic doll about 40 cm high. Jesus' light was shining on the face of the Japanese Samurai doll, which was looking at me with its right eye burning with fire.

At that moment as I was dying, trembling in fear of the doll's

Dream

burning eye, I cried to Jesus to help me from the demon who was trying to kill me. Right at that time, I heard a big cracking sound like the sound of a rifle shooting.

"I am dying now!" I thought I was dead. But I found the doll's head, cut from the body, and completely crushed into pieces. Only the headless body of the Japanese Samurai doll was standing on the wooden cabinet. On the floor I saw many broken pieces from the ceramic doll. I thought I was dead but soon I rose from death. I found it was a dream.

However what I felt was real: many tons of steel plates ing on my chest, my neck choking, and the electric current running through my whole body. Jesus' light saved me again from the demon's plan to kill me by destroying the demon completely. Evil spirits tried to slaughter me but my life was saved again by the light of Jesus. After this incident, my love and belief in Jesus was growing without limit. Since my life was saved from death by Jesus, I am now living an extra life because of Jesus' grace. I made up my mind again to serve and work more for the ministry of Jesus Christ who saved my life from the demon's attacks. The Holy Spirit led my heart to love Jesus more and worship the Almighty heavenly Father more earnestly.

3. Jesus put the evil spirits which tried to kill me into a boiling oil tank

On April 7, 1991 when I was staying at the Shila Hotel in Seoul, Korea on business for several weeks. I was sleeping, suddenly two grave stones which stood at grave in Korea appeared and they were slowly coming to me. I immediately recognized that they were evil spirits who were coming closer toward me. There was no place where I could escape from them. As they were coming closer to me, I felt the same pressure and electric currents I had the last time when the Japanese Samurai ceramic doll which tried to kill me was crushed by the light of Jesus.

As they came closer to me, I commanded them in the name of Jesus, saying "Get out of here, I command you in the name of Jesus." But they were laughing at me and coming closer to me. They tried to kill me.

I called immediately for Jesus to help me saying, "Jesus, these evil spirits are trying to kill me, Please save me from their plots to kill me." Suddenly a red fire ball like a soccer ball appeared very far in the air and it burst. When the fire ball burst, I felt a strong electric zap on my right elbow. These happened three times, one by one. Right after these fire balls burst, Jesus appeared before me.

Jesus brought one transparent glass oil tank, about 2m x 2m x 1.2m high. Inside the oil tank, oil was boiling and steam was coming from its pipes. Jesus already put those two demons into the boiling oil tank. I don't know when He put them into the transparent oil tank. I could see the two demons whose forms were changed from grave stones to snow men made of white fog, jumping at the loss in the transparent boiling oil tank.

Jesus saved me again from the demons' plot to kill me. I realized that my life depended on Jesus 100%. Wherever I live in the world, I found that it was only Jesus Christ who could save me from the evil spirits' plots to kill me. Therefore my life is not mine but it belongs to Jesus, because without Jesus' help I cannot keep myself alive even one day. So I determined strongly to believe Jesus with my life, worship Almighty God, and follow the Holy Spirit's words in deeds, as long as I live in the world. Because I have no one who can save me from Satan's plots to kill me except Jesus Christ.

Today I want to express my greatest thanks to the Triune God who always saves me from evil spirits.

4. Jesus' light melted a cobra bigger than an electric utility pole which tried to kill me

April 5, 1996 at 5:00 in the morning, I was in Korea on business.

I was riding a boat about three stories high in Umsung Reservoir, when suddenly a cobra as big as the telephone post appeared in front of me and jumped over my boat and was coming towards me to swallow me. However I began to shine it with God's green light coming from my right palm. The snake began to make a face and its tongue began to burn by God's light given to me by Jesus Christ.

The snake couldn't attack me any more but tried to run away from me. I called for Jesus' help, and this time Jesus sent me God's second weapon, round flying saw blades 2 - 3 meters in diameter, which came in large numbers and began to cut the cobra from the head of the snake, little by little into pieces.

When the cobra was almost cut into pieces, suddenly my God, Jesus, appeared with his own golden flashlight which was shining on the cobra. As soon as Jesus' golden light began to shine on the cobra, it began to melt like iron in a furnace. The cobra disappeared completely, it was melted into the furnace. Then I woke from dream.

I realized that even in my dreams, Satan is trying to kill me with all kinds of plots but the Holy Spirit and His angels protect me from evil spirits 24 hours a day without fail. Whenever I think that the Holy Spirit and His angels protect me all the time from any demon and evil spirit's attacks, I cannot but express my greatest heartfelt thanks to God. Besides this incident, there were innumerable times when Jesus saved me from fearful Satanic attacks. All the testimonies recorded in this book are real stories which I have experienced.

I am sure that God will give all the blessings of the Holy Spirit's ministries which I have experienced to the sons and daughters of God who really believe Jesus and follow in deeds the Bible's words.

Under the name of Jesus, we pray that the Almighty Heavenly Father may pour His unlimited blessings and grace to all the Christians who read this book. Amen.

CHAPTER 4

The Holy Spirit's Words about Evangelism

1. The Holy Spirit's way of training how to evangelize, while showing the spirits crying and wailing in the sea of fire of hell
2. The heaven and hell that I have seen
3. Going to the Buddhist temple to deliver Jesus' gospel to the Buddhist monks
4. How the Holy Spirit changed a person who denied God and led him to heaven
5. The Holy Spirit saved my mother-in-law who was a Buddhist believer at the last moment of death
6. The Holy Spirit saved my mother's sister who was a Buddhist and led her to heaven
7. Centurion's belief and the definition of the Bible

1. The Holy Spirit's way of training how to evangelize, while showing the spirits crying and wailing in the sea of fire of hell

It was some time in April 1996 when I was in Korea on business. When I was praying early in the morning, suddenly innumerable, many millions of people appeared before me. The place was at the entrance of the subway train station located at the intersection of Sadang Dong, Seoul, Korea. I was so surprised that I asked, "What is this?" All the sudden, Jesus Christ, embraced by the light and holding a lamb in His arms, appeared before me.

Revelation 20: 12-15 And I saw the dead, small and great, standing before God, and books were opened. And another book was opened, which is the book of life. And the dead were judged according to their works, by the things which were written in the books. The sea gave up the dead who were in it, and Death and Hades delivered up the dead who were in them. And they were judged, each one according to his works. Then Death and Hades were cast into the lake of fire. This is the second death. And anyone not found written in the book of life was cast into the lake of fire.

At the same time, the lamb in the arms of Jesus told me the following:"There are innumerable people who will be cast into the fiery sea of hell, like the spirits crying and wailing in the fire sea. They are the people who do not believe in God and didn't confess their sins to God. I want you to do your best to save such poor people in the world."

Meanwhile turning to the right with His fingers pointed, Jesus showed me a great sea whose end I couldn't see. The sea He showed me was not a blue sea like the Pacific Ocean, but it was a fiery sea where all kinds of metals and rocks are melting, like the burning furnace in a steel mill. I saw that all the people who were there were tied up with invisible ropes, and they were driven into the fire sea. They were crying, yelling and wailing but it was no use.

Many giant angels came from somewhere I don't know. They began to throw poor people bound with invisible ropes into the sulfur burning fiery lake. The people in the fiery lake are crying, wailing and lamenting that they didn't believe Jesus, but they only enjoyed their lives without paying any attention to their souls which will be cast into the fiery sea. However no one helps them. The scene was so sorrowful and miserable that I couldn't keep my eyes opened. I was wailing and weeping, while tears were continuously dripping from my eyes. The vision of the spirits crying in the fiery sea appeared in front of my eyes all day long, like on a TV screen, even if I closed my eyes.

That day was on a Sunday, the Sabbath day when all Christians in the world are going to churches to worship the Almighty God. The church where I was attending in Seoul was a small Presbyterian church which was started not long ago, located near the entrance of the subway train station at the intersection of Sadang Dong, the same place where Jesus showed me in morning prayer millions of people bound by invisible ropes and driven into the fiery sea. At the corner of the same church many bundles of leaflets advertising Jesus' gospel were stacked up high. As soon as my eyes saw them, the same scene of the sulfur burning fiery sea in which many millions of people were crying, weeping and wailing loudly appeared again before my eyes. Jesus, embraced by the light, said to me, "Read Mark 16:15-16 in the Bible."

Mark 16: 15-16 And He said to them, "Go into all the world and and preach the gospel to every creature. He who believes and is baptized will be saved; but he who does not believe will be condemned."

At the same time, Jesus, holding a lamb in His arms, said to me,

"From today I want you to give away leaflets showing Jesus' gospel to all the people passing by the entrance of the subway station, where millions of people were driven into the sea of fire." *11/15/08 And, I was just wondering which booklet to continue giving, do they make a difference*

Immediately I picked up one of the leaflets and showed it to the senior pastor of the same church and explained to him the vision of the sea of fire where millions of people were driven into, which I saw in morning prayer. Upon hearing what I said, the pastor said to me, "the Holy Spirit will train and use Chairman Joe as an evangelist for Jesus." Meanwhile he introduced me to several missionaries of the church to help me deliver leaflets for the gospel at the same place where I saw millions of people being driven into the fiery lake.

From that day until I returned to my home in America, every Sunday afternoon after Sunday morning church service for about eight months, I delivered the same leaflets introducing

Jesus' gospel with several missionaries, to the people passing
by the entrance of the subway station where the Holy Spirit
showed me millions of people bound with invisible ropes, being driven into the fiery lake. When the leaflets were all gone, I
printed more leaflets with my own money and delivered them
at the same place. Summer is very hot in Korea, and my whole
body was soaked in sweat like in a shower.

When I was tired of the summer heat and delivering leaflets,
I used to sit on the stairs of the entrance of the subway tunnel,
then the same vision of millions of people crying and weeping
in the sea of fire in hell appeared again to my eyes. Then I immediately forgot about being tired, and began to give out the
leaflets again to the people passing by.

Some people refused to accept the leaflets I gave, saying,
"We are going to a Buddhist temple to worship Buddha's
statue." Others said, "We don't believe in any god," and,
"believe God for yourself only," while throwing away the leaflets I gave. And they passed by the entrance of the subway.
Then I immediately followed them and told them that there are
surely hell and paradise after our life. I have been to heaven
and hell innumerable times. And I told them truly, "Come to
Jesus now and accept Him as your Savior Lord right now, otherwise you shall have to cry, weep and lament for not believing
in God, forever in the sulfur burning fiery lake of hell."

I have seen billions of people crying and wailing in the sea of
fire in hell, innumerable times. That's why I came to ask you to
accept Jesus as your Lord. It is only the Trinity God who can
give you eternal life in heaven. That is, the Almighty Heavenly
Father, His Son, Jesus Christ and the Holy Spirit. All the religions in the world, except the Trinity God, are worshiping idols
which were made by men who were deceived by Satan. And if

you serve the idols made by Satan, you cannot but be thrown into the fiery sea of hell, when your life is over in this world.

Revelation 21: 8 "But the cowardly, unbelieving, abominable, murderers, sexually immoral, sorcerers, idolaters, and all liars shall have their part in the lake which burns with fire and brimstone, which is the second death."

John 14: 6 Jesus said to him, "I am the way, the truth, and the life. No one comes to the Father except through Me.

I said to them, "It is up to you which church you attend, but you have to accept Jesus as your Savior Lord and you have to worship the Almighty God."

In the evening when I went home, I used to distribute the same leaflets to the people in the subway or on buses. And when I went to restaurants, banks or anywhere else, I gave out the leaflets introducing Jesus Christ to the people there. From early April until late December 1996 when I went to my home in the USA, I distributed leaflets in Korea introducing Jesus this way.

In accordance with the Holy Spirit's leading, I listened to an audio tape about "heaven and hell" witnessed by a Christian deacon. The Holy Spirit asked me to buy many copies and give them to the people who know nothing about heaven and hell. So I purchased many thousand sets and gave them to whomever I met in subway trains and buses or on the street. I always carried them in my book bag. Even on airplanes, I gave them to stewardesses, pilots and passengers, while asking them to believe in Jesus. I gave them all free without any charge. Especially when I saw old people or handicapped persons, I approached them on purpose and gave them a tape and asked them to listen and come to Jesus for their eternal life.

Whomever I met, I used to ask them whether he or she believed in Jesus. After listening to their answer, I began our conversation, keeping the focus that they should accept Jesus as their Savior Lord and believe in God.

Some people said, "You are crazy about Jesus." And some said, "Should people believe in God like you?" And some said, "Are you the only person who believes in Jesus?" Whatever they said to me, I didn't care.

But I told them that I had been to heaven and hell innumerable times. I saw billions of people crying, weeping and wailing in the sulfur burning fiery sea of hell. If you don't believe in Jesus, you also will be cast into the ever burning fiery sea which the Holy Spirit showed me. That is why, even if you hate to hear about Jesus from me, I will keep telling you about Jesus in order to save you from the fiery lake. I don't care which church you may go to, but be sure to accept Jesus as your Lord as soon as possible. And I continued my conversations with them. Most of the people listened to what I said about heaven and hell.

For many years, the Holy Spirit forced me to read only the Bible or books testifying to the Holy Spirit's miracles. Before January 1, 1990 when I was born again in the Holy Spirit, when I tried to read the Bible, I couldn't read for a long time, because I became very sleepy as soon as I held the Bible. But since I was born again in the Holy Spirit, reading the Bible gives me the taste of honey. So from early in the morning until late at night, I have been reading the Bible but I am not tired and still want to read more. Therefore while eating dinner or even in the bathroom, I have been reading the Bible.

In church on Sundays, I sit extremely close to the front and listen to the preacher's speech attentively, not to miss even one word. The words from the preacher are like the honey to my ears.

Whether I was in Korea or in the USA, I attended most of the Holy Spirit congregations being held near or far from my home. This was the Holy Spirit's spiritual training for me to evangelize the gospel to all the people in the world.

This is a lesson the Holy Spirit gives to everyone in the world: that God loves all the people and He wants to spiritually train all His children like me. Also, He wants all His children to deliver the gospel to all the creatures in the world with the Holy Spirit's power, like Jesus' disciples did in the first century. Almighty God loves each of us more than the universe. Therefore the Almighty Heavenly Father sent His only Son to us to be crucified on the cross to pardon all our sins. Accordingly, He cleansed all our sins and the Holy Spirit leads all His children who really believe in God to the eternal heaven.

If Jesus Christ was not crucified on the cross, we couldn't be cleansed from our sins and we, all the sinners, would be thrown into the fiery lake in which many billions are crying now. The Holy Spirit showed me this same fiery sea innumerable times. However Jesus Christ was crucified for our sins on the cross, so the Almighty Heavenly Father opened the way for us to be led to heaven through the Holy Spirit's guidance. All of us, whatever we do for Jesus, we cannot do even one millionth of what Jesus did for us. How can we go to the Heavenly Father, except through Jesus Christ? We all must fulfill the words of Jesus which He said before being lifted into heaven by angels.

Mark 16: 15 And He said to them, "Go into all the world and preach the gospel to every creature."

Matthew 28: 18-20 And Jesus came and spoke to them, saying, "All authority has been given to Me in heaven and on earth. Go therefore and make disciples of all nations, baptizing them in the name of the Father and of the Son and of the Holy Spirit, teaching them to observe all things that I have commanded you; and lo, I am with you always, even to the end of the age." Amen.

We must all realize the words which Jesus said at the last moment before He went up to heaven.

I have been to heaven and hell innumerable times. Therefore I put aside all the things in the world, and I followed the Holy Spirit's guidance. I had to undergo fearful spiritual training, which the Holy Spirit led me through for the last 10 years. As a result of that, the corporations which I had established and gave me great fortunes through international trade in the last 25 years disappeared. But the Holy Spirit saved me from my sins and trained me powerfully. So although I don't have any money, I am happier now in the Holy Spirit than when I was doing big business, without knowing Jesus in the world. Right now I only deliver God's word, the gospel about Jesus and His cross to everyone wherever I go.

I also testify about the Holy Spirit, who is now performing miracles through me all over the world. Leading Holy Spirit Services, I experienced many times that the Holy Spirit moved so powerfully that unbelievers, alcoholics, drug addicts and members of gangs and many such people were crying, wailing, confessing their sins, and accepting Jesus as their Savior Lord.

If you really believe in God, follow His words by your deeds and confess all your sins before Him, God will prepare for you to meet Him soon. Then all the problems you have now in your life will be solved smoothly, such as health problems, business problems, family problems, spiritual problems and whatever problems you may have will be solved completely. Because nothing is impossible with the Holy Spirit. God knows what kinds of problems you have now.

We all must do all our best in realizing, by our deeds, the last words Jesus gave us before His going to heaven.

Mark 16: 15-16 And He said to them, "Go into all the world and and preach the gospel to every creature. He who believes and is baptized will be saved; but he who does not believe will be condemned."

If we do our best to preach the gospel to every creature in the world, I am sure that Jesus will be ready for us to meet Him with solid golden crowns specially made for all of us in heaven.

The Holy Spirit's words were given in early morning prayer on June 5, 2000

2. The heaven and hell that I have seen

1) The heaven that I saw

I have been to heaven uncountable times. I have been to many different places, I cannot tell you all the places I have been to. I will tell you about one place which represents the others. The heaven that I have seen was located by the seaside which had water more clear than crystal. Along the seaside there was a road made of solid gold about 15 meters wide, which was so long that I could not see the end of the road. Along the road about 300 meters, many one or two story high buildings were standing, built with solid gold and decorated with diamonds. And in the center of these buildings, there stood a large building built of solid gold and decorated with diamonds, with a high pointed rooftop like a church.

Above the entrance of the building was a big signboard hanging on the wall. The solid gold board was about 1meter high by 3 meters wide, and the gold board was ringed with a line of innumerable red colored jewels about 10 cm wide, and in the center of this red jeweled decoration, the words of the sign were written about 10 cm wide, decorated with many uncountable diamonds on the gold board. On the tip of the rooftop, there stood a big cross made of solid gold and diamonds. The cross size was about 2m wide x 3m high but the gold board making the cross was decorated with diamonds about 15cm wide, on the face of the board. And the place where two boards meet on the cross, was dotted a big diamond which is as big as my fist. All the diamonds and gold were shining in the heavenly Father's special light.

They said, "This Cross symbolizes Jesus Christ." Soon the cross changed into a man of light. This light was much brighter than the sun. The light was so bright that no one could look at it. The form of the light was like a man. However the light was so shiny and bright that no one could recognize the man. They said, "This light shines all over heaven."

Inside this building, there was much furniture, such as chairs and tables and desks. All of the furniture was made of solid gold with decorations of diamonds, with red and blue jewels. On the right side of this village, there was a small flower mountain. The flowers on that mountain were many kinds which I don't know, and were so beautiful that I cannot explain the beauty of them in words. On the gold road, there were no cars, except one car. It was small like a Jeep, made of solid gold decorated with diamonds, with an open top in which two angels were sitting.

This car was not only running on the road but sometimes it was flying in the air like an airplane. When it was flying, the wings came out automatically. There were no other human beings, but many angels in heaven.

In addition to this, I have been to many other places. All of them are made of solid gold, decorated with diamonds. Always bright, clear and beautiful places. I have never seen any places which are so beautiful like this in the world. I have been to heaven innumerable times. If you believe Jesus with all your heart, and follow Him by your life and your acts, the Holy Spirit will show you not only heaven but also many heavenly secrets shown in Revelation Chapter 21.

Revelation 21: 10-27 And he carried me away in the Spirit to a great and high mountain, and showed me the great city, the holy

Jerusalem, descending out of heaven from God, having the glory of God. Her light was like a most precious stone, like a jasper stone, clear as crystal. Also she had a great and high wall with twelve gates, and twelve angels at the gates, and names written on them, which are the names of the twelve tribes of the children of Israel: three gates on the east, three gates on the north, three gates on the south, and three gates on the west. Now the wall of the city had twelve foundations, and on them were the names of the twelve apostles of the Lamb.

And he who talked with me had a gold reed to measure the city, its gates, and its wall. The city is laid out as a square; its length is as great as its breadth. And he measured the city with the reed: twelve thousand furlongs. Its length, breadth, and height are equal. Then he measured its wall: one hundred and forty-four cubits, according to the measure of a man, that is, of an angel. The construction of its wall was of jasper; and the city was pure gold, like clear glass.

The foundations of the wall of the city were adorned with all kinds of precious stones: the first foundation was jasper, the second sapphire, the third chalcedony, the fourth emerald, the fifth sardonyx, the sixth sardius, the seventh chrysolite, the eighth beryl, the ninth topaz, the tenth chrysoprase, the eleventh jacinth, and the twelfth amethyst. The twelve gates were twelve pearls: each individual gate was of one pearl. And the street of the city was pure gold, like transparent glass.

No one in the world can live eternally. If you are lucky, you may live 120 years. When you die, you can take nothing with you. If you believe the Holy Spirit's words and believe in Jesus Christ with all your heart and follow the Holy Spirit's guidance step-by-step, you will be led to the beautiful heaven where you will spend your eternal life, worshiping and praising the Heavenly Father forever.

However if you do not believe in Jesus Christ or if you slander Jesus Christ, the Holy Spirit, or the Heavenly Father, and do not obey the Holy Spirit's words, or if you believe idols or any other religions controlled by Satan, except the Trinity God, you will not be able to go to heaven. After you die, you will be thrown into the sulfur fire sea in hell where all kinds of metals or rocks are melting like in the furnaces of a steel mill. You will be eternally crying with screams and lamenting and deploring your having not believed in Jesus Christ when you were living in the world. However it will be too late for you to be saved, and no one will be able to save you from the sea of fire.

2) The sulphur burning fiery lake in hell

I have been to many different places in hell. The most fearful place among the places I have seen in hell was the sulfur burning fiery lake where all kinds of metals are melting like in the furnace of a steel mill. The fire sea is so big that I couldn't see the end of it, where billions of spirits are crying and wailing loudly forever and lamenting that they have not believed Jesus Christ when they were living in the world. The scene was so dreadful and miserable that no one can see them without tears in the eyes. Whenever I saw the innumerable poor spirits forever wailing and lamenting in the fire sea, tears dropped from my eyes.

Revelation 20: 12-15 And I saw the dead, small and great, standing before God, and books were opened. And another book was opened, which is the Book of Life. And the dead were judged according to their works, by the things which were written in the books. The sea gave up the dead who were in it, and Death and Hades delivered up the dead who were in them. And they were

judged, each one according to his works. Then Death and Hades were cast into the lake of fire. This is the second death. And anyone not found written in the Book of Life was cast into the lake of fire.

Why are you doing such foolish and stupid acts? I have seen innumerable things in the spiritual world, such as heaven, hell, God's final judgment, angels, Jesus, the being of light, and many others in heaven. Never be deceived by Satan and the Devil, who start with frauds and end with lies.

1 John 3: 8 He who sins is of the devil, for the devil has sinned from the beginning. For this purpose the Son of God was manifested, that He might destroy the works of the devil.

Except the Almighty God, His Son Jesus Christ and Holy Spirit, namely the Trinity God, all the other religions in the world are worshiping idols, Satan, the Devil. Therefore Jesus said the following:

John 14: 6 Jesus said to him, "I am the way, the truth, and the life. No one comes to the Father except through Me."

It means that except through Jesus, any religions or any people in the world cannot come to heaven where you can have eternal life.

Please only believe in the Trinity God: the Heavenly Father, His Son Jesus Christ and the Holy Spirit, who are telling you the only truth in the universe, and you will be saved from the fiery sea. Whatever sins you have committed so far, He will forgive all your sins. If you really believe in Jesus Christ with all your heart, and confess all your sins and repent for them before God, He will clean all your sins as white as snow.

Isaiah 1: 18-20 "Come now let us reason together," Says the Lord, "Though your sins are like scarlet, They shall be as white as snow; Though they are red like crimson, They shall be as wool. If you are willing and obedient, you shall eat the good of the land; But if you refuse and rebel, You shall be devoured by the sword"; For the mouth of the Lord has spoken.

It means that whatever sins you have committed, if you confess your sins and repent of your sins, God will forgive them all and make you as white as the snow. However if you neglect God's word and do not obey God, He will punish you fearfully. The Almighty God has created human beings. Who can talk against God, the creator of human beings, when He does everything at His will? The only thing we human beings can do for God is to worship, pray, praise, and be obedient to the Almighty God.

Brothers and Sisters!

Many times, I have seen scenes showing uncountable people crying with their loudest screams in the ever burning sulfur fire sea, lamenting, deploring of their having not believed Jesus Christ. They have to live permanently in the fiery sea of hell. The chance to live in beautiful heaven was given to them. But they chose hell by believing the wrong religion instead of Jesus Christ. Why are you going to spend your eternal life in the fiery sea of hell?

I have seen them innumerable times with my own eyes. I

have seen them so many times that I gave up all my wealth and honor in the world. I appeal to you with all my heart to believe in Jesus. I was a big businessman who was doing international trade with great amounts of money, traveling all over the world for business.

And I was elected and served as the president of "The Federation of Korean Associations in the USA" three times, representing about 2.5 million Korean-Americans in the USA. In addition to that I served two times as the chairman of "Overseas Conference Meeting of Representatives of Koreans Living Abroad" representing all 7 million Koreans abroad. I was a foolish and idiotic man who used to live while enjoying all the good things in the world, such as eating only high class and expensive food, driving only high class, expensive cars, and wearing only high class, expensive clothes.

However Jesus knows my destiny after I am dead. If I live such a life without paying much attention to God, it will be difficult for me to go to heaven. He began to drive me to the last moment of my life. That is when I was supposed to be dead by Satan's attacks. Whenever I was about to be killed by Satan's attacks, I called Jesus' name with my loudest voice, then the Holy Spirit came immediately and saved me, while killing Satan or the demons completely. This kind of incident happened not one time but many times, maybe more than 100 times in the past seven years and six months.

Therefore in my heart He trained me to think that I cannot live even one day without Jesus Christ and the Holy Spirit. He trained me to always call Jesus or the Holy Spirit in the last seven years whether I am sleeping or waking.

God loves all of us. The Holy Spirit tries to lead all of us to heaven. We are sons and daughters of the Almighty God. While we are living in the world, we have to use all our efforts to praise the Lord and deliver Jesus' gospel to all the people in the world. This is the thing which pleases the Almighty God most in the world. In order to deliver the gospel, we all have to testify boldly about the Holy Spirit Ministry before anyone.

Mark 16: 15-16 And He said to them, "Go into all the world and and preach the gospel to every creature. He who believes and is baptized will be saved; but he who does not believe will be condemned."

Brothers and Sisters!

I have seen many things in the spiritual world, such as beautiful heaven, the fiery sulfur sea and many other places in hell, the Heavenly Father's throne, the life record book, God's judgment, and many other beautiful places in heaven. I can tell you what I have seen but I cannot show you what I have seen. Believe in Jesus Christ really with all your heart, and follow in your acts, and you will receive eternal life in heaven.

I have lost all my money, which was a great amount. However right now I am with the Holy Spirit 24-hours-a-day. I can talk with Him anytime, whenever I want to, like you are talking with your friends on the phone. I am always happy, glad and peaceful, without any worry in my heart. All of these the Holy Spirit gives me, and especially His love I can never forget. I do follow all His instructions, such as receiving the Holy Spirit Messages for the pastors of big churches in Korea and the USA or other countries, or His Messages for the presidents or kings of countries. And I deliver them to the people the Holy Spirit wants to, in person or by express mail.

Right now I am much more happy and peaceful working for the Holy Spirit, than I was in the past, doing a big trading business with large amounts of money, and traveling all over the world.

My eternal life in heaven is guaranteed. I don't worry about my death. If I am dead, I will be led to heaven. When I am living in the world, I will do my best to evangelize the gospel to the world. I am always ready to go to heaven, whenever the Heavenly Father calls me to come.

Ladies and Gentlemen!

Whatever big business you own and whatever big business tycoon you are, if you do not know the place where you will be going to, and if you do not prepare the place where you will go to, after you die, you are the most foolish and idiotic person in the world and you have failed in your life. Your final destination is only the fearful, ever burning fire sea in hell. You will live eternally in the dreadful fire sea in hell, not for the short period of your current life, of about 100 years. In order to save your spirit and soul from the fiery sea of hell, the Holy Spirit asks me to deliver this universal truth, the Holy Spirit's words to you.

Chairman!

Your business and present time also are also very important

to you but prepare for your death which will come to you without fail after several decades. Your life is not guaranteed for several decades. If God calls you, you must go immediately without delaying even one day. You must go while eating your dinner, while sleeping in bed, while driving your car, or doing anything you like.

He is the God who created the universe by His words and controls everything in the universe. All the words in the Bible from Genesis to the end of Revelation are 100% God's words. The word has no fraud at all, and all the words are living, the words themselves are doing ministry and perform miracles. They are the words of the Heavenly Father, who created the universe by words.

Hebrews 4: 12 For the word of God is living and powerful, and sharper than any two-edged sword, piercing even to the division of soul and spirit, and of joints and marrow, and is a discerner of the thoughts and intents of the heart.

Believe the words of God, follow in your acts, and save your spirit. And work and serve for God's works. That is the only way which will save your eternal life in heaven.

If you are lost on the way to heaven, like the Buddhist monks and Japanese idol worshipers thrown into the fiery sea of hell, change trains immediately to the right train which will lead you to heaven without fail. If you worship any religion made by man and controlled by Satan and the Devil in this world, you will be thrown into the fiery sea when you are dead. Only the Trinity God: the Heavenly Father, Jesus Christ and the Holy Spirit, are able to lead you to heaven. I have seen innumerable things in the spiritual world. Therefore after training me for seven years and six months, the Holy Spirit sends me to deliver the universal truth, the Holy Spirit's words to you, in order to save people who are lost on the wrong way to heaven like you.

If you are lost in the wrong way to heaven, and if you want to come to the right way to heaven, please contact me. I am the Holy Spirit's servant who does work for the Holy Spirit. Whatever things He asks me to do, I am ready to do for Him to save people like you. If you want to see the ministry and miracles the Holy Spirit does with your own eyes, and if you want to experience it yourselves, please contact the Holy Spirit's envoy, who will help you to have a Holy Spirit experience yourselves for you to be led step-by-step to heaven with the Holy Spirit's guidance. Never delay the time, the most urgent and important thing you have to do today in the world is to prepare your way, leading you to heaven after you are dead. You may do your business and others later, after you finish the most important thing in your life. The Holy Spirit who will lead your eternal life wants to help you through the Holy Spirit's servant.

I pray under the name of Jesus that you may be saved and secure your ticket to heaven as soon as possible.

The Holy Spirit's words were given in prayer at 6:22 PM on July 16, 1997.

3. Going to the Buddhist Temple to deliver Jesus' gospel

The Holy Spirit's Fire came down from heaven and set the den of Satan on fire

The point of my testimony is that the Almighty Heavenly Father loves all the people in the world. God wants to save all the people who are deceived by Satan, who tells only lies. Satan wants to decoy people and to destroy their spirits completely.

1 John 3: 8 He who sins is of the devil, for devil has sinned from the beginning. For this purpose the Son of God was manifested, that He might destroy the works of devil.

Except for the Trinity God who created the universe, there are no other gods who can save a human being's spirit for eternal life. In the universe, there is only one Trinity God, the Almighty Heavenly Father, His Son Jesus Christ and the Holy Spirit, who can save our spirits for our eternity. That is the truth. If anyone serves another god in the world, he commits a great sin against God.

Exodus 20: 3-6 You shall have no other gods before Me. You shall not make for yourself a carved image - any likeness of anything that is in heaven above, or that is in the earth beneath, or that is in the water under the earth; you shall not bow down to them. For I, the Lord your God, am a jealous God, visiting the iniquity of the fathers upon the children to the third and fourth generations of those who hate Me, but showing mercy to thousands, to those who love Me and keep My commandments.

As written in the above shown Bible passage, anyone who serves their own god, except the Trinity God commits himself against the Almighty God who created the universe. Therefore the Holy Spirit spiritually trained a sinner like me and taught him what the truth was for more than 10 years, and He asked me to spread such truth all over the world, in order that people may not be deceived by Satan, who tells only lies. The Devil deceives human beings to believe in idols, commit sins against the Almighty God, and finally to decoy human beings into their destruction. God wants to save all the people who are deceived by devil, and the Holy Spirit wants to lead all such people to Jesus' salvation and to eternal life. This is God's real meaning.

Without knowing this truth, if people continuously serve idols, they will have to permanently cry in the sulfur burning sea in hell. It is God's love to prevent this tragedy and to lead such people to heaven.

Therefore the Holy Spirit spiritually trained a sinner like me for more than 10 years and He opened my spiritual eyes to see innumerable visions in the spiritual world. The Holy Spirit gave me too many experiences of the Holy Spirit's ministries. He performed innumerable miracles of the Holy Spirit through me, together with the Bible's words. The Holy Spirit showed me Satan's world too. He told me what is the real world of Satan who deceives all human beings by telling lies.

Therefore the Holy Spirit wants to save all the Buddhist monks and believers of Buddha who are deceived by Satan, by teaching and showing them the truth and facts of Satan's world. This is the purpose of my telling about the story which I experienced, when I visited a Buddhist temple.

Do not try to judge spiritual things with your flesh's eyes in the present. But try to see the eternal spiritual world with spiritual vision, which will come after your life ends in this world. Please be thankful to the Almighty God who tries to save all the people serving idols who are deceived by Satan and destined to be thrown into the ever burning fire sea in hell. God wants to save your souls and lead you to the eternal heaven where the Almighty Heavenly Father lives permanently. The Holy Spirit wants no one to be deceived by Satan's lie. We pray for God to save all the people trapped by Satan and lead them to Jesus' salvation.

1) The mission trip led by the Holy Spirit and the Holy Spirit's Miracle

From April 26, 2000 to May 25, 2000 I preached and led a daily Holy Spirit healing ministry at eight different churches in Korea. At every service the Holy Spirit led a powerful Holy Spirit service. Most of the participants in the services, saints and pastors, were blessed a lot. In the middle of the services, many of attendants were moved by the Holy Spirit. They cried and confessed their sins to God. On the days when we didn't have any official healing services, by the Holy Spirit's leading we visited unbelievers or Christians who had stopped going to churches.

My wife and I visited our friends and relatives who didn't believe in God and the people who stopped going to churches, in Seoul, Chung Buk province, Chung Nam Province, Kyung Ki Province and Kang Won Province. Most of the people we visited, when we first asked them to believe in Jesus Christ, didn't let us say anything about Jesus Christ.

Some of them said, "We believe in Buddha. Please do not tell us anything about Jesus." Some of them were gangsters who spent most of their life, from youth, as gangsters and some of them were highly educated people who didn't believe in the Almighty God, but only relied on their own ability or knowledge. The Holy Spirit led that we should deliver Jesus' gospel to such people.

Everywhere we went, the Holy Spirit performed His powerful ministry. At first, most of the people we met were very resistant against our mission of delivering Jesus' gospel. But we explained to them how the Holy Spirit changed me. We are only delivering Jesus' gospel to unbelievers in order to save their lives. Today we came to save your life, which is destined to be thrown into the fiery sea of hell.

Since I was born again on January 1, 1990, Jesus Christ has saved me from death, whenever I was confronted with the moment of death. And whenever demons tried to kill me, Jesus Christ saved me from demon attacks. Satan and evil spirits tried to kill me whenever the chance was available for them to kill me. It was not one or two times. It was many hundred times, and I cannot remember all of them. Whenever demons tried to kill me, Jesus Christ saved me from the demons' attacks.

We also told them about heaven, where all the Christians who had a really strong belief in God are going after death. They will enjoy eternal life without any worry or sorrow, while praising the Almighty Heavenly Father.

In heaven all the houses are built with solid gold, and are decorated with valuable jewels like diamonds, and all the roads are made of solid gold. The Holy Spirit showed me such a heaven too many times. (Refer: Revelation 21: 9 - 22: 5)

Revelation 21: 10-11, 18-21 And he carried me away in the Spirit to a great and high mountain, and showed me the great city, the holy Jerusalem, descending out of heaven from God, having the glory of God. Her light was like most precious stone, like a jasper stone, clear as crystal.

The construction of the wall was of jasper; and the city was pure gold, like clear glass. The foundations of the wall of the city were adorned with all kinds of precious stones: the first foundation was jasper, the second sapphire, the third chalcedony, the fourth emerald, the fifth sardonyx, the sixth sardius, the seventh chrysolite, the eighth beryl, the ninth topaz, the tenth chrysoprase, the eleventh jacinth, and the twelfth amethyst. The twelve gates were twelve pearls: each individual gate was of one pearl. And the street of the city was pure gold, like transparent glass.

I also told them about hell where the poor, miserable people who didn't believe in Jesus Christ and follow their greed to enjoy life in this world, are thrown into when their life is finished. I also told them about the souls who were crying endlessly in the sulfur burning fire sea in hell like the furnace in the steel mills. They were crying sorrowfully without end in a loud voice, lamenting that they didn't believe in God, when they were living in the world. The scene was so miserable, fearful and pitiful that no one could see them with open eyes.

Revelation 20: 12-15 And I saw the dead, small and great, standing before God, and books were opened. And another book was opened, which is the Book of Life. And the dead were judged according to their works, by the things which were written in the books. The sea gave up the dead who were in it, and Death and Hades delivered up the dead who were in them. And they were

judged, each one according to his works. Then Death and Hades were cast into the lake of fire. This is the second death. And anyone not found written in the Book of Life was cast into the lake of fire.

Revelation 21: 6-8 And He said to me, "It is done! I am the Al-Alpha and the Omega, the Beginning and the End. I will give of the fountain of the water of life freely to him who thirsts. He who overcomes shall inherit all things, and I will be his God and he shall be My son. But the cowardly, unbelieving, abominable, murderers, sexually immoral, sorcerers, idolaters, and all liars shall have their part in the lake which burns with fire and brimstone, which is the second death."

The Holy Spirit showed me innumerable souls crying endlessly with loud voices and lamenting in the fiery sea of hell for not believing in Jesus Christ.

And He trained me spiritually saying, **"In this world, there are innumerable people who are destined to be thrown into the fire sea, like the souls which you see now because of their not believing in the Almighty Heavenly Father, Jesus Christ and the Holy Spirit and not having confessed their sins committed against God. Try your best to save the souls of such people in the world."**

In addition to that, the Holy Spirit cured seven different infirmities which I was suffering from for three to four decades. He also cured three infirmities of my wife from which she was suffering for many years. Right now if we pray for sick people, the Holy Spirit cures the sickness. The Holy Spirit has cured innumerable patients through our prayers.

Mark 16: 17-18 "And these signs will follow those who believe: In My name they will cast out demons; they will speak with new tongues; they will take up serpents; and if they drink anything deadly, it will by no means hurt them; they will lay their hands on the sick, and they will recover."

If you obey the word of God and follow it in deed, the Holy Spirit will pour unlimited blessings on you.

We told them some examples in which the Holy Spirit gave unlimited blessings through our prayer.

**Deuteronomy 28: 1-14 "Now it shall come to pass, if you diligently obey the voice of the LORD your God, to observe carefully all His commandments which I command you today, that the LORD your God will set you high above all nations of the earth. And all these blessings shall come upon you and overtake you, because you obey the voice of the LORD your God: "Blessed shall you be in the city, and blessed shall you be in the country. "Blessed shall be the fruit of your body, the produce of your ground and the increase of your herds, the increase of your cattle and the offspring of your flocks.
"Blessed shall be your basket and your kneading bowl. "Blessed shall you be when you come in, and blessed shall you be when you go out. "The LORD will cause your enemies who rise against you to be defeated before your face; they shall come out against you one way and flee before you seven ways. "The LORD will command the blessing on you in your storehouses and in all to which you set your hand, and He will bless you in the land which the LORD your God is giving you. "The LORD will establish you as a holy people to Himself, just as He has sworn to you, if you keep the commandments of the LORD your God and walk in His ways. Then all peoples of the earth shall see that you are called by**

the name of the LORD, and they shall be afraid of you.

And the LORD will grant you plenty of goods, in the fruit of your body, in the increase of your livestock, and in the produce of your ground, in the land of which the LORD swore to your fathers to give you. The LORD will open to you His good treasure, the heavens, to give the rain to your land in its season, and to bless all the work of your hand.

You shall lend to many nations, but you shall not borrow. And the LORD will make you the head and not the tail; you shall be above only, and not be beneath, if you heed the commandments of the LORD your God, which I command you today, and are careful to observe them. So you shall not turn aside from any of the words which I command you this day, to the right or the left, to go after other gods to serve them."

When we testified to them of several experiences which the Holy Spirit performed through us one by one and how the Holy Spirit performed through us for other people in our family, even the people whose hearts were as hard as steel knelt down before God and accepted Jesus Christ as their Lord as Savior. According to the ways which the Holy Spirit trained us, we led many people to accept Jesus Christ as their Lord Savior on the spot.

Among the people to whom we delivered Jesus' gospel, several of them didn't accept Jesus Christ as their Lord right on the spot because of their personal pride, intelligence, knowledge and other human reasons, but accepted God's blessings through our prayer. These people also were very resistant against Jesus Christ at first, and said to us, "If you want to tell us about Jesus, don't come to our house again." Even the people who refused Jesus' gospel so strongly and ignored Christians, who were antagonistic against Christianity, Christians and churches were moved by the Holy Spirit's anointing and began to kneel down before God.

Because of the Holy Spirit's powerful anointing in the churches where I preached about the Holy Spirit's ministry, many Christians began to cry and confess to God, calling to the Almighty Heavenly Father, Jesus Christ, the Son of God, and the Holy Spirit in loud voices, at hearing my testimony about how the Holy Spirit performed miracles through me. Even the people whom we visited privately to deliver Jesus' gospel, most of them knelt before God and accepted our prayer for them one by one. My wife who saw that the Holy Spirit perform miracles strongly through me asked me to go to the Buddhist temple to deliver Jesus' gospel to her friend who was a Buddhist monk.

At first I was hesitant to go to a Buddhist temple.
But the Holy Spirit in my heart said to me, "Go to the Buddhist temple with your wife. The Holy Spirit and angels are with you, and don't worry about going to Buddhist temple. Just deliver the gospel to the Buddhist monk."

When I was a young boy, I had been to Buddhist temples many times with my grandmother or mother. I bowed innumerable times to the idol, Buddha's statue made of stone or brass, covered in golden metal. In the USA also I have visited Buddhist temples a couple of times. In the past, I visited the Buddhist temple to serve and pray to the idol, Buddha.

However this time, I visited the Buddhist temple to deliver Jesus' gospel with the power of the Holy Spirit, who is living and now performs miracles through me, to a Buddhist monk. She was my wife's friend from childhood. She was a real Buddhist monk who abandoned her life in the world four years ago.

She had her hair cut with a razor and dressed in gray Buddhist monk attire and read the Buddhist book like the Holy Bible. She already graduated from the Buddhist university and lived in the Buddhist temple believing only Buddha. The Buddhist temple where she was staying was one of the well known temples which was built 1000 years ago. That temple belongs to the Korean National Treasures.

2) The Buddhist Temple is Satan's country where innumerable big snakes live in swarms

On arriving at the temple, I was very surprised to see innumerable big snakes all over the temple. The Holy Spirit opens my spiritual eyes for me to see spiritual visions whenever the Holy Spirit wants to show me spiritual scenes. Especially when I visit sick people who are suffering from serious illness (such advanced cancer), visit Holy Spirit Services or when we pray in tongues, the Holy Spirit shows me many different spiritual visions.

In the last 10 years, the Holy Spirit has shown me innumerable spiritual visions. I was spiritually trained with so many fearful spiritual visions that I am not surprised to see small spiritual visions.

However this time was different. As soon as our car arrived at the entrance of the temple, I could clearly see innumerable big snakes sitting rolled in the spaces of the stone heaps made of small and large rocks, like a fence. They opened their mouths and the tongues of the snakes went in and out of their mouths.

Around the Buddhist temple, there were many big trees with green leaves. I was astonished again to see so many big snakes sitting rolled on the branches or creeping on the big branches of the trees. On the roof also were many big snakes creeping here and there. On the beams of the ceiling also, there were many snakes sitting rolled together. Wherever I looked, there were countless snakes all over and around the temple. So I immediately knew that place was a den of snakes.

Revelation 12: 9 So the great dragon was cast out, that serpent of old, called Devil and Satan, who deceives the whole world; he was cast to the earth, and his angels were cast out with him.

I was so scared to see so many snakes, that I didn't want to go into the temple. However my wife already entered the temple, because she couldn't see the snakes.

3) The Holy Spirit performed miracles for our gospel mission

In my heart I prayed. The Holy Spirit answered my prayer immediately.

He said to me, "Don't worry about the snakes. The Holy Spirit, the Spirit of the Almighty God who created the universe, and His angels are with you and we will protect you and help you. Just deliver boldly the words given by the Holy Spirit."

I was so encouraged by the Holy Spirit's words that I entered the temple without any fear even with innumerable snakes all over the temple, in the holes of the stone heaps like fences, on the branches of trees and on the roof and on beams under the ceiling.

Upon entering the temple, I recognized that the Holy Spirit already performed miracles for us to deliver the gospel in the Buddhist temple. This temple is a very old and well known national cultural treasure, that's why there are always about 10 to 12 Buddhist monks who stay and serve the temple year-round.

However the Holy Spirit performed a miracle, and in such a big temple, there was no one except the female monk to whom we planned to deliver the gospel. There was one more female monk but suddenly she was very sick for an unknown reason, so she couldn't come out of her bedroom. We could freely explain Jesus' gospel in the temple.

The female monk told us the following before our leaving the temple. "When other female or male monks are present in the temple, it is impossible for anyone to evangelize for Jesus and read the Bible in the Buddhist temple. In addition to that, if any Buddhist monks are found listening to Jesus' gospel, they will be chased out of the temple immediately. Therefore no one even tries to deliver the gospel in the temple." These are the unspoken rules for the Buddhist temple.

The female monk we wanted to evangelize accepted us kindly and asked us to stay at the chief monk's room, which is the best room in the temple. We didn't call her in advance that we would visit her. We visited the temple without any advance notice. However the Holy Spirit and His angels prepared everything for us to freely deliver Jesus' gospel to the female monk in the temple, while staying at the chief monk's room, the best room in the temple.

First of all, my wife began to talk about us, but soon the monk began to talk about the life in the temple and Buddha so we listened to her stories. After listening to her story, we told her that I was invited to preach and lead the Holy Spirit's healing service at eight different churches in Korea. And we finished most of the Holy Spirit healing services. Now we came to you in the temple without any advance notice to deliver you Jesus' gospel to save your soul for the eternal life. However she repeated only the words that she already made up her mind to serve Buddha, so she had her hair cut with a razor and abandoned her life in the world and came to the temple in the mountain and changed her clothes also to a Buddhist monk's gray gown to live in the temple.

Instead of accepting Jesus' gospel, she tried to persuade us to believe in Buddha. Meanwhile I was praying in my heart and my wife continuously explained that she should believe in Jesus to receive salvation. But she was not listening carefully.

4) Jesus Christ and His angels hanged Buddha's statues (bul sang) to the branches of the trees upside down and smashed them with hammers

1 Samuel 5: 1-9 Then the Philistines took the ark of God and brought it from Ebenezer to Ashdod. When the Philistines took the ark of God, they brought it into the house of Dagon and set it by Dagon. And when the people of Ashdod arose early in the morning, there was Dagon, fallen on its face to the earth before

the ark of the Lord. So they took Dagon and set it in its place again. And when they arose early the next morning, there was Dagon, fallen on its face to the ground before the ark of the Lord. The head of Dagon and both the palms of its hands were broken off on the threshold; only Dagon's torso was left of it.

Therefore neither the priests of Dagon nor any who come into Dagon's house tread on the threshold of Dagon in Ashdod to this day. But the hand of the Lord was heavy on the people of Ashdod, and He ravaged them and struck them with tumors, both Ashdod and its territory. And when the men of Ashdod saw how it was, they said, "The ark of the God of Israel must not remain with us, for His hand is harsh toward us and Dagon our god." Therefore they sent and gathered to themselves all the lords of the Philistines, and said, "What shall we do with the ark of the God of Israel?"
And they answered, "Let the ark of the God of Israel be carried away to Gath." So they carried the ark of the God of Israel away. So it was, after they had carried it away, that the hand of the Lord was against the city with a very great destruction; and He struck the men of the city, both small and great, and tumors broke out on them.

At about 6 pm in the evening, the monk told us that she would go to the Buddhist sanctum to do the Buddhist prayer. At that time, I asked her, "May I come into the Buddhist sanctum?"

She thought for a little while and said to me, "You may come in, if you want."

As soon as I entered the Buddhist sanctum, I began to pray in my heart to the Almighty God. This temple was den of snakes wherever I looked. They were sitting rolled on the branches of trees and sitting in the holes of the stone heaps like a fence. They were creeping on the beams and on the roof. With my eyes I could clearly see them creeping all over the temple.

When the monk was praying to Buddha, while sounding the Buddhist monk's wooden gong, I prayed in my heart. In the name of Jesus, with the authority of the Almighty Father and the Holy Spirit's power, bind all the demons, evil spirits, and the Devil dwelling at this temple in the name of Jesus, and throw them away into the fiery sea.

About 20 to 30 minutes after I began to pray, I saw from far away in the sky a bright beam of light shining, and Jesus, embraced by the light, and many of His angels were coming to me. Jesus and His angels came into the Buddhist sanctum and one of the angels tied up the biggest Buddha statue by the neck with a lasso like a cowboy's rope. The angels pulled the statue of Buddha and dragged it to the big tree standing at the entrance of the temple and they tied the statue upside down with the ropes.

5) Jesus burnt all the statues of Buddha and snakes with the Holy Spirit's fire from heaven

When the biggest Buddha statue was completely crushed, the angels brought all the Buddha statues in or around the temple to the same place and hanged them upside down and began to smash them with big iron hammers. Soon the Holy Spirit's fire came down from heaven and burnt all of them.

At the same time, Jesus said to Buddha's statues, "You liars, Buddha's statues, here is the so called paradise of

Buddhism that you say."

Meanwhile, all the statues of Buddha were miserably wailing and grieving without knowing what to do. I was fully filled in the Holy Spirit. Soon the Holy Spirit's fire was continuously coming down from heaven and the fire burnt all the snakes in the holes of the stone heaps, the ones sitting rolled on the branches of the trees and the ones creeping on the roof and beams. The Holy Spirit's fire from heaven was continuously coming down to all the places where the snakes were sitting rolled or creeping. The fire was burning all over the temple and the nearby mountain where snakes were in swarms. Innumerable snakes were wailing, grieving over their fate and burning in the Holy Spirit's fire.

Jesus said to the burning snakes, "This is the so called paradise of Buddhism. Don't lie to the innocent people, whom you deceived. Then they are to be thrown into the fiery sea because of your groundless deceit."

2 Kings 1: 10 So Elijah answered and said to the captain of fifty, "If I am a man of God, then let fire come down from heaven and consume you and your fifty men." And fire came down from heaven and consumed him and his fifty.

Our Savior Lord, Jesus, who came with His angels, destroyed and burnt with the Holy Spirit's fire all the evil spirits, demons and snakes who were deceiving innocent people. The Holy Spirit's fire which was continuously burning burnt the den of snakes, the Buddhist temple and nearby mountains. The scene of the Holy Spirit's fire was clearly seen by my eyes through the night. All the snakes, the evil spirits of Satan burning in the Holy Spirit's fire were wailing and lamenting endlessly through the night.

After about one hour and 30 minutes, the female Buddhist monk's prayer was finished, together with ringing the big bell. The den of snakes, Satan's home, was burnt by the Holy Spirit's fire, so the female monk seemed very depressed and powerless. She didn't try to come into our room but she was continuously doing some work outside. The demons seemed to lose all their power because of the Holy Spirit's fire. Soon dinner was ready for us.

6) The Holy Spirit's Fire coming down from heaven burnt our dinner table

When the dinner table was ready for us, we thought it is not right for God's children to eat anything at the den of Satan. So we prayed to God, whether we may eat the dinner in the country of snakes. As soon as we finished our prayer, the Holy Spirit's fire came down from heaven and burnt all the food on our table and the fire went up to heaven. The Holy Spirit showed me the scene clearly.

The Holy Spirit said to me, "All Satan's power on your dinner table was completely burnt by the Holy Spirit's fire, do not fear anything and eat the food prepared for you."

Judges 13: 19-20 So Manoah took the young goat with the grain offering, and offered it upon the rock to the Lord. And He did wondrous thing while Manoah and his wife looked on - it happened as the flame went up toward heaven from the altar - the Angel of the Lord ascended in the flame of the altar! When Manoah and his wife saw this, they fell on their faces to the

ground.

We prayed thanks to God for the wonderful food and we ate all the food prepared for us in the den of Satan. That night the monk didn't try to come to us to listen to Jesus' gospel, therefore we couldn't deliver the gospel that night.

The next morning when the breakfast food was prepared for us, we prayed again to God, whether we were allowed to eat anything in the den of Satan. Upon finishing the prayer, the Holy Spirit's fire came down from heaven and burnt everything and the fire went up again to heaven.

At the same time, the Holy Spirit said to me, "Don't worry about anything and eat all the food prepared for you."

After the prayer and fire burnt the breakfast table, we finished all the food prepared for us in the house of snakes.

1 Kings 18: 37-38 "Hear me, O Lord, hear me, that this people may know that You are the Lord God, and that You have turned their hearts back to You again." Then the fire of the Lord fell and consumed the burnt sacrifice, and the wood and the stones and the dust, and it licked up the water that was in the trench.

7) Buddhist female monk listening to Jesus' gospel by the Holy Spirit's ministry

After breakfast, the Holy Spirit asked me to deliver the gospel to the Buddhist monk. When we began to deliver the gospel, we found that she was accepting Jesus' gospel without any problem. Because the Holy Spirit had already moved the monk's mind, she accepted all the words about Jesus we delivered, as a dry sponge soaks up water. We told her the following statement: how the Holy Spirit spiritually trained and changed me so we could even come to a Buddhist temple to deliver Jesus' gospel.

1. On January 1, 1990 when I was at the moment of death, I found there were so many spirits in the world but it was only Jesus Christ who could save me from death, and Jesus saved me at the moment of my being killed. At the same time I was born again in the Holy Spirit and He spiritually trained me very hard. Therefore I abandoned all the evil and bad habits in the world and I read only the Holy Bible. The words of the Bible were sweeter to my lips than the honey to my mouth.

Therefore I read the Holy Bible from early morning to late at night everyday for many years. I was singing only Psalms and on Sundays wherever I was, in Korea, Japan or in the USA, I went to church without fail and at church I sat right in front of the pastor who preached. Because the words of God preached by the pastors were more sweet than the honey to my lips. In addition to that, I attended all the Holy Spirit's ministering services wherever they were held in the USA and Korea. I told the monk my testimony of how the Holy Spirit trained me and changed my heart.

2. The demons and evil spirits tried to kill me many times, however every time the evil spirits tried to slay me, Jesus, embraced by the light, came and saved me from the evil spirits' plot to murder me. It was not one or two times when evil spirits tried to take my life away. Demons attempted to murder hundreds of times in the last ten years.

3. I have been to Christians' paradise many hundred times. That is the heaven where good Christians who really believe and obey God in deed are going. In paradise all the houses were built with pure, solid gold and they were decorated with valuable jewels like diamonds. Therefore we determined that nothing is more important than going to heaven after our life is over in the world. So I abandoned my own business in which I was engaged for more than 25 years. We really believe the word of God, and today we visited you in the Buddhist temple to save your life for eternity.

4. The Holy Spirit showed me the sulfur burning fire sea of hell where the spirits of the people not believing in Jesus Christ are going after their life is finished in the world. I saw billions of people are wailing and lamenting everlastingly for what they didn't believe in God when they were living. The scene was so fearful and miserable that no human being can see them without tears in their eyes.

At the same time the Holy Spirit said to me, "There are innumerable people in this world who will be thrown into the fiery sea of hell like these people. Do your best to save the spirits of such people in the world."

Revelation 20: 12-15 And I saw the dead, small and great, standing before God, and books were opened. And another book was opened, which is the Book of Life. And the dead were judged according to their works, by the things which were written in the books. The sea gave up the dead who were in it, and Death and Hades delivered up the dead who were in them. And they were judged, each one according to his works. Then Death and Hades were cast into the lake of fire. This is the second death. And any-

one not found written in the Book of Life was cast into the lake of fire.

Also the Holy Spirit told me to give out leaflets of the church where I used to go in Korea, to all the people passing by the subway tunnel near the church. The leaflet was about the Holy Spirit's miracles and church ministry. I delivered the leaflets at the entrance of the subway every Sunday afternoon from April to the end of December 1996. Wherever I went, according to the Holy Spirit's instructions, I delivered the same leaflets to the people I saw at subway entrances, in subway trains, in buses, restaurants, banks, airplanes and on the roads.

Also I delivered cassettes tapes of a Christian deacon talking about heaven and hell, which he saw, to innumerable people, including many of my friends.

5. With only our prayer and the Holy Spirit's power, the Holy Spirit cured 7 different infirmities, some of which I suffered from for 30 - 40 years. He also cured my wife's three different infirmities, from which she was suffering for many years. Right now if we pray, the Holy Spirit cures other patients also. The Holy Spirit cured many patients' sickness through our prayers.

6. I said to the Buddhist monk, "If you really believe in God, the Holy Spirit will solve all your problems, such as your physical problems and illnesses, your economic problems, and your spiritual problems which you couldn't solve yourself. When I told her my testimony, her heart began to move, and she said the following several times, "You are a couple greatly blessed by God." After that, we evangelized her with the words of God. I preached to her with the words of God and my wife read the Holy Bible.

8) The Buddhist Monk trembling at the words of God

Exodus 20: 3-7 "You shall have no other gods before Me. "You shall not make for yourself a carved image-any likeness of anything that is in heaven above, or that is in the earth beneath, or that is in the water under the earth; you shall not bow down to them nor serve them. For I, the Lord your God, am jealous God, visiting the iniquity of the fathers upon the children to the third and fourth generations of those who hate Me, but showing mercy to thousands, to those who love Me and keep My commandments. "You shall not take the name of the Lord your God in vain, for the Lord will not hold him guiltless who takes His name in vain."

We gave her the above Bible passages, and explained her that if you believe in other gods, besides the Almighty Heavenly Father, you are committing more sin against Almighty God.

In addition to that, I told her one of the real stories which happened in the my hometown where I was born and raised in Korea. The country village where I was living in my young days in Korea was a small traditional agricultural village which had about 60 households in all.

There were three exorcists in my small village. The first one was very close friend of my grandmother, so we went to her very often. She had five grandsons, and among the five boys, one was three years older than me, one was my age and the other three were younger than me.

However all five of them died before they turned 40. One killed himself by drinking a poisonous liquid used for agriculture produce, after a fight between the brothers. One was killed in a traffic accident. One killed himself by committing suicide and the others died of sickness.

The second exorcist's son was my age, but he died before he turned 40, after drinking a lot of rice wine, without leaving any offspring to continue his family name after his generation.

The third exorcist's son was 2 years older than me and we went to the same middle school but he died in his forties.

As in my testimony above, all of the sons of the Buddhist exorcist in my small village died at very young ages. They were the sons of a female shaman believing and serving idols, Buddha statues in their homes. One of them had a small Buddhist temple in the mountain and the other two built small Buddhist sanctums in their home, praying always before the Buddha's statue. All three were friends of my grandmother and our family, so we used to visit them often and we knew each of them very well. But all the sons of the three families died at young ages. Because they believed in the wrong god, Buddha, not the Trinity God, that is the Almighty Heavenly Father God, Our Lord Jesus Christ and the Holy Spirit. Therefore God didn't protect them from the deceitful plot of demons to destroy and kill them at a young age and send them to hell.

If they had believed in Jesus Christ, they might not have died so early. And they might also be alive right now. Demons and evil spirits tried to kill me many hundred times but whenever they tried to slay me, I cried for Jesus to help me and every time the Holy Spirit came immediately in the form of Jesus and saved me from Satan.

That's why I am still alive. The Holy Spirit who saved me from demon attack so many times will surely save other Christians also. The Holy Spirit is always present with the good Christians who really believe in God. Therefore evil spirits can't attack the Christians who really believe in God. If evil spirits come into Christians, we pray and command in the name of Jesus to arrest the evil spirits and chase them out of the Christian patients. And the evil spirits run out of the patients crying and wailing.

However the sons of the Buddhist exorcists did not believe in Almighty God. Therefore the Holy Spirit was not present with them. So demons and evil spirits decoyed them into death at an early age and sent them to hell. I think it is very pitiful that they died at a young age because they didn't know Jesus Christ when they were living.

Refer 1 Kings 22: 51 - 2 Kings 1: 1-18 Ahaziah, the son of Ahab became king over Israel in Samaria.

2 Kings 1: 2-4 Now Ahaziah fell through the lattice of his upper room in Samaria, and was injured; so he sent messengers and said to them, "Go, inquire of Baal-Zebub, the god of Ekron, whether I shall recover from this injury." But the angel of the Lord said to Elijah the Tishbite, "Arise, go up to meet the messengers of the king of Samaria, and say to them, "Is it because there is no God in Israel that you are going to inquire of Baal-Zebub, the god of Ekron?' Now therefore, thus says the Lord: "You shall not come down from the bed to which you have gone up, but you shall surely die."' So Elijah departed.

2 Kings 1: 9-10 Then the king sent to him a captain of fifty with his fifty men. So he went up to him; and there he was, sitting on the top of a hill. And he spoke to him: "Man of God, the king has said, "Come down!"" So Elijah answered and said to the captain of fifty, "If I am a man of God, then let fire come down from heaven and consume you and your fifty men." And fire came down from heaven and consumed him and his fifty. The king sent another captain of fifty and his fifty. But fire came down from heaven and consumed the captain and his fifty men.

2 Kings 1: 13-17 Again, he sent a third captain of fifty with his fifty men. And the third captain of fifty went up, and came and fell on his knees before Elijah, and pleaded with him, and said to him: "Man of God, please let my life and the life of these fifty servants of yours be precious in your sight. Look, fire has come down from heaven and burned up the first two captains of fifties with their fifties. But let my life now be precious in your sight."

And the angel of the Lord said to Elijah, "Go down with him; do not be afraid of him." So he arose and went down with him to the king. Then he said to him, "Thus says the Lord: "Because you have sent messengers to inquire of Baal-Zebub, the god of Ekron, is it because there is no God in Israel to inquire of His word? Therefore you shall not come down from the bed to which you have gone up, but you shall surely die."" So Ahaziah died according to the word of the Lord which Elijah had spoken.

In the Bible passages above, Almighty God gives us a lesson showing that from the view point of human beings, King Ahaziah didn't do anything wrong against God. The king sent his messengers to an idol, Baal-Zabub to inquire whether he shall recover from his injury. However that was a very big sin. Therefore fire from heaven burnt two captains of fifty men and all 100 soldiers who were innocent because of the King, who died also in bed.

I said to the Buddhist female monk, "You are now serving Buddha, the idol, and your deeds serving Buddha's statue are big sins against the Almighty God." When she heard the Bible passages above and my words given by the Holy Spirit, the monk was trembling in her heart and she was uneasy and not peaceful.

However God loves you so much that He sent His only Son, Jesus Christ, to be crucified on the cross for all human beings, to forgive all our sins, including yours. In addition to that, the Holy Spirit sent us to this temple to save you from the den of Satan. If you believe in God and confess all your sins before God, He will forgive whatever you did against the Almighty God.

We asked her to accept Jesus Christ as her Savior Lord, but she said, "Right now I cannot accept Him as my Savior. But I believe all the gospel about Jesus you delivered today."

9) The female Buddhist monk accepting the Holy Spirit's healing prayer

The Holy Spirit, who knows everything in advance, performed His miracle to her eyes, and she said, "I can't see clearly." If a lady in her mid-forties cannot see clearly, it is a big problem. I said to her, "If you accept Jesus Christ as your Savior and believe in God faithfully, it will not be any problem for the Holy Spirit to cure your eyes."

Almighty God can even raise the dead to live again. Right at this moment God cures all kind of infirmities which modern medical science and doctors cannot heal. The Holy Spirit also cured innumerable sick patients through our prayer.

In order to show such miracles that the Holy Spirit performs through us, we were invited to lead the Holy Spirit healing services at many churches in Korea. And we were leading the Holy Spirit healing services by the guidance of the Holy Spirit. When she heard what we said, she said that she would accept our healing prayer. But she said that she wouldn't accept Jesus Christ as her Savior right now.

However the Holy Spirit with me said to me, "All the evil spirits which were holding her were completely bound last night by the Holy Spirit's fire and power. Give her the Holy Spirit's healing prayer."

That is, we prayed for the Buddhist female monk at the temple. She said, "I believe all the things that you are doing now in the name of Jesus Christ."

Meanwhile the Holy Spirit asked me to tell her, "If you stop believing Buddha's statue and accept Jesus Christ as your Savior Lord, and really believe in God, the Holy Spirit will cure your eyes perfectly."

So I delivered the Holy Spirit's message to her, and she said, "I know what you say."

10) The female Buddhist monk weeping and wailing without ceasing by the Holy Spirit's anointing

214 Holy Spirit, Hover Over Me

However the Holy Spirit moved her, so she confessed to us that she was a good Christian in the past.

Meanwhile the Holy Spirit said to me, "When the time comes, she will abandon Buddha's statue and she will believe in God and she will evangelize Jesus' gospel all over the world with you."

When we were leaving the temple, the female Buddhist monk was weeping and wailing continuously while waving her hand until we couldn't see her in our sight. It is because the Holy Spirit moved her heart so powerfully that she was wailing endlessly. When we came down from the mountain where the Buddhist temple was located, we took a bus going in another direction to evangelize Jesus' gospel to the people whom the Holy Spirit prepared for us.

11) The Holy Spirit's words to God's children

We went to the Buddhist temple to evangelize the Buddhist monk. There are innumerable people who believe in other idols besides Buddhism. Except for the Trinity God, that is, the Almighty God, Jesus Christ and the Holy Spirit, all other religions are idols which were made by men in the world and they will disappear. They are all idols, that is, Satan's servants who believe in Satan by the deceitful decoy of the Devil, demons and evil spirits. It is only the Holy Spirit who can lead our spirits to heaven after our life is finished in the world.

John 14: 6 Jesus said to him, "I am the way, the truth, and the life. No one comes to the Father except through Me."

As in the Bible passage above, no one can come to the Almighty Heavenly Father except through Jesus Christ. Therefore all the children of God must boldly deliver the gospel to all creation all over the world.

Mark 16: 15-16 And He said to them, "Go into all the world and preach the gospel to every creature. He who believes and is baptized will be saved; but he who does not believe will be condemned."

We Christians must tell the words of truth in the Bible which may pierce the hearts of unbelievers. We must tell them that if they don't believe in God when they are living in the world, after their life is finished, they will wail, weep and lament forever in the sulfur burning fire sea in hell for not believing in Jesus. Before it is too late, ask them to come to Jesus' salvation.

It is not easy to deliver such words to unbelievers. Telling such truthful words of God to your friends may hurt their hearts. Sometimes you may lose your friends or sometimes your friend may become your enemy. However we have to give them boldly the truth of God's words. Otherwise their spirits will have to wail and lament forever in the ever burning fire sea in hell, for not believing in Jesus Christ when they were living. This is the only way we can save their lives from the fire sea.

I have been to heaven and hell innumerable times, maybe hundreds of times. We must deliver Jesus' gospel boldly to all the people believing in any idol except the Trinity God: the Almighty God, Jesus Christ and the Holy Spirit. If we deliver the gospel boldly to people who believe in idols, the Holy Spirit will prepare a way through which we can smoothly and successfully deliver the gospel.

The Buddhist temple we visited to deliver Jesus' gospel was a den of Satan, where innumerable big snakes were swarming. The person to whom we visited to evangelize was a Buddhist monk, who thought that Christians were her enemy. However the angels of the Holy Spirit prepared a way through which we could deliver the gospel successfully.

The Holy Spirit prepared for us to deliver the gospel to the monk, while staying in the best room in the temple, which belonged to the chief monk. In addition to that, the Holy Spirit's fire from heaven burnt all the statues of Buddha and innumerable snakes in the temple. However none of Buddha's statues or innumerable snakes challenged Jesus and His angels who were burning them, but all of them were burning wailing, weeping and lamenting, burning like dead wood in the Holy Spirit's fire from heaven.

This testifies that the statues of Buddha were idols which were made by men, and they had no power to save the spirits of human beings from hell after death. If Buddha's statue knew in advance that we were coming to the temple, they might have stopped us from delivering the gospel in the Buddhist temple. However they had no defense at all.

We visited the temple without any advance notice. However, the Holy Spirit led us to the temple and He prepared for us to deliver the gospel smoothly, by moving all 10-12 monks who were living in the temple everyday, and leaving only the one monk whom we planned to evangelize. There was one other monk there, but the Holy Spirit ministered miracles on her. She was suddenly so sick that she couldn't come out of her bedroom.

This proves that the Holy Spirit moves even the hearts of unbelievers like monks at His will. The Holy Spirit knew in advance that the monk whom we visited would not accept Jesus' gospel, so He made a miracle that she couldn't see clearly with her eyes. Consequently she had to accept the Holy Spirit's healing prayer. This fact proves that all these are things which we cannot establish without the Holy Spirit's power.

The God in whom we believe is the Almighty Heavenly Father God who created the heavens, the earth and all the creatures in the universe. He is the Most High of all gods in the universe. He is the Almighty God who can do anything in the universe. All idols are nothing but dead wood before the Almighty God. Therefore the Holy Spirit prepared the road through which we could establish our aim of evangelizing the gospel to the Buddhist monk in the den of snakes. All these prove again that our God is the Most High King of all kings in the universe.

We are sure that if you deliver the gospel boldly to unbelieve -rs, the Holy Spirit will prepare all the roads through which you can deliver the gospel successfully, wherever you are in the world. We have experienced such things too many times. This is the lesson that the Holy Spirit gives us today.

12) The Holy Spirit's words to the unbelievers who know nothing about Jesus

The God we believe in and serve is the Almighty God who created the universe. (Refer to Genesis Chapters 1 & 2.) God even created the forefather of human beings. God created you, too. The Almighty God is your father and He loves you more than your parents who bore and raised you. In order to save you from sin and death, God allowed His only Son, Jesus Christ, to be crucified on the cross. God waits for you to come into His arms. There are no gods who can save you from death and hell in the world except the Trinity God, that is, the Almighty Father, His Son, Jesus Christ and the Holy Spirit. It is only Jesus who can save you from your sins and the fiery sea of hell.

All the religions in the world except the Almighty God, are idols which were made by Satan's deceitful lures. And Satan has no power to save you from sin and sulfur burning fire sea in hell. If you believe in idols to the end, you will be thrown into the ever-burning fiery lake of hell after your life is finished.

I have been to heaven and hell innumerable times. I know that you will be shocked to hear what I say about the spiritual world. However if I don't tell you the truth about Satan, the Devil will tell only lies to you to decoy you to permanent destruction in hell.

And after you are abandoned into the fiery lake in hell, it is too late for you to be saved but you have to be eternally weeping, wailing and lamenting for not having come to Jesus. God loves you. You have committed great sins against the Almighty God by believing and serving idols. But God loves you. If you come to Jesus and really believe in God and confess all your sins before God, all your sins will be cleansed like crystal.

Isaiah 1: 18-20 "Come now, and let us reason together," Says the LORD, "Though your sins are like scarlet, They shall be as white as snow; Though they are red like crimson, They shall be as wool. If you are willing and obedient, You shall eat the good of the

land; But if you refuse and rebel, You shall be devoured by the sword"; For the mouth of the Lord has spoken.

1. Some people say that if anyone believing in Buddha changes their religion to Jesus, his home will perish and disasters will happen to his family members. These kinds of words are groundless lies made by Satan, who lies to the people believing in Satan not to believe in Jesus. The God we believe in is the Almighty God who is the most high among all gods in the universe. All the creatures in the universe are the created by God. It is only the Almighty Father God whom all the people in the world have to serve.

Exodus 12: 12 For I will pass through the land of Egypt on that night, and will strike all the firstborn in the land of Egypt, both man and beast; and against all the gods of Egypt I will execute judgment; I am the Lord.

As in the Bible passages above, the Lord God is the most powerful and Most High God who can punish all the gods in the world at one time. Therefore Satan, evil spirits and demons want to kill you and hurt you. However they cannot hurt you with their power, because the Holy Spirit, the Spirit of the Most High is always with you and protects you and leads you wherever you go. You don't have to worry about such things.

Therefore when Christians pray for sick people, they command in the name of Jesus to arrest all the evil spirits which cause the patients to be sick and chase them away from the patients. And then the evil spirit bound in the name of Jesus goes out of the patients while crying sorrowfully and wailing. And the patients recover immediately from their sickness.

Mark 16: 17-18 "And these signs will follow those who believe: In My name they will cast out demons; they will speak with new tongues; they will take up serpents; and if they drink anything deadly, it will by no means hurt them; they will lay their hands on the sick, and they will recover."

I have experienced innumerable spiritual ministries. Evil spirits and demons tried to slaughter me more than a few hundred times. Whenever evil spirits tried to kill me, Jesus Christ, embraced by the light, came to me and arrested and bound all the evil spirits and threw them into the fiery lake.

However Buddhist monks or sorcerers cannot command the evil spirits to go out of these patients, because demons or evil spirits are more powerful than the idols whom you are believing. Therefore if you command them to get out of the patients, they will try to kill you. In addition to that, the idols whom you serve do not have the power to chase the evil spirits out of the patients, so you sacrifice rice cakes, heads of pigs, money and other food to the demons and evil spirits and you beg the evil spirits and demons to leave the patients for many days.

This proves that the idols you serve are not powerful, because you are begging the other evil spirits to go out of the patients. If you believe in the Almighty God, you don't need to beg other evil spirits to go out. But just command in the name of Jesus the evil spirit causing the illness to go out of the patient immediately and the evil spirit will go out of him immediately, while wailing.

If you want to prove what I say, please visit prayer houses or churches where the Holy Spirit ministers powerfully, and watch how the pastors or Christians pray for other patients.

You will see many evil spirits going out of patients while crying loudly and wailing. All these are miracles the Holy Spirit is ministering. Therefore to save your spirit from sin and hell, you have to come to Jesus Christ, the Son of the Almighty God who created the universe.

2. Some Buddhist believers insist, "Jesus and Buddha are brothers. And we believe in God." Therefore it is same whether we believe Buddha or Jesus. It sounds plausible to unbelievers. However you should know that it is a groundless deceitful lie which was made by Satan.

The Almighty God prophesied about the coming of Jesus Christ many thousand years ago, before Jesus Christ was born in the world. That is, in the Old Testament which was written before Jesus was born, God told many times about the coming of Jesus through prophets. Namely the Old Testament is the word of God which promised the coming of Jesus. In addition to that, God prophesied that Jesus will be born and be crucified on the cross to cleanse the sins of all human beings in the world.

Isaiah 7: 14-15 Therefore the Lord Himself will give you a sign: Behold, the virgin shall conceive and bear a Son, and shall call His name Immanuel. Curds and honey He shall eat, that He may know to refuse the evil and choose the good.

God prophesied that Jesus would come to the world to save all the human beings, 700 years before Jesus was born in the world, through the prophet Isaiah.

Isaiah 9: 6-7 For unto us a Child is born, Unto us a Son is given; And the government will be upon His shoulder. And His name

will be called Wonderful, Counselor, Mighty God, Everlasting Father, Prince of Peace. Of the increase of His government and peace There will be no end, Upon the throne of David and over His kingdom, To order it and establish it with judgment and justice From that time forward, even forever. The zeal of the Lord of hosts will perform this.

As shown in Bible passage above, about 700 hundred years before Jesus was born in the world, the Almighty God said the above through a prophet. Besides the above examples, there are innumerable times that God told of the coming of Jesus.

About 1400 years before Jesus was born in the world, God prophesied the coming of Jesus through the mouth of Moses.

Acts 3: 22-23 For Moses truly said to the fathers, "The Lord your God will raise up for you a Prophet like me from your brethren. Him you shall hear in all things, whatever He says to you. And it shall be that every soul who will not hear that Prophet shall be utterly destroyed from among the people.'

In addition to that, after Jesus was born in the world, Almighty God proved many times that people can be saved only through Jesus.

John 1: 1-4 In the beginning was the Word, and the Word was with God, and the Word was God. He was in the beginning with God. All things were made through Him, and without Him nothing was made that was made. In Him was life, and the life was the light of men.

The light mentioned above is Jesus. The Bible says that all was made through Him. As shown above, Jesus is God. He is also the only Son of God.

John 14: 6 Jesus said to him, "I am the way, the truth, and the life. No one comes to the Father except through Me."

The Bible says that people can go to the Almighty Heavenly Father only through Jesus Christ. Also, when Jesus was living in the world, Jesus showed innumerable miracles which modern medical science cannot prove.

He raised dead people to life.
Refer John 11: 1-44 Lazarus who was dead and buried in the tomb for four days and there was stench because his body was spoiled. However when Jesus cried with a loud voice, "Lazarus, come forth!"

John 11: 44 And he who had died came out bound hand and foot with graveclothes, and his face was wrapped with a cloth. Jesus said to them, "Loose him, and let him go."

Luke 7: 12-15 And when He came near the gate of the city, behold, a dead man was being carried out, the only son of his mother; and she was a widow. And a large crowd from the city was with her. When the Lord saw her, He had compassion on her and said to her, "Do not weep." Then He came and touched the open coffin, and those who carried him stood still. And He said, "Young man, I say to you, arise." So he who was dead sat up and began to speak. And He presented him to his mother.

He cured innumerable patients completely with only His words.

John 5: 6-9 When Jesus saw him lying there, and knew that he already had been in that condition a long time, He said to him,

"Do you want to be made well?" The sick man answered Him, "Sir, I have no man to put me into the pool when the water is stirred up; but while I am coming, another steps down before me." Jesus said to him, "Rise, take up your bed and walk." And immediately the man was made well, took up his bed, and walked. And that day was the Sabbath.

Matthew 15: 30-31Then great multitudes came to Him, having with them the lame, blind, mute, maimed, and many others; and they laid them down at Jesus' feet, and He healed them. So the multitude marveled when they saw the mute speaking, the maimed made whole, the lame walking, and the blind seeing; and they glorified the God of Israel.

Jesus fed 5000 people with 5 loaves of bread and two fish, and 12 baskets full of bread was left over.

John 6: 9-13 "There is a lad here who has five barley loaves and and two small fish, but what are they among so many?" Then Jesus said, "Make the people sit down." Now there was much grass in the place. So the men sat down, in number about five thousand. And Jesus took the loaves, and when He had given thanks He distributed them to the disciples, and the disciples to those sitting down; and likewise of the fish, as much as they wanted. So when they were filled, He said to His disciples, "Gather up the fragments that remain, so that nothing is lost." Therefore they gathered them up, and filled twelve baskets with the fragments of the five barley loaves which were left over by those who had eaten.

However Jesus was crucified on the cross for the sins of all the people in the world.

Refer Matthew Chapter 27
Matthew 27: 35-36 Then they crucified Him, and divided His garments, casting lots, that it might be fulfilled which was spoken by the prophet: "They divided My garments among them, And for My clothing they cast lots." Sitting down, they kept watch over Him there.

Matthew 27: 45-46 Now from the sixth hour until the ninth hour there was darkness over all the land. And about the ninth hour Jesus cried out with a loud voice, saying, "Eli, Eli, lama sabachthani?" that is, "My God, My God, why have You forsaken Me?"

Matthew 27: 50-54 And Jesus cried out again with a loud voice, and yielded up His spirit. Then, behold, the veil of the temple was torn in two from top to bottom; and the earth quaked, and the rocks were split, and the graves were opened; and many bodies of the saints who had fallen asleep were raised; and coming out of the graves after His resurrection, they went into the holy city and appeared to many. So when the centurion and those with him, who were guarding Jesus, saw the earthquake and the things that had happened, they feared greatly, saying, "Truly this was the Son of God!"

But He was resurrected and now He is with the Almighty Heavenly Father.

(Refer Matthew Chapter 28)
Matthew 28: 1-10 Now after the Sabbath, as the first day of the week began to dawn, Mary Magdalene and the other Mary came to see the tomb. And behold, there was a great earthquake; for an angel of the Lord descended from heaven, and came and rolled back the stone from the door, and sat on it. His countenance was

like lightning, and his clothing as white as snow. And the guards shook for fear of him, and became like dead men. But the angel answered and said to the women, "Do not be afraid, for I know that you seek Jesus who was crucified.

He is not here; for He is risen, as He said. Come, see the place where the Lord lay. And go quickly and tell His disciples that He is risen from the dead, and indeed He is going before you into Galilee; there you will see Him. Behold, I have told you." So they went out quickly from the tomb with fear and great joy, and ran to bring His disciples word. And as they went to tell His disciples, behold, Jesus met them, saying, "Rejoice!" So they came and held Him by the feet and worshiped Him. Then Jesus said to them, "Do not be afraid. Go and tell My brethren to go to Galilee, and there they will see Me."

Matthew 28: 16-20 Then the eleven disciples went away into Galilee, to the mountain which Jesus had appointed for them. When they saw Him, they worshiped Him; but some doubted. And Jesus came and spoke to them, saying, "All authority has been given to Me in heaven and on earth. Go therefore and make disciples of all the nations, baptizing them in the name of the Father and of the Son and of the Holy Spirit, teaching them to observe all things that I have commanded you; and lo, I am with you always, even to the end of the age." Amen.

After He was resurrected from death, Jesus was taken up to heaven.

Refer Acts 1: 9-11 Now when He had spoken these things, while they watched, He was taken up, and a cloud received Him out of their sight. And while they looked steadfastly toward heaven as He went up, behold, two men stood by them in white apparel, who also said, "Men of Galilee, why do you stand gazing up into heaven? This same Jesus, who was taken up from you into heaven, will so come in like manner as you saw Him go into heaven."

After Jesus went up to heaven, the Holy Spirit came down from heaven and even now He does all kinds of miracles, such as were done by Jesus.

Acts 2: 1-8 When the Day of Pentecost had fully come, they were all with one accord in one place. And suddenly there came a sound from heaven, as of a rushing mighty wind, and it filled the whole house where they were sitting. Then there appeared to them divided tongues, as of fire, and one sat upon each of them. And they were all filled with the Holy Spirit and began to speak with other tongues, as the Spirit gave them utterance. And there were dwelling in Jerusalem Jews, devout men, from every nation under heaven. And when this sound occurred, the multitude came together, and were confused, because everyone heard them speak in his own language. Then they were all amazed and marveled, saying to one another, "Look, are not all these who speak Galileans? And how is it that we hear, each in our own language in which we were born?

Right now, the Holy Spirit performs all kinds of miracles which modern medical science cannot understand, such as healing all kinds of infirmities which medical doctors or hospitals cannot cure, like cancer, AIDS and other human diseases. Nothing is impossible with the Holy Spirit. If you want proof of what I say, please visit any prayer house or church where the Holy Spirit ministers powerfully.

There are many places all over the world. In such prayer houses or churches where the Holy Spirit ministers powerfully, you will be able to see that the Holy Spirit performs miracles on the spot which you can see with your own eyes. He changes impossible things into possible things. Nothing is impossible with the Holy Spirit. Surely I plead for you to come to Jesus Christ, who loves you. We want you not to be deceived any more by Satan, who tries to destroy you permanently in hell. That is the only way through which you can save yourself for eternal life to be with God in heaven.

3. The Bible testifies that only the name of Jesus can save human beings for eternal life in heaven.

Acts 4: 7-12 And when they had set them in the midst, they asked, "By what power or by what name have you done this?" Then Peter, filled with the Holy Spirit, said to them, "Rulers of the people and elders of Israel: If we this day are judged for a good deed done to a helpless man, by what means he has been made well, let it be known to you all, and to all the people of Israel, that by the name of Jesus Christ of Nazareth, whom you crucified, whom God raised from the dead, by Him this man stands here before you whole. This is the "stone which was rejected by you builders, which has become the chief cornerstone.' Nor is there salvation in any other, for there is no other name under heaven given among men by which we must be saved."

The Holy Spirit says the following:
"All the religions, including Buddhism, made by men in the world are idols made by Satan's groundless lies, and there are no paradises of Buddhism after life. There is no transmigration, which Buddhism teaches, in the universe.

"In order to prove the truth, the Holy Spirit sent you to the Buddhist temple where so many snakes were dwelling

and all of them were burnt by the Holy Spirit's fire from heaven, which you saw with your spiritual eyes. Jesus Christ is the only Savior who can save human beings for the eternal life in heaven."

The Holy Spirit testifies to the above statements.

We truly ask you to come to Jesus Christ immediately without being deceived any more by Satan.

Genesis 3: 1-7 Now the serpent was more cunning than any beast of the field which the Lord God had made. And he said to the woman, "Has God indeed said, "You shall not eat of every tree of the garden'?" And the woman said to the serpent, "We may eat the fruit of the trees of the garden; but of the fruit of the tree which is in the midst of the garden, God has said, "You shall not eat it, nor shall you touch it, lest you die."' Then the serpent said to the woman, "You will not surely die. For God knows that in the day you eat of it your eyes will be opened, and you will be like God, knowing good and evil."
So when the woman saw that the tree was good for food, that it was pleasant to the eyes, and a tree desirable to make one wise, she took of its fruit and ate. She also gave to her husband with her, and he ate. Then the eyes of both of them were opened, and they knew that they were naked; and they sewed fig leaves together and made themselves coverings.

Genesis 3: 13-15 And the Lord God said to the woman, "What is this you have done?" The woman said, "The serpent deceived me, and I ate." So the Lord God said to the serpent: "Because you have done this, You are cursed more than all cattle, And more than every beast of the field; On your belly you shall go, And you shall eat dust All the days of your life. And I will put enmity Be-

tween you and the woman, And between your seed and her Seed; He shall bruise your head, And you shall bruise His heel."

As the Bible passages above show, Satan, the serpent, only lies. The serpent told a lie to the first woman, the mother of all human beings, and as a result of that, she ate the fruit of the tree in the midst of the garden which God told Adam not to eat. Eve was deceived by the serpent's lie, therefore the first parents of human beings, Adam and Eve, were driven out by God from the garden of Eden. Satan always lies like this to everyone, in order to destroy them in hell. If you read Genesis Chapter 3, you will understand fully how the serpent deceived Eve.

1 John 3: 8 He who sins is of the devil, for the devil has sinned from the beginning. For this purpose the Son of God was manifested, that He might destroy the works of the devil.

As in the Bible passages above, Satan, the Devil, always lies and sins against God. Therefore one reason why Jesus was manifested was to destroy the works of the Devil. We want you never be deceived by Satan, the snake. In order to save you from Satan's lie, we give you Jesus' gospel. God loves you and wants to give His unlimited blessings to you.

Deuteronomy 28: 1-6 "Now it shall come to pass, if you diligently obey the voice of the Lord your God, to observe carefully all His commandments which I command you today, that the Lord your God will set you high above all nations of the earth. And all these blessings shall come upon you and overtake you, because you obey the voice of the Lord your God: "Blessed shall you be in the city, and blessed shall you be in the country. "Blessed shall be the fruit of your body, the produce of your ground and the increase of your herds, the increase of your cattle

and the offspring of your flocks. "Blessed shall be your basket
and your kneading bowl. "Blessed shall you be when you come in,
and blessed shall you be when you go out."

If you really believe in God, faithfully worship Him and follow Jesus in your deeds, the Holy Spirit will give you God's
unlimited blessings as shown above. God loves you so much
that He wants to give you all the blessings above. We want you
to receive all the blessings God gives to you. However if you
do not obey the words of God and if you continuously believe
idols, the Holy Spirit says, "I will curse you as follows."

**Deuteronomy 28: 15-21 "But it shall come to pass, if you do not
obey the voice of the Lord your God, to observe carefully all His
commandments and His statutes which I command you today,
that all these curses will come upon you and overtake you:
"Cursed shall you be in the city, and cursed shall you be in the
country.
"Cursed shall be your basket and your kneading bowl.
"Cursed shall be the fruit of your body and the produce of your
land, the increase of your cattle and the offspring of your flocks.
"Cursed shall you be when you come in, and cursed shall you be
when you go out. "The Lord will send on you cursing, confusion,
and rebuke in all that you set your hand to do, until you are destroyed and until you perish quickly, because of the wickedness of
your doings in which you have forsaken Me. The Lord will make
the plague cling to you until He has consumed you from the land
which you are going to possess."**

God loves you. God never wants to curse you as above. But
if you disobey the words of God, and do not worship God, and
if you believe other idols, the Holy Spirit said, **"I will curse
you as mentioned in the Bible passage."**

Do not be deceived by Satan and devils any more but come to Jesus immediately, who will save you from Satan's plot to destroy you. The Holy Spirit will give you God's unlimited blessings from Deuteronomy 28: 1-14. After you finish reading the testimonies in this book, we want everyone, such as unbelievers, the people who stopped believing God because of Satan's obstructions, or people worshiping idols, to come to Jesus immediately.

Almighty God will pardon all your sins, if you confess them before God. Do not hesitate any more, please go to a Christian church near your home and accept Jesus as your Savior Lord. And the Holy Spirit will lead you to eternal life in heaven. The church must be a Christian church which worships the Trinity God, Almighty Heavenly Father, His Son, Jesus Christ and the Holy Spirit. As long as you believe in the Trinity God mentioned above, it doesn't matter what denomination of church you attend. All are the same to God.

Under the name of Jesus, we pray for the Almighty God to bless all the readers of this book without limit. Amen

The Holy Spirit words were given at early morning prayer on July 1, 2000

4. How the Holy Spirit changed a person who denied God and led him to heaven

Mark 16: 16 He who believes and is baptized will be saved; but he who does not believe will be condemned.

One day in the summer of 1995 when I went to a restaurant with my wife for dinner, I found that the owner of the restaurant was suffering from severe liver cancer. The Holy Spirit asked me to visit his home, where he was resting. After driving about 30 minutes, we reached his home and I introduced Jesus to him and I played an audio tape to him about heaven and hell, the testimony recorded by Deacon P., for about 60 minutes. However the patient named P. said to me, "I cannot believe in Jesus." Because I graduated from Seoul National University, the most well-known university and the most difficult university to apply to in Korea. How can I believe that a virgin without a man can conceive a baby?

I answered him as follows; "Not only the graduates of Seoul National University, but also Ph.D.'s and medical doctors believe in Jesus, and even the professors who teach the Ph.D.'s and medical doctors believe in Jesus." There must be a heaven and hell. I have been to heaven and hell innumerable times. No one in the world knows about the secrets of the Heavenly Father, whether they are doctors, scientists or professors. How can they know the miracles performed by the Holy Spirit, such as healing incurable diseases like cancer, curing paralytics to rise immediately, healing the blind to see, and chasing out demons from demon possessed people?

All these kinds of miracles are being performed right at this moment all over the world, by the Holy Spirit in congregations and churches led by pastors inspired by the Holy Spirit. I can show you such miracles performed by the Holy Spirit. All the miracles are performed in the name of Jesus by the Holy Spirit's power and the Almighty Heavenly Father's word. Whether you believe in God or not, heaven, hell and God's judgment will not be removed at all. You or anyone in the world cannot avoid God's judgment deciding where you will be sent to, heaven or hell. The people believing in God will be sent to heaven, but the people not believing in Jesus will be sent to the fiery lake of burning sulfur.

After telling him this, I gave him several audio tapes and books of testimonies written by Missionary K., Pastor C., & Deacon P. who experienced the spiritual world deeply and had seen heaven and hell. And I told him, "If you read all these books and finish listening to the tapes I give you now, you will be able to understand the truth about God who is going to help you. After I gave him a long heartfelt prayer, I left him. After several days, I visited him and gave him several more books telling the testimonies about the Holy Spirit's miraculous ministry. After that, I left for Korea and Japan.

When I called my home from Japan, my wife told me that Mr. P. died. However about one week before he died, he called all his family members, including his wife and all his children, and while he was crying, asked, "All of you, my wife and children and all my family members, really believe in Jesus, even if I die. I want to see a Christian pastor, call a pastor for me." So they invited Pastor K. who introduced Jesus to him and baptized Mr. P. in the name of the Father and of the Son and of the Holy Spirit. When I heard the news that the same Mr. P. who had refused Jesus so drastically when I first visited him, finally accepted Jesus and died, I was so moved that I began to cry in my hotel room in Tokyo, Japan. And tears began to drop from my eyes continuously. After that, when I prayed for him, the Holy Spirit informed me that Mr. P. went to heaven under the guidance of the Holy Spirit.

The Holy Spirit knew exactly when Mr. P. would die, so He sent me to introduce Jesus to him. If the Holy Spirit had not asked me to go to Mr. P., he might have died without knowing Jesus. If Mr. P. had died without knowing Jesus, he might have been thrown into the fiery sea in hell. However the Holy Spirit knew in advance when he would die, so He sent His envoy to introduce Jesus to him. Finally the Holy Spirit moved Mr. P. to accept Jesus at the last moment of his life, so he was sent to heaven after he died. Now Mr. P. is in heaven because of the Holy Spirit's help.

5. The Holy Spirit saved my mother-in-law who was a Buddhist believer at the last moment of death

Whenever I talked about Jesus to my mother-in-law, she used to hate hearing what I said, and she was very uneasy and restless.

Luke 23: 39-43 Then one of the criminals who were hanged blasphemed Him, saying, "If You are the Christ, save Yourself and us." But the other, answering, rebuked him, saying, "Do you

not even fear God, seeing you are under the same condemnation? And we indeed justly, for we receive the due reward of our deeds; but this Man has done nothing wrong." Then he said to Jesus, "Lord, remember me when You come into Your kingdom." And Jesus said to him, "Assuredly, I say to you, today you will be with Me in Paradise."

Some time in April 1996 when I was praying, a vision of my mother-in-law appeared before me. That is, when she was praying before Buddha, suddenly four or five fearful giant demons with spears in their hands surrounded her completely, and at the same time a giant snake appeared in front of her. It was about 1 meter thick and its length was so long that I couldn't tell how long it was. After that, the same snake bit my mother-in-law with his mouth and swallowed her whole, then flew away into the sky. I was so scared that I couldn't move my body. After returning home, I told my wife about the vision of my mother in law which I had seen in prayer. And I told her, "My mother-in-law, your mother, will be killed and swallowed by Satan. We must pray more for her."

Several months after this vision appeared, she became very sick. We did our best to introduce Jesus to her, but she was so stubborn that she refused all our efforts. It was so pitiful. But we continued our prayers for her. Before she died, she was unconscious for about two weeks. When I was praying for her, suddenly the Holy Spirit's tongue began to come out of my mouth and from my eyes, tears were streaming.

At the same time the Holy Spirit showed me the vision that I, instead of her, was confessing all the sins she had committed to God in the Holy Spirit's tongue.

The vision was as this: she was sitting in front of a nicely made grave in the bright sunlight and about 10 female Buddhist monks in gray gowns were walking around her while praying in Buddhist style.

I was continuously praying for her in the heavenly tongue, and suddenly Jesus dressed in a long white gown with several angels appeared and they pushed away all the female monks and took my mother-in-law by her hands with them and took her to the Buddhist temple she used to attend when she was healthy. She threw something black like soil to Buddha, and Jesus began to speak to Buddha.

"You liars, the statues of Buddha! Where is the paradise that you promised to people?"

Turning around, He pointed with His right finger to the fiery lake of sulfur burning in hell. And He continued to say that the fire sea in hell you see over there is the paradise you promised to people. Jesus and the angels crushed all the statues of Buddha with hammers and threw them all into the fiery sea. Now the statues of Buddha were crying and screaming in the fiery sea in burning sulfur.

While I was continuously speaking in the Holy Spirit's tongue for a long time, Jesus and His angels took my mother-in-law to every Buddhist temple she used to go to, one by one, and crushed all the statues of Buddha with hammers and threw all of them away into the fiery sea in hell.

At the same time the statues of Buddha were crying and screaming in the fiery sea of burning sulfur, but no one could help them. After they finished breaking and crushing all the statues of Buddha and threw them away into the fiery sea, they put a large hat with the words **"JESUS' VICTORY"** on my mother-in-law's head.

After that they gave my mother-in-law a long white dress and put a gold crown on her head, and Jesus took her in His arms and flew to heaven in the shining light.

In the meantime, while she was unconscious, my sister-in-law invited a Catholic Father, who baptized her in the name of the Heavenly Father, Jesus Christ, and the Holy Spirit.

After she died, the Holy Spirit in the shape of my mother-in-law appeared to me, and He said to me, "Because of your heartfelt prayer, your mother-in-law was saved and she is now in heaven. Tell all her eight sons and daughters and all her grandchildren not to believe in the statue of Buddha any more, but they all must believe in Jesus with heartfelt worshiping to God."

He gave me my mother-in-law's will to all her children.

That is, "When they are alive, they should not follow only money, but do their best to believe in God, and the Holy Spirit will give all of them eternal life. Otherwise they will be thrown away into the fiery sea in hell like the statues of Buddha which were shown to the Holy Spirit's envoy."
At the same time He showed me the fiery sea in hell again.

Revelation 20: 12-15 And I saw the dead, small and great, standing before God, and books were opened. And another book was opened, which is the Book of Life. And the dead were judged according to their works, by the things which were written in the books. The sea gave up the dead who were in it, and Death and

Hades delivered up the dead who were in them. And they were judged, each one according to his works. Then Death and Hades were cast into the lake of fire. This is the second death. And anyone not found written in the Book of Life was cast into the lake of fire.

The Holy Spirit showed me heaven where my mother-in-law was. There was a giant stadium, about 10 times bigger than the Olympic stadium, floating high in the air. It was made of solid gold, with ceilings and chairs which were made of pure gold with diamond decorations. Inside the stadium, there was a big stage in front, lower than the seats, all made of pure gold. On this stage many angels and human spirits who went to heaven were singing in a choir praising the Heavenly Father, and they had all kinds of musical instruments like a professional orchestra.

My mother-in-law, my mother, my grandmother and many angels who were sitting in the audience were singing and praising Jesus Christ who was standing in the center of the angels on the stage. They all seemed to be very happy, without any of the worries of human life.

Revelation 21: 10-27 And he carried me away in the Spirit to a great and high mountain, and showed me the great city, the holy Jerusalem, descending out of heaven from God, having the glory of God. Her light was like a most precious stone, like a jasper stone, clear as crystal. Also she had a great and high wall with twelve gates, and twelve angels at the gates, and names written on them, which are the names of the twelve tribes of the children of Israel: three gates on the east, three gates on the north, three gates on the south, and three gates on the west. Now the wall of the city had twelve foundations, and on them were the names of

the twelve apostles of the Lamb. And he who talked with me had a gold reed to measure the city, its gates, and its wall.

The city is laid out as a square; its length is as great as its breadth. And he measured the city with the reed: twelve thousand furlongs. Its length, breadth, and height are equal. Then he measured its wall: one hundred and forty-four cubits, according to the measure of a man, that is, of an angel. The construction of its wall was of jasper; and the city was pure gold, like clear glass. The foundations of the wall of the city were adorned with all kinds of precious stones: the first foundation was jasper, the second sapphire, the third chalcedony, the fourth emerald, the fifth sardonyx, the sixth sardius, the seventh chrysolite, the eighth beryl, the ninth topaz, the tenth chrysoprase, the eleventh jacinth, and the twelfth amethyst. The twelve gates were twelve pearls: each individual gate was of one pearl. And the street of the city was pure gold, like transparent glass.

But I saw no temple in it, for the Lord God Almighty and the Lamb are its temple. The city had no need of the sun or of the moon to shine in it, for the glory of God illuminated it. The Lamb is its light. And the nations of those who are saved shall walk in its light, and the kings of the earth bring their glory and honor into it. Its gates shall not be shut at all by day (there shall be no night there). And they shall bring the glory and the honor of the nations into it. But there shall by no means enter it anything that defiles, or causes an abomination or a lie, but only those who are written in the Lamb's Book of Life.

Revelation 22: 1-5 And he showed me a pure river of water of life, clear as crystal, proceeding from the throne of God and of the Lamb. In the middle of its street, and on either side of the river, was the tree of life, which bore twelve fruits, each tree yielding its fruit every month. The leaves of the tree were for the healing of

the nations. And there shall be no more curse, but the throne of God and of the Lamb shall be in it, and His servants shall serve Him. They shall see His face, and His name shall be on their fore- heads. There shall be no night there: They need no lamp nor light of the sun, for the Lord God gives them light. And they shall reign forever and ever.

The Holy Spirit emphasized several times that no one can enter the kingdom of God except through Jesus Christ. And He asked all her eight children and her grandchildren to believe in Jesus, that is the only way to heaven.

John 14: 6 Jesus said to him, "I am the way, the truth, and the life. No one comes to the Father except through Me.

I recorded all the truth which the Holy Spirit had told me, and delivered all of it to her sons and daughters. The Holy Spirit saves even non-Christians like my mother-in-law by making them unconscious for some time and He leads someone to confess their sins for them, if you pray continuously for your family members or parents who are not Christian.

Please pray continuously for your beloved sons and daugh- ters or parents who do not believe in God. The Holy Spirit will save them even at the last moment of their life. The Holy Spirit wants to save all of you regardless of who you are.

If you want to lead them to Jesus Christ immediately, Please give them *Holy Spirit, Hover Over Me* to read. While they read the book, the Holy Spirit will move them powerfully with Holy Spirit's anointing and they will come to church to confess their sins immediately. They will continuously come to church in the power of Holy Spirit. And they will be changed into really good Christians by the Holy Spirit supernatural miracle.

6. The Holy Spirit changed my aunt, my mother's elder sister, who was Buddhist and took her with Him to heaven

After my aunt accepted Jesus as her Savior Lord, the Holy Spirit took her to heaven. My aunt was a Buddhist believer and she didn't know anything about Jesus.

Matthew 1: 21 "And she will bring forth a Son, and you shall call His name Jesus, for He will save His people from their sins."

My aunt was suffering from paralysis for several years in the last part of her life. I prayed with all my heart many times for her, several months before she died. When I visited my aunt with a pastor named L., who was very powerfully inspired by the Holy Spirit, she was very sick and couldn't move her body herself but had to fully depend upon her children. At that time, she really accepted Jesus in her heart and Pastor L. baptized her under the name of the Heavenly Father, Jesus Christ, and the Holy Spirit. She was saved at that time.

Human beings act and think just like children, thinking about whether he or she will die or live and abandoning all his or her greed and hope, only when the last days of life come close. The prayers coming from the mouth of a patient facing death are really from his heart. The prayers from the patients at such a time really move the Holy Spirit and Jesus and the Heavenly Father. The prayers, confessing of sins, and forgiving of others spoken by patients in the last days of their life come from a real belief in God. Once their sins are forgiven by God in the last days of their life, they are clean until they die, because they do not have any more chance to commit sin, but are suffering from their sickness to the last moment of life.

Before the moment of death, people are stammering in speech like little children. They do not lie but only tell the truth, and they desire God's kingdom powerfully in their hearts. Therefore, they are well accepted by God in the last moment of their life. The Holy Spirit knows all human beings' hearts, conditions, and circumstances very well. Therefore, the Holy Spirit uses the last days of their life to change patients to accept Jesus as their Savior and to give them eternal life in heaven. The people who accepted Jesus and are saved in the last days of their life are the most lucky and blessed people.

My Beloved Readers!

If your parents or beloved ones do not believe in Jesus, please pray to the last moment of their life. The Holy Spirit will arrange a chance for them to accept the Heavenly Father, Jesus Christ, and the Holy Spirit, and He will save them to heaven. After my aunt died, when I prayed to God, the Holy Spirit showed me a vision showing Jesus carrying her. She was in His arms, dressed in a long white gown with a gold crown on her head and flew surrounded in a bright light to heaven. Jesus asked me to tell what I saw to her children, and I told all that I saw to my cousin, my aunt's son.

7. The centurion's belief and the definition of the Bible

At 9: 28 at night on April 21, 1997 when I was praying, the Holy Spirit gave the following Holy Spirit words to all the Christians in the world.

Matthew 8: 8-9 The centurion answered and said, "Lord, I am not worthy that You should come under my roof. But only speak a word, and my servant will be healed. For I also am a man under authority, having soldiers under me. And I say to this one, "Go,' and he goes; and to another, "Come,' and he comes; and to my servant, "Do this,' and he does it."

When I finished reading the above statements, the Holy Spirit told me the following.

This man is a gentile but his faith is many times larger than Jewish people's. Jewish people, whether Sadducee or Pharisee, are talking only about God's law. But this man believed Jesus' words 100%.

Therefore after seeing his belief, Jesus said, "Go your way; and as you have believed, so let it be done for you."

And his servant was healed at that very hour. Today innumerable Christians do not believe as this man did. After calculating in advance, if they find benefits for them, they believe and if they cannot find any benefits, they do not believe God. There are too many of these kind of opportunist believers in the world. Heaven is not guaranteed for such believers.

No matter who talks against you, you have to believe in God wholly as it was written in the Bible. Regardless of when it was written or by whom, all the words in the Bible were dictated by the Holy Spirit, word by word, to the prophets or men of God when they were fully filled in the Holy Spirit or the Holy Spirit miracles which the prophets or men of God experienced.

2 Timothy 3: 16-17 All Scripture is given by inspiration of God, and is profitable for doctrine, for reproof, for correction, for instruction in righteousness, that the man of God may be complete, thoroughly equipped for every good work.

That is, the same as you writing the words dictated by the Holy Spirit word-by-word. Therefore the words in the Bible are living and life breathing, and are doing ministry by themselves.

Hebrews 4: 12-13 For the word of God is living and powerful, and sharper than any two-edged sword, piercing even to the division of soul and spirit, and of joints and marrow, and is a discerner of the thoughts and intents of the heart. And there is no creature hidden from His sight, but all things are naked and open to the eyes of Him to whom we must give account.

As shown in the above Bible passages, the Bible's words are living and powerful, therefore the Holy Spirit performs miracles together with the Bible's words. The Bible is the word of God, therefore no man in the world can deduct any words from it or add any words to it.

Revelation 22: 18-19 For I testify to everyone who hears the words of the prophecy of this book: If anyone adds to these things, God will add to him the plagues that are written in this book; and if anyone takes away from the words of the book of this prophecy, God shall take away his part from the Book of Life, from the holy city, and from the things which are written in this book.

As shown in the above Bible passages, no one is allowed to translate the meaning of the Bible according to his own thoughts. Of course, in translating the Bible, there happened to be some mistakes in the translation between the languages. However the Holy Spirit knows the original meaning. He explains the mistakes corrected in the original meanings and/or He explains the mistakes as they are. That is, even with mistaken words, the Holy Spirit does ministry, knowing the mistakes. Therefore the mistakes made in translating between the languages cannot create any problems, because the Holy Spirit uses the Bible as it was written, with mistakes.

That is why the Bible has the authority and does ministry as the words say. Therefore all Christians in many different countries pray to God, while meditating on the meaning of the words in the Bible written in their own language. Even the New International Version of the Holy Bible, which is translated into familiar language, also does ministry when you read it.

However the Bibles written by heretics according to their own beneficial thoughts and ideas for their own religious sects' interests or powers do not have any value at all as the word of God. Such books are not the Bible but are story books. They are dead books which do not do any Holy Spirit ministry. The Holy Spirit does not do any ministry when you read such books. Now you understand the truth about the Bible, and whenever anyone asks you about the Bible, reply as follows.

The Holy Spirit doesn't care about the little differences made in translating from one language to another language. He does the Holy Spirit's ministry as the Bible was written. However, the Holy Spirit does not do any ministry with the Bibles which were written and corrected by heretics for the purpose of their own interest and power. In such books, usually the founders of the heretical religious sects are pretending to be sons of God instead of Jesus and they do not believe in the Holy Spirit's ministry either.

There are innumerable religious groups like this in the world. In the future I want you to also evangelize to such heretics and teach them the Holy Spirit's words and lead them to the Heavenly Father God and Jesus, according to the Holy Spirit's guidance. Such heretics are committing the biggest sins to God. It is exactly the same as the fearful and miserable scenes which you saw at God's angry final judgments.

I want you to tell them the fearful scenes which you have seen at God's final judgments and persuade them to follow the Holy Spirit's guidance. All heretics, heretical groups or sects are the same. Regardless of whomever you meet in the world, you should guide them to God. This is the truth and the way leading you to heaven, carrying the cross on your back, step-by-step per the Holy Spirit's guidance.

The Holy Spirit's words were given in prayer at

9:28 pm on April 21, 1997.

CHAPTER 5

The Holy Spirit's words and ministry about me and my family members

1. The Holy Spirit changed my unlimited greed
2. A man going anywhere Holy Spirit services are performed
3. The Holy Spirit who guides my way
   1) When I was going to a restaurant on Kelly Drive
   2) When I was on the way to a Holy Spirit Revival meeting in the Pocono
   3) When I was on the way to pray for Pastor C. who was sick
   4) When I was on the way to Westminster Theological Seminary

1. The Holy Spirit changed my unlimited greed

John 3: 3, 5 Jesus answered and said to him, "Most assuredly, I say to you, unless one is born again, he cannot see the kingdom of God." Jesus answered, "Most assuredly, I say to you, unless one is born of water and the Spirit, he cannot enter the kingdom of God.

There is a great difference, like heaven and earth, between what I am now and what I was before I was born again. In the past all I knew was business and money. I tried to value everyone and everything in the world by money. In addition to that, my greed for money was so enormous that no one could control it. Whether I was at home, at my company or on a business trip, I used to think only about business. Therefore at home my wife and children might have thought that her husband and their father was a man who knows only money and business.

Even when all our family, for once, went on vacation, I couldn't spend time with my children and wife. Instead, I used to think about the business. I used to be a man with a fiery, impatient character. Whenever any good business idea came up to my mind I tried to establish the business project immediately without waiting. When any person didn't agree with me or stood against me, I couldn't fight my hot temper. I had to win over him by any means. I was one of the most selfish people who knew only the benefits or interests for myself or for my family.

When I was a young student in middle school, high school and university, I was very selfish for my own benefits. I didn't even serve the school. Sometimes the school administration decided that all the students should do some work on a certain day, such as planting trees in spring, or cutting grass or weeds to make grass compost in summer. On such days I used to be absent from school or I sneaked out of class without giving any notice to my teachers. And I did my own work at home or played with my friends not going to school.

I was a selfish man who knew only himself. My whole life, I always worked for my own profit and benefit. I was also one of the most greedy men in society. I cannot explain how greedy I used to be. My greedy mind for business was so great that I did everything with all my effort and power without sleeping. I couldn't afford to lose anything to other people in business. In order to increase my own profits, I used to invest more money than I needed.

But after I was saved from death by Jesus Christ on January 1, 1990, I realized that I was one of the most foolish men in the world. I was a such a greedy man, that in the last 60 years of my life I had never worked as an employee of another company. Whenever I did business, big or small, I used to be the owner of the business.

I used to start businesses as the owner, President and employee, doing all the work for myself. When the business grew gradually, I used to expand the business more and more for more profits and my own interests and honor. Some people in the world called me a successful businessman. However from God's viewpoint, I was one of the most foolish and miserable men in the world, who knew only today's profit, while knowing nothing about eternal life which will come after life is finished.

By the Holy Spirit's powerful ministry and anointing, all the greed disappeared from my heart. Accordingly I was born again and changed by the Holy Spirit's power. My impatient character and greedy mind for money and business were completely re-moved by the Holy Spirit's powerful baptism. In replacement of them, the fruit of the Holy Spirit appeared.

Galatians 5: 22-23 But the fruit of the Spirit is love, joy, peace, longsuffering, kindness, goodness, faithfulness, gentleness, self-control. Against such there is no law.

I am still a baby from God's point of view, but comparing myself today with what I was before I was born again in the Holy Spirit, I have changed greatly. I am full of the fruit of the Holy Spirit and God's grace. I am totally under the control of the Holy Spirit.

Furthermore I was changed into a son of God who always tries to do only the things that will glorify the Heavenly Father. In the past, I was a man who worked only for my own profit and interests. Now I am a man of God who works only for the glory of God. This is the Holy Spirit's greatest miracle for me. Without Jesus Christ I could not even dream of this kind of change. My wife also says all the time, "Your change of heart by the Holy Spirit is the greatest of the Holy Spirit's miracles we have ever experienced.

2. A man going anywhere Holy Spirit services are performed

Acts 2: 1-4 When the Day of Pentecost had fully come, they were all with one accord in one place. And suddenly there came a sound from heaven, as of a rushing mighty wind, and it filled the whole house where they were sitting. Then there appeared to them divided tongues, as of fire, and one sat upon each of them. And they were all filled with the Holy Spirit and began to speak with other tongues, as the Spirit gave them utterance.

When I was in Korea, I went to all the different churches and prayer houses where the Holy Spirit's ministry was going on, and prayed through the night with the Holy Spirit. Since I returned home to the USA, I have been going to all different churches where the Holy Spirit's ministry is, not only in Philadelphia, but even to a Church in Closter, N. J. once a week for nine months, where the Holy Spirit moves most powerfully in the Eastern part of the USA. It takes about three hours one way from my home and takes about 12 hours if I finish all the church service and return home.

In addition to that, I have been to Toronto Airport Christian Fellowship Church for nine days which is about 500 miles away from my home, where the Holy Spirit moves the most powerfully in the world. And I received the Holy Spirit's Power greatly wherever I went.

Because of the Holy Spirit's leading in my heart, I have been to many churches and prayer houses where the Holy Spirit's

ministry is performed. Right now also I go to all the churches
where the Holy Spirit's ministry is performed in Philadelphia
and its surrounding area. The people without the Holy Spirit
cannot go to so many churches where the Holy Spirit moves so
powerfully.

When I am at home, I watch video tapes showing the Holy
Spirit's ministry, read the Bible, and communicate with the
Holy Spirit all day long except in the sleeping hours. The Holy
Spirit was teaching the Bible to me and He was biblically
teaching me how to discern between the Holy Spirit and demons for many years, and He has been spiritually training me
according to the Bible.

3. The Holy Spirit who guides my way

The Holy Spirit showed a green arrow sign for me to follow,
when I got lost on the road.

**Refer Acts 8: 26-31, 35-39 Now an angel of the Lord spoke to
Philip, saying, "Arise and go toward the south along the road
which goes down from Jerusalem to Gaza." This is desert. So he
arose and went. And behold, a man of Ethiopia, a eunuch of great
authority under Candace the queen of the Ethiopians, who had
charge of all her treasury, and had come to Jerusalem to worship,
was returning. And sitting in his chariot, he was reading Isaiah
the prophet. Then the Spirit said to Philip, "Go near and overtake
this chariot." So Philip ran to him, and heard him reading the**

prophet Isaiah, and said, "Do you understand what you are reading?" And he said, "How can I, unless someone guides me?" And he asked Philip to come up and sit with him.

Then Philip opened his mouth, and beginning at this Scripture, preached Jesus to him. Now as they went down the road, they came to some water. And the eunuch said, "See, here is water. What hinders me from being baptized?" Then Philip said, "If you believe with all your heart, you may." And he answered and said, "I believe that Jesus Christ is the Son of God." So he commanded the chariot to stand still. And both Philip and the eunuch went down into the water, and he baptized him. Now when they came up out of the water, the Spirit of the Lord caught Philip away, so that the eunuch saw him no more; and he went on his way rejoicing.

1) When I was going to a restaurant on Kelly Drive

In the summer of 1997, when I was going to a meeting at a Korean restaurant located on Kelly Drive in Philadelphia, I knew the address but I did not know the way.

At that time the Holy Spirit showed me a large green arrow sign, about one meter by five meters, showing me the way to follow. And He told me to follow the green arrow. I followed the green sign and soon I found the same restaurant at my left of the road. I thanked the Holy Spirit again who even helped me find my way on the road.

2) When I was on the way to a Holy Spirit Revival

meeting in the Pocono

On July 4, 1997 when we were on the way to the Pocono
prayer house where a Holy Spirit service was to be performed
by Rev. Y., I thought we had passed the prayer house, so I tried
to turn my car in the opposite direction but the Holy Spirit told
me, "Go more." And when I followed the Holy Spirit's instruction, we soon arrived at our destination. God knows the whole
world. There is no place in the world that the Holy Spirit does
not know.

3) When I was on the way to pray for Pastor C. who was sick

Sometime in September 1998 when I was on the way to pray
for Pastor C. who was recovering at his home from major heart
surgery, I was looking for his home in the wrong direction.
Suddenly the Holy Spirit showed me a big green arrow sign
pointing in the direction where his home was located. I followed the Holy Spirit's sign and I found Pastor C.'s home easily
on my right.

4) When I was on the way to Westminster Theological Seminary

In May 1998 when our second son graduated from Westminster Theological Seminary, the commencement ceremony was
not held at the school campus, but it was held at a big church.
After the graduation ceremony we were invited to lunch at the
campus.

When we were on the way to Westminster, I thought I had to follow 73 West, but my wife said, "73 East." But when I tried to follow 73 West, the Holy Spirit showed me a big green sign pointing to 73 East. I followed the Holy Spirit's sign and we arrived at our destination.

The Holy Spirit showed me my way whenever I got lost on the road. The angels of the Holy Spirit always lead and protect the children of Christians all over the world, who really believe in God. Our Almighty Heavenly Father always loves all of His children and leads them one by one through the Holy Spirit, when they are lost on the road. When they face unexpected impossible problems, Jesus Christ solves all the problems for the children of God.

We must always express thanks for the Almighty God who loves all of us, and we have to follow the way the Holy Spirit leads, to any place all over the world.

CHAPTER 6

The Holy Spirit's healing ministry about my flesh

1. The Holy Spirit completely healed my 36-year stomach ulcer
2. The Holy Spirit who healed a 50-year-old hole in my left eardrum
3. The Holy Spirit cured my 45-year chronic nose inflammation
4. The Holy Spirit completely cured the severe back pain from which I was suffering for many years
5. The Holy Spirit healed the athlete's foot I had for 40 years
6. The Holy Spirit's fire healed the chronic rash on my right ankle, from which I was suffering for many years
7. When I have pain in my body, I pray with my hand on the area where the pain is, then the pain disappears immediately
8. The Holy Spirit immediately cured the pain in the joints of my upper thigh

1. The Holy Spirit completely healed my 36-year stomach ulcer

**Mark 1: 32-34 At evening, when the sun had set, they brought
to Him all who were sick and those who were demon-possessed.
And the whole city was gathered together at the door. Then He
healed many who were sick with various diseases, and cast out
many demons; and He did not allow the demons to speak, because
they knew Him.**

I was suffering from a severe stomach ulcer for 36 years,
from the time I was 21 to 57. Because of this severe ulcer, I
was hospitalized several times in the USA and Korea. I took
many different medicines which the doctors recommended on
and off for 36 years. When I took them, the pain disappeared
for a few months. However when the ulcer symptoms came
back, with severe pain in the upper part of my stomach, I was at
a loss of what to do.

What I was most afraid of was that the chronic ulcer would
turn into cancer. In some of my friends who had been sick with
stomach ulcers for many years, the ulcer later turned into cancer and they died of stomach cancer. Whenever I saw such
friends dying of stomach cancer which began from ulcers, I
was terribly scared because I also had a stomach ulcer which
might change to cancer at any time. There are many people
who died like this in Korea and the USA. I thank God that He
saved me completely from the ulcer before changing it to can-

cer.

In January 1997 when I was praying to God early in the morning, Jesus appeared, embraced by the light in a long white robe and He said to me, **"I am healing your digestive organs."**

At the same time, two angels dressed in medical gowns with round mirrors on their foreheads took another person who was exactly the same as me, laid him down on a long operating table and cut open his stomach. They cut out his stomach and a piece of his bowel about one foot long and replaced it with a new one they brought from a chest and put it into his open belly. They stitched and sealed up the cut part, sprayed it with something, and held his hand to help him stand. Then they disappeared.

Since that time more than eight years have passed, but I have had no more symptoms of the ulcer. And my digestive organs work very powerfully, like when I was in my late teens or twenties. I am very thankful to the Holy Spirit and Jesus who healed my ulcer completely. I want to turn all the glory to the Heavenly Father for healing my ulcer completely.

2. The Holy Spirit who healed a 50-year-old hole in my left eardrum

Mark 2: 1-12 And again He entered Capernaum after some days, and it was heard that He was in the house. Immediately many gathered together, so that there was no longer room to receive them, not even near the door. And He preached the word to them. Then they came to Him, bringing a paralytic who was carried by four men. And when they could not come near Him because of the crowd, they uncovered the roof where He was. So when they had broken through, they let down the bed on which the paralytic was lying.

When Jesus saw their faith, He said to the paralytic, "Son, your sins are forgiven you." And some of the scribes were sitting there and reasoning in their hearts, "Why does this Man speak blasphemies like this? Who can forgive sins but God alone?" But immediately, when Jesus perceived in His spirit that they reasoned thus within themselves, He said to them, "Why do you reason about these things in your hearts?

Which is easier, to say to the paralytic, "Your sins are forgiven you,' or to say, "Arise, take up your bed and walk'? But that you may know that the Son of Man has power on earth to forgive sins"--He said to the paralytic, "I say to you, arise, take up your bed, and go to your house." Immediately he arose, took up the bed, and went out in the presence of them all, so that all were amazed and glorified God, saying, "We never saw anything like this!"

When I was a little boy, maybe around four or five-years-old, I used to play with friends my age in the water of a small brook in Korea. Sometimes a lot of water went into my ears, while swimming. I had a bad infection in my left year for a long time. However at that time Korea was under Japanese colonialism. And since my family was poor and lived in a small agricultural village in Korea, we could not afford to go to the hospital. At that time when a man was very sick, he was sent to the hospital for matters of life or death. But patients with ear infections could not even dream of going to the hospital in poor traditional Korean farming villages.

Since that time I have had a big problem hearing with my left year. Later when I had it checked by a medical doctor, he told me that I had a hole in my eardrum. I couldn't hear telephone conversations, so I always answered the phone with my right ear.

But sometime in June 1997, in prayer to God early in the morning, the Holy Spirit told me that, **"I am now healing your left ear."** So I answered, **"Thank you, God."**

And I found that I could hear very well. All of the sudden in early July 1997, a woman from the Delaware Valley Hearing Center called me. She asked me whether we had any person with a hearing problem in our family, so I told her that I had a hole in my ear drum, so I couldn't hear clearly.

She gave me an appointment and sent an ear technician to my home. Later in early August 1997, a hearing test technician with an electronic machine like a computer visited my home. When I was with my wife, he checked and found a big hole in my left ear. When he checked both ears' hearing power with that machine, he was very surprised to find that my left ear also was very normal in hearing.

So I found out right away that the Holy Spirit cured my left ear. I prayed and asked the Holy Spirit about my ear. He answered that in order to prove that the Holy Spirit completely cured my ear, He sent an ear technician to my home when my wife was at home. At the same time the Holy Spirit showed me the scene in which a couple of angels dressed in doctor's white gowns with mirrors on their foreheads were working on my left ear to heal my hearing.

On November 21, 1997, my family doctor checked my left ear and told me that he found a scar on my left ear drum showing that the hole was healed, and at the bottom of the ear drum there was a tiny hole. When I asked the Holy Spirit in prayer, He told me that He was repairing the hole in my left ear drum. But He left the scars to prove that the Holy Spirit healed it. I thank the Holy Spirit and Jesus Christ so much for having healed my left ear. I want to turn all the glory to the Heavenly Father for completely healing my left ear.

3. The Holy Spirit cured my 45-year chronic nose inflammation

Mark 3: 1-5 And He entered the synagogue again, and a man was there who had a withered hand. So they watched Him closely, whether He would heal him on the Sabbath, so that they might accuse Him. And He said to the man who had the withered hand, "Step forward." Then He said to them, "Is it lawful on the Sabbath to do good or to do evil, to save life or to kill?"

But they kept silent. And when He had looked around at them with anger, being grieved by the hardness of their hearts, He said to the man, "Stretch out your hand." And he stretched it out, and his hand was restored as whole as the other.

266 Holy Spirit, Hover Over Me

I have had phlegm since I was in my teens, so I have always felt as if something was blocking my throat. The medical doctor told me that I had a chronic inflammation in my nose. I was taking special medicine for that problem on and off for many years, but no medicine could cure it completely. I had to take two tablets and nasal sprays every day.

In February 1997, when I was praying early in the morning, the Holy Spirit told me that He was curing the chronic inflammation in my nose, and showed me two angel doctors working on my nose and throat, checking them with a doctor's mirror and flashlight and touching them with a pair of tweezers.

They put some ointment on my throat and inside my nose, and they were gone. The Holy Spirit asked me to throw the medicine I was taking into the trash can, so I threw it away. Since that time, my sickness has gone away, and I take no more medicine for that purpose at all.

Eight years passed since the Holy Spirit's angels cured the sickness in my nose, and no symptoms of the chronic inflammation have reappeared. It was cured completely.

Human beings cannot prove the Holy Spirit's power with their science or medicine. How easily the Holy Spirit healed all the chronic diseases from which I was suffering from, my whole life! When I tell my friends how the Holy Spirit healed all my chronic diseases, many of them do not believe what I say. But I myself and all of my family members know everything about the sicknesses which the Holy Spirit cured.

Some people try to prove the Holy Spirit's Miracles with human science or medicine. Except for the Christians who experienced the Holy Spirit's miracles, no one can understand the Holy Spirit's power.

Even Christians who experienced the Holy Spirit's miracles do not know how the Holy Spirit cures patients. Even the pastors who spend a lot of time praying every day to God do not understand how the Holy Spirit cures sick people. We only know by seeing the patients who came lying on a bed because of their illnesses, who say their sicknesses were cured and all their pain is gone. And they feel so happy that they praise the Lord and dance on the floor.

This is the Holy Spirit's healing ministry. I express my greatest thanks to the Holy Spirit and Jesus Christ for having cured my 45-year chronic inflammation in my nose and turn all the glory to the Heavenly Father.

4. The Holy Spirit completely cured the severe back pain from which I was suffering for many years

Since 1982 I have had severe back pain for several years. I took many different medicines which medical doctors and Chinese herbal medicine doctors recommended, but nothing cured my back pain. Terrible pains began to go down to my left leg from my back. My pain was so severe that I had to limp on my left leg for a couple of years.

268 Holy Spirit, Hover Over Me

Therefore I had to take four tablets of aspirin every day, and these aspirins caused more stomach pains. I could not take any more aspirin, so my doctor recommended that I take coated aspirins, but that did not help the pain from my stomach ulcer.

I had acupuncture applied to my back many times, but that did not help my pain at all. I had the area where pain came from cauterized with moxa treatment by a herbal medicine doctor. That did not help the pain go away, either.

Some people said to me, "The bear gallbladder is the best medicine for back pain, so I went bear hunting with my American friend in Oregon, where we hunted bear. Then I dried the gallbladder and drank a strong whiskey mixed with the gallbladder power. But nothing helped my back pain go away.

Some people said to me, "Wild boar's blood is good medicine for back pain," so I drank a lot of wild boar's blood in Tennessee, where we went wild boar hunting. But nothing helped cure my back pain.

In hospitals and rehabilitation centers I had lots of different treatments, such as heat massage and back movements, but no one could cure my back pain. So I was always very nervous, and I had to limp on my left leg. Accordingly, at home I was always lying on the hard floor.

After several years of severe pain in my back, I met finally a church pastor who was fully inspired by the Holy Spirit. He laid his hands on my back and prayed and touched my back bones. It felt very nice and I felt some of the misplaced bones moving into the right place. Miraculously and immediately, my back pain was gone. The Holy Spirit knows which bone was misplaced, so He moved the misplaced bone to its original place. Since that day I have stopped taking aspirin for back pain. My left leg, which was lame, was cured normally.

Today, more than 15 years after my back pain was cured, I have not had to take any aspirin for back pain. I was wondering how the Holy Spirit perfectly healed the back pain from which I was suffering from for so many years. Only people who experienced it, can understand the Holy Spirit's miracles.

I want to express my thanks again to the Holy Spirit and Jesus Christ for having cured my back. I want to turn the glory to my Heavenly Father who cured my back pain.

5. The Holy Spirit healed the athlete's foot I had for 40 years

Mark 1: 40-45 Now a leper came to Him, imploring Him, kneeling down to Him and saying to Him, "If You are willing, You can make me clean." Then Jesus, moved with compassion, stretched out His hand and touched him, and said to him, "I am willing; be cleansed." As soon as He had spoken, immediately the leprosy left him, and he was cleansed. And He strictly warned him and sent him away at once, and said to him, "See that you say nothing to anyone; but go your way, show yourself to the priest, and offer for your cleansing those things which Moses commanded, as a testimony to them." However, he went out and be-

gan to proclaim it freely, and to spread the matter, so that Jesus could no longer openly enter the city, but was outside in deserted places; and they came to Him from every direction.

Since I was a teenager, I have had athlete's foot, and I used many different medicines for it. After I used some medicine, it went away for a while, but came back again soon. Sometimes when it was severely itchy, I could not endure it. However hard I scratched on the area, I still felt itchy. I couldn't do anything but scratch the itching area until blood came out. Even after it started bleeding, I still felt itchy. I lived like this for more than 40 years.

But one day in March 1997, when I was praying early in the morning, the Holy Spirit told me,

"I am now curing your foot pain,"
and He showed me two angel doctors dressed in white gowns working on my feet. They checked my feet with a mirror and a flashlight and they cleaned my feet with a cotton ball soaked in alcohol, held by tweezers.

They put on some kind of ointment and applied a bandage to my feet and then said to me, **"Your athlete's foot was completely healed."**
Eight years have passed since that time, and I haven't had to use any medicine for athlete's foot pain. The athlete's foot which was so itchy was completely healed. People who did not experience the Holy Spirit's miracles cannot understand it. I myself cannot understand God's miracles.

When I command in the name of Jesus the evil spirits causing pain to leave immediately, with the words of the Almighty

Heavenly Father and the authority of the Holy Spirit, the pain of patients leave immediately, and the patients begin to praise God by singing and dancing, saying that all their pain is gone. I feel very pleased to see such miracles performed by the Holy Spirit. Some people try to judge the Holy Spirit's miracles with human reason and science. God's power cannot be decided or judged by the human reason or science. Only the Holy Spirit knows about it.

I want to express my biggest thanks to the Holy Spirit and Jesus Christ for having cured my athlete's foot. I want to turn all the glory to my Heavenly Father who cured my athlete's foot.

6. The Holy Spirit's fire healed the chronic rash on my right ankle, from which I was suffering for many years

Mark 5: 25-35 Now a certain woman had a flow of blood for twelve years, and had suffered many things from many physicians. She had spent all that she had and was no better, but rather grew worse. When she heard about Jesus, she came behind Him in the crowd and touched His garment. For she said, "If only I may touch His clothes, I shall be made well." Immediately the fountain of her blood was dried up, and she felt in her body that she was healed of the affliction. And Jesus, immediately knowing in Himself that power had gone out of Him, turned around in the crowd and said, "Who touched My clothes?"

But His disciples said to Him, "You see the multitude thronging

You, and You say, "Who touched Me?"' And He looked around
to see her who had done this thing. But the woman, fearing and
trembling, knowing what had happened to her, came and fell
down before Him and told Him the whole truth.

And He said to her, "Daughter, your faith has made you well.
Go in peace, and be healed of your affliction." While He was still
speaking, some came from the ruler of the synagogue's house who
said, "Your daughter is dead. Why trouble the Teacher any further?"

I had suffered from a chronic rash, of about 1¼ inch diameter, right above my ankle joint inside my right leg for several
years. This rash was inflammatory, blistered, itchy, and sometimes it bled. It was very itchy, and sometimes it was sore and
stung terribly, when it was inflamed. When it began to itch, I
used to scratch it until it was bleeding, but still it was itchy. I
applied many different kinds of medicines which the doctors
recommended on it, many times for many years. But no medicine could cure it at all, so I had to suffer from this rash for
many years.

Sometime in July 1997, after washing the foot, I prayed to
God to cure that infection with my right palm about one inch
above the rash. I found the following day that all the blistered
rashes had broken open and were drying and being healed. And
I didn't feel any itching on the rash. After several days, I found
that all the blistered rashes were gone completely. From my
palm special, powerful Holy Spirit heat comes out, and if I
place my palm above such infections, they are healed miraculously. After that the place where the rash was became very soft
skin like a baby's skin.

More than seven years have passed since the Holy Spirit

cured the rash, which never returned. It was completely cured. God's healing power is a supernatural miracle which no human being can prove with science or medicine.

Whenever I think that all my diseases were cured by the Holy Spirit's miraculous healing power, I cannot but express the greatest thanks to God for giving me His unlimited grace and love.

Again I want to thank Jesus and the Holy Spirit who cured the chronic rashes on my ankle from which I was suffering for many years and I want to turn all the glory to the Almighty God who healed the rashes.

7. When I have pain in my body, I pray with my hand on the area where the pain is, then the pain disappears immediately

Since the rashes on my ankle were cured, when I am sick or have pains on some part of my body, I do not go to the doctor, hospital or drug store, but I pray to the Holy Spirit with my right hand placed on the sick area, then the sickness or pain goes away immediately. I experienced such Holy Spirit miracles innumerable times.

In the past when I was sick, I used to visit the doctor or go to the drug store for medicine. However now I pray to God to cure any sickness I have, such as a cold, not feeling well, fever or anything, and it goes away immediately. I found that all of these miracles were performed by the Holy Spirit who is always with me.

It is pitiful and miserable to see some Christians who do not have the Holy Spirit's experience and do not believe the miracles performed by the Holy Spirit. God loves all the Christians in the world. If you really pray hard for the Holy Spirit's miraculous power, God is always willing to bestow to you the same Holy Spirit anointing that He gave to me. The Holy Spirit gives the Holy Spirit's power to all Christians who love God and are obedient to Jesus.

God's power heals anything miraculously. No human science or doctors can find the Holy Spirit's miracle to cure diseases. That works only for Christians who really believe in God. God wants to cure sick people through you also.

8. The Holy Spirit immediately cured the pain in the joints of my upper thigh

It was sometime in February 2001. At church when I was going down some stairs, though they were covered with carpet, I misplaced my left foot and slipped down two stairs. I did not notice anything wrong immediately, but when I came home, I began to feel severe pain coming from the joints of the upper part of my thigh. The pains were so severe that I could not do anything else and I could not endure the pain.

When I prayed to God, the Holy Spirit asked me to sit straight up on a hard wooden chair, according to the Holy Spirit words. When I sat with my back straight up on a hard wooden chair in our kitchen, the Holy Spirit asked me to do the following.

"Put your two hands on the joints of your upper thigh where the pain comes from, bind the evil spirits which caused you to slip on the stairs in the name of Jesus, and command them to get out of your body immediately. And command the joints, nerves, discs and muscles in your thigh to move to the original place where they were before. And command the pain to be removed immediately and all the damaged places to be healed immediately in the name of Jesus."

According to the words of the Holy Spirit, I sat with my back straight up on the wooden chair. And I placed two hands on the joints where the pain came from and I commanded everything exactly as the Holy Spirit asked me to do.

Immediately within one minute, I felt the joints on the upper part of my thigh where the pain came from were moving up and down and turning and shaking. At the same time I felt some of the misplaced joints move to their original place. Immediately the pain in the joints of the upper part of my thigh disappeared. I was so glad and happy to experience my pain healed immediately by the Holy Spirit's power. It was marvelous to see the

Holy Spirit cure the misplaced joints of my thigh.

I stood up from the chair and praised God with tears falling from my eyes, raising my hands up high and dancing by myself. And I thanked Him again for His wonderful miracles. This is the Holy Spirit's healing power. When I see Christians who did not experience such Holy Spirit Miracles and do not believe in the power of God, I cannot understand them.

You must always listen to the small voice spoken by the Holy Spirit in you.

1 Kings 19: 12-13 and after the earthquake a fire, but the Lord was not in the fire; and after the fire a still small voice. So it was, when Elijah heard it, that he wrapped his face in his mantle and went out and stood in the entrance of the cave. Suddenly a voice came to him, and said, "What are you doing here, Elijah?"

If the Holy Spirit says anything to you, you have to follow exactly per the Holy Spirit's words, like a little child. And then the Holy Spirit will perform His miracles for you.

If you decide and doubt the Holy Spirit's miracles with human reason, knowledge, and wisdom, the Holy Spirit will not perform any miracles for you. You have to act like little children.

Mark 10: 15-16 Assuredly, I say to you, whoever does not receive the kingdom of God as a little child will by no means enter it." And He took them up in His arms, laid His hands on them, and blessed them.

I want to express the greatest thanks to the Almighty Heavenly Father who immediately healed the pain in the joints of my upper left leg.

CHAPTER 7

The Holy Spirit's healing of my wife

1. The Holy Spirit healed my wife's severe headaches
2. The Holy Spirit healed my wife's indigestion
3. The Holy Spirit cured cramps in my wife's body
4. The Holy Spirit pulled a gall stone out of a patient

Mark 16: 17-18 "And these signs will follow those who believe: In My name they will cast out demons; they will speak with new tongues; they will take up serpents; and if they drink anything deadly, it will by no means hurt them; they will lay hands on the sick, and they will recover."

1. The Holy Spirit healed my wife's severe headaches

My wife was suffering from severe chronic headaches for many years. Many doctors at several hospitals examined her with modern equipment, but no one could find any cause for the pain, so she was taking pain killers for many years.

2. The Holy Spirit healed my wife's indigestion

For many years, my wife's digestive organs couldn't digest the food she ate, so she always complained about pain in the upper part of her stomach. All the doctors who checked her thoroughly with modern equipment could not find the cause of her indigestion. Therefore she had to take digestive medicine for many years.

3. The Holy Spirit cured cramps in my wife's body

My wife used to easily get cramps in her legs, sometimes when she was sleeping, sitting, or lying down. Medical doctors checked her thoroughly with modern equipment but they couldn't find the reason for the cramps. She was suffering from these cramps for many years.

When I prayed to God about my wife's illnesses, the Holy Spirit said to me immediately, **"She is too arrogant. She does not believe in the Holy Spirit's miraculous ministry and she believes in God according to her own human reason, thought, knowledge and selfishness. Therefore the Holy Spirit caused these sicknesses on purpose."**

My wife has been believing in God in traditional Presbyterian churches in Korea and the USA for many decades since she was young. But she didn't attend any Holy Spirit revival services, where the Holy Spirit is really performing miracles. She was a good Christian who really believed in God's word, but not like the Christians who are fully filled in the Holy Spirit. However she spent lots of time reading the Bible.

Since I was saved from death by Jesus on January 1, 1990 and was born again in the Holy Spirit, I put aside all my business and read the Bible from early morning until late at night.

And from the morning, I sang hymns loudly, prayed in a loud voice, and attended all the Holy Spirit congregations near or far from my home every day. She was very surprised at what I was doing according to the Holy Spirit's words.

Therefore whenever I testify about the Holy Spirit's miracles which I experienced, she didn't like to hear about it and always said something against the Holy Spirit's ministry.

Therefore the Holy Spirit said to me, **"In order to train her spiritually, He gave her special illnesses."**

I immediately told her everything that the Holy Spirit had said to me about her being sick. She began to pray to the Holy Spirit while crying, and confessed all her sins against God.

About one week later, when I prayed, the Holy Spirit said to me, **"I saw her crying and tears, now I will cure all her sickness."**

At the same time the Holy Spirit showed me that angels were curing her. After I prayed for her, all her illnesses and pain began to disappear one by one from her body. Now she doesn't have to take any pain killers or digestive medicine any more. Now she is healthy. Sometimes when her body is sick, she asks me to pray for her, or when I am busy she prays for herself. Then the Holy Spirit miraculously cures the pain or sickness in her body immediately.

After the Holy Spirit cured her illnesses, she never complained about the Holy Spirit's ministry. In addition, whenever any Holy Spirit services are to be performed, she goes first, ahead of me. She never says no to the Holy Spirit's request. The

Holy Spirit trained her spiritually in this way.

Now when she meets any of her friends in the company where she works or in the church who are sick, she prays for them, and they get well. Already many of them got well because of her prayers.

4. The Holy Spirit pulled gallstones out of a patient

It was sometime in 1998. At the company where my wife used to work, there was an employee who was suffering very severely from pain caused by gallstones.

At the hospital the doctors said to him, **"The gallstones were found in an X-ray of his body."**

He was scheduled for a gallstone operation the next day. One day before the surgery, my wife prayed for him at her company. The Holy Spirit performed His miracles immediately.

When he was admitted to the hospital the next day, he had many X-rays taken to find the exact location for surgery. However the doctors couldn't find the gallstones, which disappeared from their original location. But the doctors found some scars which were made when the gallstones were pulled from his body. The Holy Spirit cured his pain miraculously by moving the gallstones from his body before the doctors removed them by surgery in the hospital.

This is the Holy Spirit's healing miracle.

CHAPTER 8

The Holy Spirit's healing of others through my prayers

1. The Holy Spirit healed brain paralysis
2. The Holy Spirit cured stomach cancer
3. The Holy Spirit healed liver cancer
4. The Holy Spirit healed an 80-year-old man's sickness
5. The Holy Spirit healed an 80-year-old lady's trembling hands
6. The Holy Spirit healed an 86-year-old lady who was partially blind and deaf
7. The Holy Spirit immediately healed a 40-year-old lady's deaf ear
8. The Holy Spirit healed a kidney which needed to change blood three times weekly
9. The Holy Spirit cured an 80-year-old lady's uneasy heart
10. The Holy Spirit who healed severe back pain immediately
11. The Holy Spirit who healed intolerable pain in the chest immediately
12. The Holy Spirit who healed a 12-year-old chronic arthritis
13. The Holy Spirit who saved a missionary speaking in Satanic tongues
14. The Holy Spirit who caught an evil spirit which tried to deceive a missionary

John 11: 32-44 Then, when Mary came where Jesus was, and saw Him, she fell down at His feet, saying to Him, "Lord, if You had been here, my brother would not have died." Therefore, when Jesus saw her weeping, and the Jews who came with her weeping, He groaned in the spirit and was troubled. And He said, "Where have you laid him?" They said to Him, "Lord, come and see." Jesus wept. Then the Jews said, "See how He loved him!" And some of them said, "Could not this Man, who opened the eyes of the blind, also have kept this man from dying?" Then Jesus, again groaning in Himself, came to the tomb.

It was a cave, and a stone lay against it. Jesus said, "Take away the stone." Martha, the sister of him who was dead, said to Him, "Lord, by this time there is a stench, for he has been dead four days." Jesus said to her, "Did I not say to you that if you would believe you would see the glory of God?" Then they took away the stone from the place where the dead man was lying.

And Jesus lifted up His eyes and said, "Father, I thank You that that You have heard Me. And I know that You always hear Me, but because of the people who are standing by I said this, that they may believe that You sent Me." Now when He had said these things, He cried with a loud voice, "Lazarus, come forth!" And he who had died came out bound hand and foot with grave-clothes, and his face was wrapped with a cloth. Jesus said to them, "Loose him, and let him go."

1. The Holy Spirit healed brain paralysis

Once when one of my friends in Korea was running for congress, after he found that he lost the election, he became a paralytic and went into a coma. When I was praying in the morning, my friend appeared, dressed in all black and crying before me, asking me to help him, and the Holy Spirit asked me to call him. When I called him, I found out he was hospitalized.

I called the hospital where he was. When I prayed to God for him on the phone, the Holy Spirit performed His miraculous ministry. Therefore he gradually recovered from his paralysis.

This is the Holy Spirit's ministry. For God distance is no limit. I called and prayed on the phone from the USA where I was staying, for my friend who was hospitalized in Korea. Accordingly the Holy Spirit performed miracles for my friend in Korea. For God there is nothing impossible in the world. This is the Holy Spirit's miracle.

2. The Holy Spirit cured stomach cancer

Sometime in the summer of 1998, when I was praying early in the morning, a man named L. appeared and asked me to help him while crying before me. Sometime after, Jesus, embraced in the light, appeared before me and asked me to visit him and pray for him. When I called him, he said to me, **"I am suffering from stomach cancer."**

When I told him everything that happened in the morning prayer, he said, **"God replied my prayers through you."**

While I was praying with my right hand placed on his stomach, the Holy Spirit immediately showed me a very big red snake which was rolled in his stomach, and at his home several giant black demons were walking here and there and evil spirits tried to take him with them to some place, pulling him by force. I was so surprised to see them.

At the same time the Holy Spirit said to me, **"Don't worry about them at all, but boldly bind the evil spirits in the name of Jesus and command them to get them out of him immediately. The Holy Spirit and His angels are always with you."**

When I tried to pray, God's tongue automatically came out of my mouth. I was fully filled with the Holy Spirit and I prayed in heavenly tongues for about ten minutes. I didn't tell him about the spiritual things that I saw at his home, but I told to my wife about the things that I saw.

On his next trip to the hospital, he had many X-rays taken. But the doctors couldn't find any symptoms of cancer. His stomach cancer was completely cured. He is now healthy and goes to church as a normal healthy man. I want to express the greatest thanks to God who cured stomach cancer of Mr. L.

3. The Holy Spirit healed liver cancer

One day in February 1999, when I was praying in the early morning, the wife of an elder of a church, dressed all in black, was crying before me. Soon Jesus appeared before me, embraced by the light, and said to me, **"You know her, help her with Holy Spirit's power."**

After prayer, when I called her, I found that she was suffering from liver cancer. We visited her home and found that all the hair on her head was gone because of the radiation treatment. And her belly was large, like a pregnant woman's. She said because of the liquid, her stomach was full. She said that when the pain comes, she could not tolerate the pain, so she rolled all over the room, crying. Painkillers didn't stop her pain.

I gave her the necessary words from the Bible, and prayed for her. Soon the Holy Spirit's power was present with her, and she fell on the floor. After the prayer, we came home. The same night she threw out a lot of dirty liquid from her stomach, and her husband said that something like ping pong balls made of phlegm mixed with blood, two of them, came out of her stomach through her mouth.

After that, her stomach shrank to normal and her pain was gone. She was very happy. She was recovering from her cancer. This is the Holy Spirit's miracle. Because of her strong belief in God and our prayer, the Holy Spirit performed His miracle ministry. Such people must continuously pray to God for their health and they have to tell their testimony that God cured their cancer to other people, for the glory of God. And they have to spread the gospel for God. And then the cancer will not return. I want to turn all the glory to the Heavenly Father for healing her liver cancer.

4. The Holy Spirit healed an 80-year-old man's sickness

Mr. & Mrs. P. were senior citizens in their eighties. The wife was healthy but the husband was sick all over. Therefore he couldn't come to church for many weeks. Sometime in the summer of 1997, when I was praying early in the morning, the senior man, dressed in all black, appeared before me and asked me to help him, while crying and weeping. The Holy Spirit asked me to help him.

In accordance with the Holy Spirit's words I visited him with my wife and we prayed for him. After our prayer he said, **"I am feeling very good and my heart is in peace and I am**

very pleased."

He recovered his health immediately and he was healthy again. From the next week he began to come to church as normal. This is the Holy Spirit's healing ministry.

The Holy Spirit asked me to visit such old and sick people in their homes and pray for them. And to bind all the evil spirits in the name of Jesus and cast them out of such old people with the authority of the Holy Spirit and with the words of the Almighty Heavenly Father, in the name of Jesus. We follow all the instructions of the Holy Spirit, and then He cures the sick people immediately with the Holy Spirit's powerful miracle.

5. The Holy Spirit healed an 80-year-old lady's trembling hands

It was in the fall of 1997, when a woman in her eighties who was suffering from hand tremors asked me to pray for her. She was attending a Catholic church.

She said to me, **"I contacted my family doctor but he told me that this disease is specially carried by senior people, and there is no special medicine for it."**

According to the Holy Spirit's words, I visited her apartment with my wife, and we prayed for her hand tremors to be cured by the Holy Spirit's power. After our prayer, her hands stopped trembling. When we prayed, we were fully filled with the Holy Spirit, and she was crying and pleased to experience the Holy Spirit's miracles. Two years after our prayer, now she is healthy and enjoys normal life.

Whenever her sons or daughters got sick, she asked me to pray for them. The Holy Spirit performed miracles for her children also. God performs miracles in such a way. The people who experienced the Holy Spirit's healing miracles believe more faithfully in God than before they experienced the Holy Spirit's ministry.

6. The Holy Spirit healed an 86-year-old lady who was partially blind and deaf

Sometime in winter 1998, an 86-year-old woman who was suffering severely from diabetes became partially blind and deaf. She was a really good Christian, faithfully believing in God. When I prayed for her and commanded to bind the evil spirits causing the diabetes in the name of Jesus. I also commanded her blind eyes and deaf ears to be cured immediately in the name of Jesus, with the authority of the Holy Spirit and with the words of Almighty God.

After my prayer, she could read the Bible immediately and hear what I said in Korean. She was so happy that she rose from her bed, and she was praising God and singing hymns and danced before God.

She said to me, "My eyes are clear to see and my ears can clearly hear what you say. I am so happy that I praise God now." She began to go to church as usual.

7. The Holy Spirit immediately healed a 40-year-old lady's lady's deaf ear

A middle-aged lady who was partially deaf came to me to receive the Holy Spirit's powerful anointing. She was going to a Catholic church. When I rebuked the evil spirit causing her deafness and commanded to arrest all the evil spirits in her body in the name of Jesus, she fell on the floor because of the Holy Spirit's powerful anointing.

When she rose again from the floor, her deaf ear was cured. She could hear clearly all that I said to her.

She was so happy that she was praising God while weeping and crying.

8. The Holy Spirit healed a kidney which needed to change change blood three times weekly

A man named C. always calls me and asks me to pray for him, whenever he is sick. One day in January 2001, he called me again and said to me, **"My doctor called me today and asked me to be hospitalized right away. My kidney is inflamed, so my blood should be changed three times a week, otherwise it is dangerous to my life. Urine also doesn't come out easily, because my bladder also is inflamed."**

After talking with his doctor, he called me right away. And he told me that he said this to his doctor: **"I will come to your hospital after talking with Almighty God."**

When I was fully filled in the Holy Spirit by reading a Holy Spirit testimony book, he called me to pray for him. As soon as I picked up the phone to pray for him, the heavenly tongue was coming out of my mouth, and I saw a vision that the angels were working on him. I told him that the angels who came embraced by the light were working on him.

After my prayer, he said to me, **"I am feeling as if all the pain is gone and I am very pleased now."**

From the next day he could urinate smoothly. Within several days, his urination was normal. He didn't go to the hospital to which his doctor asked him to be hospitalized immediately. But six months after his doctor asked him to be hospitalized, when he went to visit his doctor in good condition, his doctor was very surprised to see him and said to him, **"I thought you were dead."**

He said to his doctor, **"The Holy Spirit cured my illness. And now I am alright."**

His doctor said to him, **"You don't have to come to me any more."** The Holy Spirit performs miracles like this. God heals all the diseases or sicknesses for His children who always pray to God.

9. The Holy Spirit cured an 80-year-old lady's uneasy heart

One senior lady in her eighties was suffering from severe uneasiness in her heart, so she was taking pain killers everyday. When I prayed for her, I commanded to bind all the evil spirits causing her uneasiness in the name of Jesus and cast them out of her immediately.

The Holy Spirit was present immediately, and she fell on the floor. About ten minutes later, she rose from the floor and said, **"All the evil spirits which were causing uneasiness in her heart were gone, and now I am very peaceful."**

She began to praise the Lord and to sing hymns and dance on the floor.

10. The Holy Spirit who healed severe back pain immediately

An unmarried young lady in her mid-twenties was suffering from severe back pain. To relieve the pain she was taking aspirin every day. When she had X-rays taken at the hospital, the doctor told her that one of the discs between her back bones was dislocated. When I prayed for her, the Holy Spirit cured her pain immediately. She said to me, **"All the pain was gone immediately and I am very peaceful in my heart."**

After she came back from her vacation, she said to me, **"All the pain is completely gone."**

God cures pain like this. She was a highly educated lady, so she didn't believe in the Holy Spirit's miracles. However she cannot say anything before God who cured her pain immediately. She said, **"Now I really believe in God and His Holy Spirit's miraculous power."**

Almighty God ministers in such a way.

11. The Holy Spirit who healed intolerable pain in the chest immediately

There was a retired pastor in his seventies. When he was young, he was sent to foreign countries as a missionary and he delivered Jesus' gospel to innumerable people in the world. Right now also he is active in delivering the gospel.

He said, **"I have severe pain in my chest and it is intolerable. For the last several years since the pain began to occur, I had a lot of different treatments from doctors, but nothing helps relieve the pain. I am continually suffering from pain."**

He came to me to get the Holy Spirit's prayer. After heartfelt prayer, I commanded to bind all the evil spirits causing the severe pain in his chest and cast them out of him. I also rebuked the pain and commanded the pain to be healed immediately in the name of Jesus, and he fell on the floor due to the Holy Spirit's powerful presence.

Some time later, he rose up from the floor and said that all the pain in his chest was completely gone. He wondered how the Holy Spirit performed miracles for him. No human beings can understand how powerful the Holy Spirit's miracles are. He was happy and began to praise the Lord, and began to dance and sing hymns. We thanked God again for His healing the pain of an old pastor.

He said, **"God loves a sinner like me so much that He cured the pains in my chest immediately. However when I think about the innumerable pastors and Christians who do**

**not experience the Holy Spirit's miracles and do not ask
God to cure their sicknesses. But they are going to hospitals
and drug stores instead of God, it is pitiful and miserable."**

We have innumerable people whom the Holy Spirit cured
through our prayers, but we cannot mention all of them. No
man can prove the Holy Spirit's miracles with the world's science or medicine. Only the Holy Spirit knows how He performs miracles for sick people. Even I, who pray for sick people to be cured by the Holy Spirit, do not know anything about
how He cures the sick. We just believe in God and follow the
words of the Holy Spirit which are given to me by the Holy
Spirit.

We believe, **"If anyone who believes really in God, follows
the words of God in deed, reads the Bible a lot, prays a lot
and receives much of the Holy Spirit's power by attending
the Holy Spirit's meetings, confesses all his or her sins and
pardons all the people who sinned against him or her in the
past, and really asks God to give them the Holy Spirit's
power, God will gladly give the Holy Spirit's power to him
or her."**

We knew nothing about the Holy Spirit's miracles before, but
He who gave us His power surely will give the same thing to
other Christians. You have to endure for a long time, until you
receive the Holy Spirit's power. You need a lot of prayer and
patience to receive the Holy Spirit's power.

12. The Holy Spirit who healed a 12-year-old chronic arthritis

A chronic rheumatic patient who was suffering in all the joints in her body for 12 years was completely cured by the words of the Almighty Heavenly Father, in the name of Jesus Christ, and by the authority of the Holy Spirit. She was attending a Catholic Church.

May 6, 1999 by Kyu Im Kim in Pennsylvania

Praise Jesus!

Hallelujah! I want to turn all the glory to the Almighty Heavenly Father. And I want to express the greatest thanks to my Lord, Jesus, and the Holy Spirit. The Holy Spirit performed a miraculous healing ministry through all the parts of my body, but I cannot understand it and my heart is still beating hard. I have read many religious testimonies showing the Holy Spirit's miracles but I never thought that I would write such a testimony, myself. It seems like a dream.

I was a patient who was suffering from chronic rheumatic disease for 12 years. I had all kind of treatments to cure it, in the last 12 years. Nothing could cure it and disappointment grew inside me more and more. I tried many different medi-

cines, physical therapies and exercise, with hope. My sickness
was not healed but because of my addiction to the medicines, I
had a lot of blood flow.

Therefore I had to receive a blood transfusion three times.
Sometimes I stopped taking the medicine but instead I received
more than 100 bee stings a day on my rheumatic joints. I had to
suffer from intolerable pain for many years. I also received
moxa treatments. This treatment is to inflame the rheumatic
joints to make the purulent matter come out of the rheumatic
joints.

Sometimes they burnt the rheumatic joints with lighted cigarettes, and put medicine into the burnt area to inflame the purulent matter. I received every kind of therapy and medical treatment available but I realized that no medicine or modern medical science could cure the rheumatic disease. I gave up hope of
curing my disease with any medicine or therapy. I realized that
only the Almighty Heavenly Father can cure this disease, but I
visited other hospitals and began to take another medicines.

The discs between the bones were inflamed and damaged
because of the purulent pus, so I couldn't use my hands and
legs. The pain was so severe that I couldn't move at all, and I
had to take pain killers every day. I had to fight against fear and
my condition was too miserable to be seen by others. I was
baptized in 1979 in the name of Father, Son, and the Holy
Spirit in the Catholic Church, but my belief in God was crushed
and I was wandering in fear, complaint, and coldness.

However I had a hope that Jesus could cure anything in the
world. In the meantime I confessed all my past wrong doings
and asked Him to forgive all my sins and I repented everything

I did wrong to God. Troubles also happened in my family because of my chronic illness. Our family lost many assets because of my sickness. I myself lost confidence in everything. I was in despair, but the Lord planned to send us to the USA. In His plan I thought there might be a change in my family and a way to cure my sickness, so I prayed continuously to God. Not from my point of view but from God's point of view, I began to pray.

We sent our children to the USA first. It was a big risk, but we believed God would help our children and prepare our way to follow. Six months after our children's departure for the USA, we boarded the airplane for the USA. Accordingly we arrived safely. From that day we began to live in a house surrounded by a large green garden all around.

At the end of December 1998, as soon as we came to the USA, the owner of the house introduced me to the Chairman of the Whole Race Gospel & Missionary Service, Missionary Do Shick Joe, who always read the Bible and prayed. He visited us in our home and he was moved to see me, suffering from chronic rheumatic disease, and he planted a big belief in my heart.

"Nothing is impossible with God. The Bible is the word of of God and all of it is true. The words themselves are living and they perform miracles. We must follow the words as they are written in deed. Then the Holy Spirit will perform His miracles."

And he read John 11: 1-44, where Lazarus was dead for four days and buried in the tomb, but Jesus called him to rise and he rose from death according to Jesus' command. The Holy Spirit who raised the dead from his tomb will surely cure your rheumatic sickness. In order to make me believe in Almighty God faithfully and sincerely, he showed me a video showing the Holy Spirit miracles.

And he said to me, **"I will pray for the Holy Spirit to be present in you and cure your sickness completely. Please believe everything that I say in prayer, like little children, and then the Holy Spirit will surely cure your pains miraculously."**

"The Holy Spirit performed all kinds of the miracles which were same the Holy Spirit's miracles written in The book of Acts in the new testament, which were performed through the disciples of Jesus in the first century, today, through me. The Holy Spirit is curing all kinds of sicknesses miraculously through our prayers everyday. The Holy Spirit performs miracles through the angels also, which we cannot understand. It is not my power but they are being performed by the Holy Spirit who is always with me."

"We command the evil spirits to be bound and chase them out of the sick in the name of Jesus. And command the sick person to be healed completely in the name of Jesus, by the words of Almighty God and the authority of the Holy Spirit, and then the sick person is cured completely by the power of God."

Mark 16: 17-18 And these signs will follow those who believe: In My name they will cast out demons; they will speak with new tongues; they will take up serpents; and if they drink anything deadly, it will by no means hurt them; they will lay hands on the

sick, and they will recover."

   Mark 11: 24 Therefore I say to you, whatever things you ask when you pray, believe that you receive them, and you will have them.

   In addition to the above mentioned Bible passages, he gave me many other words from the Bible and said to me, **"Please read the Bible, the new testament from the beginning of Matthew to the end of Acts, four times, and then your belief will grow and the Holy Spirit will perform the miracles for you."**

   "It is nothing for the Holy Spirit who cures the dead to heal your rheumatic disease. Nothing is impossible with God. When I prayed for you, already the Holy Spirit went into your heart. Do not doubt at all but believe all that I say to you. And just believe that the Holy Spirit will surely cure your chronic rheumatic pain. Please confess all your sins from your childhood, and repent of all your sins before God in prayer. In addition to those, forgive all the people who did anything wrong against you in the past. And obey the words of God."

   When I heard his prayers and preaching, I was very pleased and I felt as if my sickness would be cured immediately and my heart was very peaceful. After that there were some difficulties but I was continuously peaceful in my heart everyday.

   I confessed all my sins which I did wrong against God from my childhood until now before God and repented of all my sins in prayer. And I prayed for Almighty God to change my heart in order to obey God's words. I also prayed for the Lord to lead the way for my future.

I emphasized the positive instead of negative and yes instead
of no in my prayers. Also I prayed and asked for the forgiveness of the people against whom I did wrong before God. And I
forgave all the people who did wrong against me in the past in
front of the Almighty Heavenly Father. I reconciled with my
body which I didn't take care of for a long time. Because I did
not care about my health for a long time before my sickness.
While doing the above mentioned things, I read the Bible
which Chairman Joe asked me to read.

Sometime in March 1999 he called me, saying to me, **"The
Holy Spirit asked me to pray on the phone for you. And he
said to me, 'Stop taking any more medicines.'"**

I thanked him for his prayer and stopped taking the medicines. But I couldn't endure it for more than a couple of days.

**However while reading John 14: 20 At that day you will know
that I am in My Father, and you in Me, and I in you.**

The Bible's words touched me and began to move me. And
when I was reading **Acts 3:6**
**Then Peter said, "Silver and gold I do not have, but what
I do have I give you: In the name of Jesus Christ of Nazareth, rise up and walk."**

the above Bible passages touched me and moved me greatly,
and the Holy Spirit began to perform the miracles in my body.
Peter's prayer was changed to my prayer and while I was praying, Chairman Do Shick Joe called again and said to me, **"The
Holy Spirit asked me to pray for you on the phone,"** and

after his heartfelt prayer, he commanded in the name of Jesus to immediately heal the rheumatic pains in the joints of my body.

By the telephone prayer of Missionary Joe, the Holy Spirit began to heal the rheumatic pain in my body. Three or four days after the telephone prayer of Chairman Joe, when I rose up from my bed in the morning, I didn't feel any pain at all, and I could walk freely without any pain, even if I didn't take any medicines. My body felt very light. I was so surprised that I touched my whole body to see if I was in a dream. I couldn't believe that I had received the greatest blessing of my life from the Almighty Heavenly Father. It was not a dream but it really happened to my body by the Holy Spirit's power. Hymns praising the Lord were coming from my mouth automatically, and I danced joyfully before God continuously. However I couldn't tell this to other people.

If I told my testimony to them, they would doubt and not believe what I said. I couldn't express my feelings at that moment. After several days of this, I visited a medical doctor, who checked my blood. As a result of the blood test, the doctor confirmed to me, "The rheumatic inflammation was completely cured. Rheumatic sickness also shows some symptoms such as high blood pressure and diabetes." However my body didn't show any symptoms of the rheumatic sickness. This is the greatest victory Jesus Christ won for me.

I cried and wept loudly without end. Crying for joy now and crying and weeping for the sorrow and sadness in the past were all mixed, so I cried and kept thanking Jesus Christ who healed my pains completely. I cried and prayed and thanked God continuously for this miraculous healing of my pains from which I was suffering for the last 12 years, while hugging my children and husband.

I began to think of my future. How can I please the Lord who cured my sickness with Jesus' love? There is nothing I can do for Him. I prayed to God to lead my life to the way God is most pleased and also to lead me to turn all the glory to the Almighty Heavenly Father and to evangelize Jesus' gospel to all the people I will meet in the future. I thanked Chairman Do Shick Joe again, who faithfully and sincerely prayed to the Holy Spirit who cured my sickness. I believe that the Holy Spirit who completely cured my chronic rheumatic disease can heal any pain or sickness from anyone that believes in God faithfully.

In the name of Jesus, I pray for God to give His unlimited blessings to Pastor Do Shick Joe who always visits the poor and sick people and prays for them, and who delivers food for the poor homeless people begging in the streets of Philadelphia, USA.

Amen
May 6, 1999 by Kyu Im Kim in Pennsylvania

13. The Holy Spirit who saved a missionary speaking in Satanic tongues

In a small church in Seoul, Korea when a missionary who was leading a night church service spoke in Satanic tongues, the Holy Spirit asked me to pray in heavenly tongues. When I spoke in God's tongue, the missionary fell to the ground and was in a coma like dead man, but I prayed again to the Holy Spirit not to kill him. Accordingly he recovered again from his coma, but he knew nothing about what happened to him.

It was one night in September 1996 in Seoul, Korea. When I entered the church, all the people were praying in loud voices, some people were praying in God's tongue and others in human language. It was so noisy that I couldn't even hear the person next to me.

But the Holy Spirit inside of my heart said to me, **"The missionary leading the whole church by singing at the front with a guitar and microphone is speaking now in Satan's tongue,"** and He asked me to pray in God's tongue against him.

So I told what Holy Spirit told me, to the pastor serving in the church, exactly as Holy Spirit told me. The pastor asked me to pray in God's tongue against Satan's tongue as the Holy Spirit asked me. So I sat by the pastor at the last seat in the back and as soon as I opened my mouth to pray in God's tongue, the missionary who was speaking in a loud voice became mute and couldn't say anything and he laid down his guitar on the floor. And when I prayed for about one minute, he fell down on the floor.

The pastor who asked me to pray in God's tongue was scared if anything would happen, so she asked me to stop praying, and she went to the missionary and I saw he was in coma like dead man while moving his tongue in and out like a snake. So she prayed for him and I prayed to the Holy Spirit not to kill him. About 30 minutes later he woke up, but he didn't know what happened to him.

The congregation which is being led by the preacher possessed by evil spirits cannot continue. If a Christian or a pastor fully filled in the Holy Spirit prays in God's tongue in silence, the preacher speaking in Satanic tongue will fall to the ground and will die on the spot.

The Holy Spirit knows exactly who speaks in Satanic tongues even in large congregations where tens of thousands of people are listening to the preacher. Meanwhile the Holy Spirit binds evil spirits with His power and chases them out of Christians and He saves Christians from Satan's traps.

14. The Holy Spirit who caught an evil spirit which tried to deceive a missionary

Sometimes pastors or missionaries who received gifts of prophecy from the Holy Spirit call me to check whether the prophecy he or she received are from the Holy Spirit or not.

One day in October 1999 a female missionary said to me, **"The Holy Spirit gave me His words in prayer: Pray for your nephew who was suffering from cerebral paralysis, and stop all the medicine which he is taking now. And then**

I will cure his sickness completely."

The innocent missionary who knows nothing about how to discern between the Holy Spirit and evil spirits believed that all the words given spiritually in prayer were from the Holy Spirit. She stopped giving all the medicines to her 20-year-old nephew.

She said to me, **"The first day he was staggering here and there. On the second day, he slept all day long without eating anything. But on the third day he was just sleeping without waking up, even when I tried to wake him up several times, he could not wake up. I am scared to death."**

Therefore she called me to pray for her and her nephew, and she said, **"If he does not take this medicine, his brain cells will slowly die."**

When I prayed for him, the Holy Spirit told me that the female missionary was deceived by evil spirits. The Holy Spirit said to me, **"It was not the Holy Spirit who spoke to her in prayer but it was an evil spirit that spoke to her in her prayer."**

I told her all the things the Holy Spirit told me. And I asked her to place the telephone receiver on the ear of her nephew who was sleeping, and then I will bind the evil spirit in the name of Jesus, by the authority of the Holy Spirit, and the words of the Almighty Heavenly Father, and will cast the evil spirits out of your nephew.

Immediately I commanded the evil spirits bound in the name of Jesus and chased them out of the patient in the name of Jesus. And according to the words of the Holy Spirit who told me how to, I said to her, **"If the patient does not wake up within 30 minutes, take him to the emergency room in the hospital. If you do not do as I say now, the patient will die."**

He didn't wake up within 30 minutes, so she took him to the hospital emergency room.
She said to me, "He woke up in the hospital emergency room but about one week has passed. He hasn't recovered fully, yet, but he was recovering gradually."

Evil spirits always try to deceive faithful Christians for the purpose of destroying those Christians in the society where the sons and daughters of God are working for the Lord. If the female missionary had stopped giving the medicine for several days more, while believing that the Holy Spirit would cure his sickness, her nephew would have died.

As the result of that incident, she might have been sentenced as the killer of her nephew and she would have been sent to prison. However she was continuously praying to God, so the Holy Spirit moved her to call Pastor Do Shick Joe who was in the USA. In such a way, the evil spirits always attempt to hurt the good Christians and destroy you. Therefore you have to learn how to discern between the Holy Spirit and evil spirits.

CHAPTER 9

God's love and blessing

1. God's love
1) Jesus loves the poor
2) The sheep helping the poor will be sent to heaven
3) The Holy Spirit produced enough bread for 400,000 to 450,000 people with two or three dozen donuts
4) The Holy Spirit's Message to all homeless people living on the streets of the U. S. A.
2. Almighty God gives His great financial blessings to His children who really believe in Jesus Christ.
1) The Holy Spirit raised price of a $0.50 stock to over $136.00
2) The Holy Spirit caught a lot of fish for a fisherman and moves him to bring all the fish to my home for nothing
3) The Holy Spirit also sends kimchi to my home
4) The Holy Spirit sends money for all expenses of a Holy Spirit meeting
3. Almighty God who gives His unlimited blessing
4. The Holy Spirit comforted a sick man at the moment of his death and led him to heaven

1. God's love

1) Jesus loves the poor

This is the Holy Spirit's message given in early morning prayer on January 5, 2001.

God loves you. In order to save the whole human race, which is supposed to be thrown into the fiery lake because of sin, Almighty God sent His beloved, only Son, Jesus Christ, to us. However, the religious leaders of the Israelites persecuted, treated Him contemptuously, and finally crucified Him on the cross. All human sin was cleansed by the precious blood of Jesus Christ. God loves us so much that He sent His only Son to us. Is there any one who will give his only son to be crucified in order to forgive our sins in the world?

God wants to save the life of the poor people born in poor countries who are starving to death because of hunger, and He wants to lead them to Jesus Christ. The poor people starving to death want to work but no jobs are available. Because they don't have any food, they maintain their life by eating the weeds and roots of plants or the bark of trees but because of malnutrition, they get sick and soon die.

There are innumerable poor people in the world. Some people are sick but they can't go to the hospital because of money, so they sleep on the streets while begging for food. Finally their lives are finished on the street. There are innumerable such poor beggars in the world.

There are innumerable poor people who are frozen to death, while sleeping on the streets because they don't have any shelter or money. There are innumerable young children born in poor families without any money who are begging for food on the street. They try to find anything to eat in trash cans all over the cities. But they cannot find anything to eat and they finally get sick and die eternally.

The Almighty Heavenly Father loves the rich and the poor equally. God wants to save such poor people abandoned from society. God wants you to throw away your greed to make only you and your own family rich and satisfied. The Heavenly Father wants you to save such poor dying people.

Luke 16: 19-31 "There was a certain rich man who was clothed in purple and fine linen and fared sumptuously every day. But there was a certain beggar named Lazarus, full of sores, who was laid at his gate, desiring to be fed with the crumbs which fell from the rich man's table. Moreover the dogs came and licked his sores. So it was that the beggar died, and was carried by the angels to Abraham's bosom.

The rich man also died and was buried. And being in torments in Hades, he lifted up his eyes and saw Abraham afar off, and Lazarus in his bosom. "Then he cried and said, 'Father Abraham, have mercy on me, and send Lazarus that he may dip the tip of his finger in water and cool my tongue; for I am tormented in this flame.' But Abraham said, 'Son, remember that in your lifetime you received your good things, and likewise Lazarus evil things; but now he is comforted and you are tormented. And besides all this, between us and you there is a great gulf fixed, so that those

who want to pass from here to you cannot, nor can those from
there pass to us.'

"Then he said, 'I beg you therefore, father, that you would send
him to my father's house, for I have five brothers, that he may
testify to them, lest they also come to this place of torment.'

Abraham said to him, 'They have Moses and the prophets; let
them hear them.' And he said, 'No, father Abraham; but if one
goes to them from the dead, they will repent.' But he said to him,
'If they do not hear Moses and the prophets, neither will they be
persuaded though one rise from the dead.'"

Jesus said this in the Bible. The rich man who neglected the
poor and didn't help the poor beggar dying of hunger only tried
to satisfy his own greed. When he died, he was cast into the
ever burning fiery lake to cry and lament eternally in torment.
However when the beggar Lazarus died, though he was poor
and begging at the gate of the rich man's house, he was carried
to heaven by the angels and he enjoys eternal life in heaven.

Jesus only tells the truth. He never tells a lie. In order to go
to heaven, we should all believe Jesus Christ and all that Jesus
said.

The Whole Race Gospel and Missionary Service is managed
by the Holy Spirit's leading and is doing the ministry of helping
such poor beggars like Lazarus who were abandoned by society, and leads them to Jesus.

2) The sheep helping the poor, dying spirits will be sent to heaven

Matthew 25: 31-46 "When the Son of Man comes in His glory, and all the holy angels with Him, then He will sit on the throne of His glory. All the nations will be gathered before Him, and He will separate them one from another, as a shepherd divides his sheep from the goats. And He will set the sheep on His right hand, but the goats on the left.

Then the King will say to those on His right hand, 'Come, you blessed of My Father, inherit the kingdom prepared for you from the foundation of the world: for I was hungry and you gave Me food; I was thirsty and you gave Me drink; I was a stranger and you took Me in; I was naked and you clothed Me; I was sick and you visited Me; I was in prison and you came to Me.'

"Then the righteous will answer Him, saying, 'Lord, when did we see You hungry and feed You, or thirsty and give You drink? When did we see You a stranger and take You in, or naked and clothe You? Or when did we see You sick, or in prison, and come to You?'

And the King will answer and say to them, 'Assuredly, I say to you, inasmuch as you did it to one of the least of these My brethren, you did it to Me.'

"Then He will also say to those on the left hand, 'Depart from Me, you cursed, into the everlasting fire prepared for the devil and his angels: for I was hungry and you gave Me no food; I was thirsty and you gave Me no drink; I was a stranger and you did not take Me in, naked and you did not clothe Me, sick and in prison and you did not visit Me.'

"Then they also will answer Him, saying, 'Lord, when did we see You hungry or thirsty or a stranger or naked or sick or in prison, and did not minister to You?'

Then He will answer them, saying, 'Assuredly, I say to you, inasmuch as you did not do it to one of the least of these, you did not do it to Me.'

And these will go away into everlasting punishment, but the righteous into eternal life."

Jesus, who judges all the spirits of all human beings, dead or living in the world, said the above words in the Bible. Jesus said that passing by poor and starving people without paying any attention to them and not helping them with what they need is the same as passing by Jesus when He is in trouble, without paying any attention to Jesus and not helping Jesus at all. Jesus said, **"Depart from Me, you who are cursed, into the eternal fire prepared for the devil and his angels."**

The Heavenly Father not only wants to save the starving people but He also wants to lead the starving people to Jesus to save their spirits for eternity. Jesus wants to save all people, regardless of what they are: drug addicts abandoned by society, being lured by Satan into self destruction; poor, starving people without any money or food; or lawbreakers such as murderers, contract killers, or rapists who commit all kinds of sins in the world without knowing that they will be judged according to what they have done by God's fearful punishment.

In addition to that, God wants to save all the people who are deceived by Satan's heresies and are wandering in darkness. Whatever sins people have committed, God wants to cleanse their sins and lead them to Jesus, if they will return to Jesus and confess all their sins.

God wants to cure all sickness, such as drug addiction, alcoholism, and incurable diseases with the Holy Spirit's power and change them into real sons and daughters of God and lead them to heaven where they can enjoy eternal life.

The Whole Race Gospel and Missionary Service is doing God's ministry, curing sick patients with the Holy Spirit's power and leading them to Jesus.

In order to do God's ministry, a lot of money is required. Any amount of money you contribute to God's ministry will be used for saving such souls abandoned by society and leading them to Jesus to save their eternal life. While you are reading "God's Love", innumerable people are starving to death because they don't have food to eat.

The money you donate will save many starving people and lead them to Jesus to send them to heaven. God wants you to donate any amount you want from deep in your heart.

God will bless you and your family and your offspring through generations, your business and whatever you do with your hands 1000 times more than the amount you donate to God's ministry.

3) The Holy Spirit produced enough bread for 400,000 to 450,000 people with two or three dozen donuts

Matthew 14: 13-21 When Jesus heard it, He departed from there by boat to a deserted place by Himself. But when the multitudes heard it, they followed Him on foot from the cities. And when Jesus went out He saw a great multitude; and He was moved with compassion for them, and healed their sick.

When it was evening, His disciples came to Him, saying, "This is a deserted place, and the hour is already late. Send the multitudes away, that they may go into the villages and buy themselves food." But Jesus said to them, "They do not need to go away. You give them something to eat."

And they said to Him, "We have here only five loaves and two fish." He said, "Bring them here to Me." Then He commanded the multitudes to sit down on the grass. And He took the five loaves and the two fish, and looking up to heaven, He blessed and broke and gave the loaves to the disciples; and the disciples gave to the multitudes. So they all ate and were filled, and they took up twelve baskets full of the fragments that remained.

Now those who had eaten were about five thousand men, besides women and children.

My wife is moved by the Holy Spirit to always bring food to our church for the pastors and church members whenever anyone brings food to us. In the fall when we collect many chestnuts, or someone brings sweet potatoes, tomatoes, fish or any food as gifts to our home, she always wants to bring them to church first, while thinking about the pastors and church members.

In fall 2000, on our way home from the theological seminary where we study, several times we purchased two or three dozen donuts at the Dunkin' Donuts store. We ate a few and brought the balance to our church and cut them in half and served them for the church members to eat after Sunday or Wednesday church services.

However Dunkin' Donuts closes at about 10 PM, and we couldn't go before the store closed. In addition to that, due to a shortage of money, we couldn't buy enough donuts for all the church members. The Holy Spirit knows the heart of my wife who wants to buy donuts to serve the church, even if she doesn't have any money.

So He moved my wife's heart and gave the Holy Spirit's words to her. **"Go to the man of the company the Holy Spirit recommends and tell him. 'Help us, we need food to serve God's church and homeless people sleeping on the street.'"**

Whenever the Holy Spirit tells to us to do anything, we immediately follow the Holy Spirit's words, by our deeds.

In early morning prayer the next day, the Holy Spirit confirmed His words to me, so I wrote a letter to the man whom the Holy Spirit recommended. We went to him and explained our situation and gave our letter to him written according to the Holy Spirit's instructions.

The Holy Spirit already moved the man whom we met, and he approved for us to take baked goods once a week. We were waiting for the day of the week when we could take the free bakeries. We began to receive two to three shopping carts full of many kinds of bread a week. We served the church after services on Sunday and Wednesday. On Monday, Tuesday, and Thursday, we served the food for the students and professors of our theological seminary where we study.

We gave the cakes and pies to the churches in which the Holy Spirit revival services were being held. We shared the food with many other churches and pastors and church members. Sometimes we gave bread to our neighbors, who were very pleased to receive it. We said to everyone who took our food, "These are gifts given by Jesus.

We received this food as a gift without any charge, so we give it free without any charge to you. Believe in Jesus and thank God who gave you the food." Everyone was very pleased to receive it. There were many kinds of baked goods, such as pies, donuts, cakes, muffins, breads, and cookies.

On the afternoon of Christmas Eve, the Holy Spirit asked us to give them to the homeless people begging and sleeping on the streets of Philadelphia. We gave a shopping bag of bread with the Holy Spirit's messages which were especially given to the homeless people, to every homeless person begging on the street whom we met. They were thankful beyond expression for the bread. Some of the homeless people gave us the addresses of shelters where homeless people were living together.

At first we donated the baked goods to two different shelters where homeless people were living together. But soon the shelters grew to four and five. There were 50 to 250 homeless people living together in one shelter. So we were short of food. However the Holy Spirit moved the heart of the manager of the company which donated the bread. We received food three times a week instead of once a week.

Except for the time when I went abroad on a mission trip to

preach Jesus' gospel, we haven't missed even one shopping cart allocated for us, in the last four years and five months.

We brought all of them home and donated all the food to the churches and shelters where homeless people were living together.

During early morning prayer on the day when I had to deliver the food, the Holy Spirit would tell me, **"Go and pick up the food and give it to the poor, homeless people begging and sleeping on the streets."**

Therefore I could not miss even one day of picking up the baked goods in the last four years and seven months.

When we added up everything, we were very surprised to find out how much food we delivered to the churches and homeless people. Since we received donations three times a week for the past four years and seven months, it was enough to feed about 400,000 to 450,000 people.

We were very surprised to find such a great quantity of bread. When the Holy Spirit saw that my wife was buying two or three dozen donuts for the church, even when she didn't have any money, the Holy Spirit moved her and performed a miracle for us to get such a large quantity of food.

The Holy Spirit increased the donuts for ten people by 40,000 to 45,000 times the original quantity. The corporation which the Holy Spirit recommended donated enough food to feed 400,000 to 450,000 people in the past four years and seven months.

In the meantime, we delivered and donated all of it to shelters where homeless people were living together, churches in which the Holy Spirit meetings were being held, and many other people. As long as we receive the food and deliver it to the shelters for homeless people and churches, the quantity of baked goods produced by the Holy Spirit's miracle will grow without limit.

The Heavenly Father performs miracles in this way. When we really want to help poor people, the Holy Spirit performs miracles in this way. The Holy Spirit wants to feed all the poor, homeless people begging and sleeping on the streets all over the world in this way or in many other ways and lead them to Jesus for eternal life. This is the same as the Holy Spirit miracle in which Jesus fed five thousand people with five loaves of bread and two fish.

Today also we received much of bread, pies, cakes and all kinds of baked food from a big company in the USA and delivered it to the poor, starving people begging for food on the street, in accordance with the Holy Spirit's instructions. We gave them bread, the Holy Spirit's message for the homeless people sleeping on the street, and we gave water to the people who asked for something to drink.

The Holy Spirit asks us to give food to poor churches, pastors and Christians. In addition to these people, the Holy Spirit asks us to deliver most of the baked goods to shelters where the poor homeless people who are sick and begging on the street are living together. Therefore according to the Holy Spirit's words, however busy we are, we put aside all other things, and regardless of weather, whether it is raining, snowing, is hot or cold, we deliver food to the shelters where homeless people are living together.

We deliver the food which the Holy Spirit gives us to five different shelters. God loves all people equally, regardless of color: white, black and Asian people. Some people ask me who gives us these baked goods? My answer is as follows:

The Holy Spirit gave us all this bread and Jesus loves you so much that the Holy Spirit tells me to deliver this bread to you without fail in morning prayer on the day when we receive it. It is about a 60 - 70 miles round trip from my home to the shelters and it takes about three hours when we finish the deliveries to five shelters. When the traffic is heavy, it takes three to four hours round trip.

However busy we are, we put aside all other work and whether it is raining, snowing, is hot or cold, we deliver the food together with the Holy Spirit's messages given to the homeless people, to the shelters where starving, poor homeless people live. We tell them that all these baked goods were given by the Holy Spirit to you, so please thank Jesus and the Heavenly Father.

When I go on a delivery, sometimes the Holy Spirit moves me so powerfully that tears continuously fall from my eyes all the way to the shelters and back home. God loves human beings so much that He sent His only Son to be crucified on the cross to save all human beings from sin.

In addition to that, in order to save the poor homeless people abandoned by society and lead them to Jesus, the Holy Spirit loves them so much that He arranged for a sinner like me to receive a lot of food and let me deliver it to the poor homeless people.

**When I think how the Holy Spirit so powerfully moves
me to deliver such food, tears fall from my eyes endlessly.**

While most of the people in the world are working hard for
their own or their family's interests to satisfy the greed of their
flesh, God asks me to deliver food to the poor homeless people
to save their souls. Whenever I think of how much the Holy
Spirit loves the poor people, tears fall from my eyes.

When I was a big businessman, what did I do for God's ministry? I feel a strong remorse that I worked hard only for my
own interests, while committing all kinds of sins to satisfy my
unlimited greed. The people who receive the bread given by the
Holy Spirit thank me beyond expression.

I say to them, **"Don't thank me but thank Jesus who told
me to deliver the food to you every week."**

I reply to them as follows: **"It is Jesus who prepared the
food for you and it is the Holy Spirit who asked me to deliver it to you. Almighty God loves you so much that He
asks me to deliver the bread to you in early morning prayer
in the day it is time for me to pick up the bakeries without
fail."**

Sometimes the Holy Spirit asks us to visit sick elderly patients without family who are suffering from chronic diseases
and to pray for them with the Holy Spirit's power. The Holy
Spirit always comforts them and asks them to go to Jesus for
eternal life.

The Holy Spirit cured innumerable patients with His power.
Sometimes senior patients who were healed by the Holy Spirit

get up from their sick beds and dance joyfully in the Holy Spirit's power.

Sometimes God asks us to visit the shelters where drug addicts are living and to pray for them and cure the drug addiction with the Holy Spirit's power and lead them to Jesus.

Sometimes the Holy Spirit asks us to visit dying patients in his or her last moment of life and to tell them that God loves them so much that He sent us to tell them about heaven, which the Holy Spirit showed me many times. And God asks me to tell them that they will be led to heaven after their life and not to worry about death but just believe in Jesus. They die peacefully with Jesus.

When we meet young gangsters wandering on the streets, the Holy Spirit asks us to tell them about heaven and hell, burning in sulfur fire, and testify to them about how the Holy Spirit performs miracles today. He asks us to lead them to Jesus. When they hear my testimony about how the Holy Spirit works and I testify to them that the Holy Spirit performs miracles, then they confess their sins while crying with tears from their eyes. And they come to Jesus. And the Holy Spirit changes their life from gang members to real Christians.

Sometimes the Holy Spirit leads us to deliver Jesus' gospel to people who are worshiping idols because they are deceived by Satan, and God asks us to testify about how the Holy Spirit does His miraculous ministry, to lead these people to Jesus. God changes them to come to Jesus.

Sometimes the Holy Spirit asks us to visit the mental asylums and pray for the patients there and cast out the demons and evil spirits from them in the name of Jesus and the Holy Spirit's power and lead them to Jesus.

This is God's love. The Heavenly Father loves souls like these that are abandoned by society, and He takes care of them very carefully and leads them to Jesus.

Almighty God asks you to participate in God's ministry of saving poor people and leading them to Jesus for eternal life. God asks you to support God's ministry financially or with your time. The funds raised will be used for the following ministries.

The Holy Spirit told me to use the funds to revitalize the Worldwide Holy Spirit Revival Movement.

John 3: 3, 5 Jesus answered and said to him, "Most assuredly, I say to you, unless one is born again, he cannot see the kingdom of God."
Jesus answered, "Most assuredly, I say to you, unless one is born of water and the Spirit, he cannot enter the kingdom of God."

In the world there are innumerable missionaries, pastors and servants of God who evangelize Jesus' gospel to all creation. And they want to build churches and grow the churches bigger and bigger by spreading the gospel more and more. However because of the lack of funds, many pastors of the poor churches in the world can't do the ministry of spreading the gospel.

Even in the USA there are many churches which can't afford to pay the rent for the church building and to support the living expenses of the pastor. The Holy Spirit wants to arrange Holy

Spirit meetings in such churches in order to pour the Holy Spirit's power to the pastors and Christians of such poor churches to revitalize the Holy Spirit movement in the areas where such poor churches are located.

And God wants to use all such pastors and Christians of the poor churches who are full of the Holy Spirit, as the men of God like Jesus' apostles in the first century, to revitalize the Holy Spirit Revival Movement in the areas where such poor churches are located.

Acts 1: 8 But you shall receive power when the Holy Spirit has come upon you; and you shall be witnesses to Me in Jerusalem, and in all Judea and Samaria, and to the end of the earth."

There are too many churches which cannot hold the Holy Spirit's meetings because of money. God wants to support such poor churches until they can stand for themselves by pouring the Holy Spirit's anointing onto the pastors of such churches and the church members. God loves equally all the people in the world, regardless of race: white, black, or Asian. God loves all people equally regardless of the denomination of the church. God loves all the churches and Christians who worship the Trinity God: Father, Son, and the Holy Spirit, as their Lord.

Therefore regardless of the country or denomination they belong to, God wants to anoint all Christians with the Holy Spirit's strong power and change all of them into real good sons and daughters of God and send them into the world to deliver the gospel and lead all the people to Jesus. In addition to that, God wants all such real Christians to be born again by the Holy Spirit to revitalize the Holy Spirit movement in the areas where they are living and to deliver the gospel to all the people.

Born again Christians filled with the Holy Spirit's anointing, when they meet people who don't believe in God, cannot pass unbelievers without evangelizing to them. This is because such Christians filled with the Holy Spirit know the destiny of unbelievers, to be cast into the ever burning fiery lake when their life is finished in the world. This is because the Holy Spirit works strongly with God's love in the heart of Christians filled with the Holy Spirit. The Holy Spirit changes innumerable Christians and uses them to preach Jesus' gospel to every creature in the world.

Mark 16: 15-16 And He said to them, "Go into all the world and and preach the gospel to every creature. He who believes and is baptized will be saved; but he who does not believe will be condemned."

The Holy Spirit asked me to use the funds for saving poor people and leading them to Jesus for their eternal life. The Holy Spirit wants to save many poor people who are starving to death, and give them food and lead them to the Holy Spirit's meetings led by pastors who are strong with the Holy Spirit's power.

God wants them to experience the Holy Spirit's ministry, receive the Holy Spirit's anointing, and all their sickness to be healed by the Holy Spirit. He also wants to lead them find new jobs and start new lives with hope in Jesus.

At the same time, it is God's will that all such Christians saved by the Holy Spirit believe Jesus in good faith and preach the gospel to all creation and revitalize the Worldwide Holy Spirit Revival Movement. The funds will be used for saving such poor souls.

John 14: 16-17, 26 And I will pray the Father, and He will give you another Helper, that He may abide with you forever--the Spirit of truth, whom the world cannot receive, because it neither sees Him nor knows Him; but you know Him, for He dwells with you and will be in you. But the Helper, the Holy Spirit, whom the Father will send in My name, He will teach you all things, and bring to your remembrance all things that I said to you.

The Holy Spirit told me to use the funds to raise and educate servants of God to revitalize the Worldwide Holy Spirit Revival Movement and to preach the good news to all creation. The Heavenly Father wants all men of God to fully receive the Holy Spirit's powerful baptism and anointing, before serving God.

Men of God who didn't receive the Holy Spirit's strong power cannot preach the gospel boldly to the world, even if they have served for many years. The Apostle Peter, who had lived with Jesus for three years, denied Jesus three times in one night before he was baptized powerfully by the Holy Spirit. He was baptized strongly by the Holy Spirit on the day of Pentecost in Acts chapter 2, and after receiving the Holy Spirit's power, he preached the good news so boldly to the Israelites that he could lead more than 3,000 to Jesus in one day. This is the reason why the Holy Spirit wants to revitalize the Holy Spirit Revival Movement and to baptize all Christians strongly with the Holy Spirit's power. Christians filled with the Holy Spirit boldly preach the gospel to the world and such Christians cure all kinds of sickness and solve all problems with the Holy Spirit's power.

Matthew 12: 28 But if I cast out demons by the Spirit of God, surely the kingdom of God has come upon you.

This is the word of Jesus. If you drive out the demons by the Holy Spirit, then the Kingdom of God has come upon you. It is the heavenly Father's will that you have to participate actively in the Worldwide Holy Spirit Revival Movement and to be baptized strongly by the Holy Spirit and to experience the Holy Spirit's ministry and to preach the good news to all creation.

1 Corinthians 4: 19-20 But I will come to you shortly, if the Lord wills, and I will know, not the word of those who are puffed up, but the power. For the kingdom of God is not in word but in power.

These are the Bible's words. The Kingdom of God is not in word but in power. Almighty God wants to give you the Holy Spirit's strong power. Therefore, before sending the servants of God into the world to preach the gospel to every creature, Almighty God wants to lead all the men of God who will be dispatched into the world to Holy Spirit meetings and to baptize them in the Holy Spirit's ministry. He only wants to select Christians who are fully filled with the Holy Spirit's power, to send them into the world to preach the good news to all creation.

Mark 16: 17-18 "And these signs will follow those who believe: In My name they will cast out demons; they will speak with new tongues; they will take up serpents; and if they drink anything deadly, it will by no means hurt them; they will lay hands on the sick, and they will recover."

Christians filled in the Holy Spirit's power can boldly preach the gospel to anyone in the world. The Holy Spirit is always present with such men of God and the Holy Spirit performs all kinds of miracles through them.

The funds will be used for raising and training men of God to receive the Holy Spirit's strong power and send them to preach the good news to all creation. The men of God who receive the Holy Spirit's power and follow only the Holy Spirit's leading seem to be foolish and innocent like babies to the people in the world, because they don't know how to tell lies or how to deceive other people, but they only follow the way of truth by the Holy Spirit's leading.

Mark 10: 15 "Assuredly, I say to you, whoever does not receive the kingdom of God as a little child will by no means enter it."

The above shown Bible words are the words of Jesus. It means that only Christians who are innocent like children and follow God's word in their deeds can enter the kingdom of God. When you are strongly baptized by the Holy Spirit, you will be changed like a child. Therefore such Christians do not try to deceive others and they cannot tell lies. The Holy Spirit, who is always present in their hearts, knows what they think in advance and leads them only to the way of truth. Therefore they cannot tell lies or act in deceitful ways.

1 Corinthians 3: 16-17 Do you not know that you are the temple of God and that the Spirit of God dwells in you? If anyone defiles the temple of God, God will destroy him. For the temple of God is holy, which temple you are.

If anyone deceives others, he did not receive the Holy Spirit's power. Christians filled with the Holy Spirit's powerful anointing know that if they deceive the Holy Spirit, they will be severely punished.

Acts 5: 1-11 But a certain man named Ananias, with Sapphira his wife, sold a possession. And he kept back part of the proceeds, his wife also being aware of it, and brought a certain part and laid it at the apostles' feet.

But Peter said, "Ananias, why has Satan filled your heart to lie to the Holy Spirit and keep back part of the price of the land for yourself? While it remained, was it not your own? And after it was sold, was it not in your own control? Why have you conceived this thing in your heart? You have not lied to men but to God."

Then Ananias, hearing these words, fell down and breathed his last. So great fear came upon all those who heard these things. And the young men arose and wrapped him up, carried him out, and buried him.

Now it was about three hours later when his wife came in, not knowing what had happened. And Peter answered her, "Tell me whether you sold the land for so much?" She said, "Yes, for so much." Then Peter said to her, "How is it that you have agreed together to test the Spirit of the Lord? Look, the feet of those who have buried your husband are at the door, and they will carry you out."

Then immediately she fell down at his feet and breathed her last. last. And the young men came in and found her dead, and carrying her out, buried her by her husband. So great fear came upon all the church and upon all who heard these things.

The men of God who have received the Holy Spirit's strong

power and follow the Holy Spirit's leading cannot lie or deceive other people. Therefore God selects only such Christians filled in the strong Holy Spirit Power and entrusts them with God's special ministry.

Revelation 2: 7 "He who has an ear, let him hear what the Spirit Spirit says to the churches. To him who overcomes I will give to eat from the tree of life, which is in the midst of the Paradise of God."

Revelation 2: 11 "He who has an ear, let him hear what the Spirit says to the churches. He who overcomes shall not be hurt by the second death."

Here the word "churches" means "human beings". Only the ones who follow the Holy Spirit's words in their deeds will eat from the tree of life in the paradise of God. It means that only Christians with such great faith, followed by deeds, will be able to go to the paradise of God.

The ones who do not follow the Holy Spirit's words will be abandoned into the second death, the ever burning fiery lake in hell.

Revelation 21: 8 "But the cowardly, unbelieving, abominable, murderers, sexually immoral, sorcerers, idolaters, and all liars shall have their part in the lake which burns with fire and brimstone, which is the second death."

As shown in the above Bible words, participating in the Worldwide Holy Spirit Revival Movement is not optional, in which if you want, you may participate, or if you don't want, you may not participate.

The above Bible words said, "Those who do not follow the Holy Spirit's leading will be cast into the second death, the fiery lake of burning sulfur."

These are the words given by Jesus, who was resurrected from death, while He was showing Himself to the Apostle John on the island of Patmos, when John was in the Spirit. (Refer to Revelation chapters 1-3.)

Our Lord Jesus said the above. No one can deny the words of truth spoken by Jesus. In order to receive salvation, we should all obey what Jesus said. Obeying Jesus means that we obey Almighty God, the Heavenly Father who sent Jesus to us. When we follow the Holy Spirit, that means that we obey the Heavenly Father who sent the Holy Spirit to us. God loves us so much that the Holy Spirit leads us to Heaven for eternal life. We all must follow the way the Holy Spirit leads.

All the funds you donate from your heart will be used for saving innumerable poor souls abandoned by society and leading them to Jesus.

Almighty God will give unlimited blessings to you and your children's generations, more than 10,000 times than the amount you donate to God's ministry.

The Holy Spirit performed miracles and gave us enough bread for 400,000 to 450,000 people to eat in the last 4 years and 7 months, when He saw us buying a few dozen donuts for our church, even when we didn't have any money.

If the donuts we served to our church were for seven peo-

ple to eat, the Holy Spirit performed miracles and gave us food 57,000 to 64,000 times bigger than what we served to our church.

We have had a lot of financial difficulties but didn't ask anyone for any financial support. But in early morning prayer, we asked God to send us the necessary funds. As a result of our prayers, the Holy Spirit, who knows everything about our financial difficulties, has continuously moved other Christians to send the money necessary for us to do God's ministry.

We will deliver baked goods to the homeless people as long as the Holy Spirit provides them for us to deliver. In the years to come, the quantity of the food given by the Holy Spirit will grow without limit. It will be enough to feed many hundreds of thousands to millions of poor people not only in Philadelphia but all over the world.

God wants to feed all the poor homeless people all over the world in the Holy Spirit's numerous ways and lead them to Jesus to save their lives for eternity. God needs great support from many people all over the world, including you, to feed the innumerable poor homeless people all over the world.

God loves you. God wants you to participate in God's ministry of saving the poor homeless people all over the world and leading them to Jesus for their eternal life.

If you participate in God's ministry of saving innumerable poor homeless people all over the world which pleases the Trinity God, Almighty God will give unlimited heavenly blessings to you and your children for generations.

While you are reading this testimony about the Holy Spirit's miracle, whatever you want to donate to God's ministry according to your heart being moved by the Holy Spirit, the Holy Spirit will be very pleased.

Mark 12: 41-44 Now Jesus sat opposite the treasury and saw how the people put money into the treasury. And many who were rich put in much. Then one poor widow came and threw in two mites, which make a quadrans. So He called His disciples to Himself and said to them, "Assuredly, I say to you that this poor widow has put in more than all those who have given to the treasury; for they all put in out of their abundance, but she out of her poverty put in all that she had, her whole livelihood."

God will be pleased to see any amount you donate to God's ministry. Any amount you donate to God's ministry to save the poor homeless people all over the world and lead them to Jesus will be saved for your own treasure in heaven for your eternal life.

Matthew 6: 19-21 "Do not lay up for yourselves treasures on earth, where moth and rust destroy and where thieves break in and steal; but lay up for yourselves treasures in heaven, where neither moth nor rust destroys and where thieves do not break in and steal. For where your treasure is, there your heart will be also."

We believe that God's miraculous blessings from Holy Spirit are the same as the miracle which fed 5,000 men with five loaves of bread and two fish, with 12 baskets full of leftover bread. The Holy Spirit will give you heavenly miraculous blessings 10,000 times bigger than any amount you donate to God's business.

The Holy Spirit wants you to participate in God's ministry to save the poor homeless people all over the world and lead them to Jesus. God wants to pour heavenly blessings on you and your family members and children for generations.

Malachi 3: 10-12 "Bring all the tithes into the storehouse,
That there may be food in My house,
And try Me now in this," Says the Lord of hosts,
"If I will not open for you the windows of heaven And pour out for you such blessing
That there will not be room enough to receive it.
"And I will rebuke the devourer for your sakes,
So that he will not destroy the fruit of your ground,
Nor shall the vine fail to bear fruit for you in the field,"
Says the Lord of hosts;
"And all nations will call you blessed,
For you will be a delightful land," Says the Lord of hosts.

Deuteronomy 28: 1-14 "Now it shall come to pass, if you diligently obey the voice of the Lord your God, to observe carefully all His commandments which I command you today, that the Lord your God will set you high above all nations of the earth.
And all these blessings shall come upon you and overtake you, because you obey the voice of the Lord your God:
"Blessed shall you be in the city, and blessed shall you be in the country. "Blessed shall be the fruit of your body, the produce of your ground and the increase of your herds, the increase of your cattle and the offspring of your flocks.
"Blessed shall be your basket and your kneading bowl.
"Blessed shall you be when you come in, and blessed shall you be when you go out.
"The Lord will cause your enemies who rise against you to be

defeated before your face; they shall come out against you one way and flee before you seven ways.

"The Lord will command the blessing on you in your storehouses and in all to which you set your hand, and He will bless you in the land which the Lord your God is giving you.

"The Lord will establish you as a holy people to Himself, just as He has sworn to you, if you keep the commandments of the Lord your God and walk in His ways.

Then all peoples of the earth shall see that you are called by the name of the Lord, and they shall be afraid of you. And the Lord will grant you plenty of goods, in the fruit of your body, in the increase of your livestock, and in the produce of your ground, in the land of which the Lord swore to your fathers to give you.

The Lord will open to you His good treasure, the heavens, to give the rain to your land in its season, and to bless all the work of your hand.

You shall lend to many nations, but you shall not borrow. And the Lord will make you the head and not the tail; you shall be above only, and not be beneath, if you heed the commandments of the Lord your God, which I command you today, and are careful to observe them. So you shall not turn aside from any of the words which I command you this day, to the right or the left, to go after other gods to serve them."

The Holy Spirit wants you to receive all the heavenly blessings given to you from financially supporting God's ministry with any amount you feel in your heart, moved by the Holy Spirit.

Under the name of Jesus, we pray every morning for God to give unlimited heavenly blessings to all His sons and daughters who support God's ministry financially to save the poor and lead them to Jesus, more than 10,000 times the amount they donate to God's business.

Almighty God loves all of us and He wants to give His unlimited blessings to all of us.

The Holy Spirit words about God's miracles were given in early morning prayer on March 18, 2002.

4) The Holy Spirit's Message to All the Homeless People Living on the Streets of the U.S.A.

To the Homeless People!
At 12:07 in morning prayer on February 25, 1998, the Holy Spirit gave me the following message to all the homeless people sleeping on the streets in the cities of America.

Brothers and Sisters!
Hallelujah! God sent me today to save you from sin and lead you to heaven. I have been to heaven and hell many times in the last eight years. The Bible words He gives you today are:

Luke 16: 19-31 "There was a certain rich man who was clothed in purple and fine linen and fared sumptuously every day. But there was a certain beggar named Lazarus, full of sores, who was laid at his gate, desiring to be fed with the crumbs which fell from the rich man's table.

Moreover the dogs came and licked his sores. So it was that the beggar died, and was carried by the angels to Abraham's bosom.

The rich man also died and was buried. And being in torments

in Hades, he lifted up his eyes and saw Abraham afar off, and Lazarus in his bosom.

"Then he cried and said, 'Father Abraham, have mercy on me, and send Lazarus that he may dip the tip of his finger in water and cool my tongue; for I am tormented in this flame.'

But Abraham said, 'Son, remember that in your lifetime you received your good things, and likewise Lazarus evil things; but now he is comforted and you are tormented. And besides all this, between us and you there is a great gulf fixed, so that those who want to pass from here to you cannot, nor can those from there pass to us.'

"Then he said, 'I beg you therefore, father, that you would send him to my father's house, for I have five brothers, that he may testify to them, lest they also come to this place of torment.'

Abraham said to him, 'They have Moses and the prophets; let them hear them.'

And he said, 'No, father Abraham; but if one goes to them from the dead, they will repent.' But he said to him, 'If they do not hear Moses and the prophets, neither will they be persuaded though one rise from the dead.'"

As told in this Bible passage, God loves you more than anyone else, because in your lifetime you are living in agony.

John 3: 16 "For God so loved the world that He gave His only begotten Son, that whoever believes in Him should not perish but have everlasting life.

The Heavenly Father wants to take all of you to Heaven.
To lead you to the eternal life in heaven, the Holy Spirit wants you to do the following;

1. You have to believe in Almighty God who created the

heavens and the earth and all the creatures in the universe, and that Jesus, the Son of God, died on the cross to pay for your sin and you were forgiven of your sin. Jesus was resurrected from death on the third day after He was crucified on the cross.

2. You must accept Jesus Christ as your Savior and Lord and you must believe and follow the Holy Spirit who controls you and empowers your daily life, your witness, and leads you to heaven. This is the Trinity God.

3. You have to believe the Bible 100% as it was written. The Bible is God's word. Therefore it is living and the Holy Spirit is performing miracles with it. Believe in the Bible 100% as it says.

4. Go to the churches near your residence where the Holy Spirit does ministry. That is, the churches where the Holy Spirit inspired pastors lead the service by the Holy Spirit's guidance. Your physical problems and sickness will be cured by the Holy Spirit. That is why I ask you to go to the Holy Spirit inspired churches instead of normal churches.

5. In such churches being led by the Holy Spirit inspired pastors. If you are an alcoholic, the Holy Spirit will save you from your alcohol problem.
If you are a drug addict, He will save you from your drug problem. If you have any other diseases you are suffering from, He will heal your diseases.
He is Almighty God who can heal any kinds of diseases you might have. He can raise even the dead.

John 11: 38-44 Then Jesus, again groaning in Himself, came to

the tomb. It was a cave, and a stone lay against it. 39Jesus said, "Take away the stone." Martha, the sister of him who was dead, said to Him, "Lord, by this time there is a stench, for he has been dead four days."

Jesus said to her, "Did I not say to you that if you would believe you would see the glory of God?" Then they took away the stone from the place where the dead man was lying.

And Jesus lifted up His eyes and said, "Father, I thank You that that You have heard Me. And I know that You always hear Me, but because of the people who are standing by I said this, that they may believe that You sent Me." Now when He had said these things, He cried with a loud voice, "Lazarus, come forth!" And he who had died came out bound hand and foot with grave-clothes, and his face was wrapped with a cloth. Jesus said to them, "Loose him, and let him go."

As in the above mentioned statements, God can save you from any problems you might have now. Right now also, the Holy Spirit performs the same miracles all over the world, which were shown by Jesus 2,000 years ago.

The Holy Spirit is doing all kind of ministries in Holy Spirit inspired churches all over the world. He raises the dead and heals any kind of incurable diseases according to their belief, today. Just believe Him as the Holy Spirit leads you, and you will be saved from your troubles.

Once you are saved from your chronic problems, try to get a job to solve your living problems. Be very faithful to your job, and start your new life with God. Never go back to your old bad habits, like drinking alcohol and taking drugs. But you must keep going to Holy Spirit inspired churches. And follow the Holy Spirit's instructions, He will help you solve all your problems.

When you are completely saved from your current troubles

by the help of the Holy Spirit, you may go to any normal church near your home regularly. From that time you must testify to how God, Jesus and the Holy Spirit saved you from your old troubles in your church and to any people you meet. Then the Heavenly Father will give you more blessings. And you can guide more homeless people to God in exactly the same way that He did for you, until there are no more homeless people sleeping on the street in the cities of the U.S.A.

If you are depressed because you have no money, compare yourself with the people who are in a worse condition than you are in now.

There are innumerable, great many people who are in poorer and more miserable conditions than you are in the world. There are countless, handicapped people who want to work but cannot work because of their physical conditions: blind people, paralyzed people who have to lie down their whole lives, or sick people suffering from incurable diseases.

You are citizens of the U.S.A., the richest and most powerful country in the world. You are getting some money from the U.S. government also. But there are innumerable, poor people in poor countries who want to work but no jobs are available and they get nothing from their governments. They starve to death. Many tens of millions of people are starving to death every year in the world. Compared to them, you must be very proud and rich and happy.

Get a new hope that you will go to heaven where houses are made of solid gold and diamonds. Whenever you are depressed because of money, think of your home in heaven as mentioned below, then you will be happy and encouraged.

Your lifetime is very limited but your eternal life is permanent. The balance of your life is nothing compared to your eternal life in Heaven. I have been to the heaven many, many times. You will live your eternal life in such a beautiful home.

Revelation 21: 18-21 The construction of its wall was of jasper; and the city was pure gold, like clear glass. The foundations of the wall of the city were adorned with all kinds of precious stones: the first foundation was jasper, the second sapphire, the third chalcedony, the fourth emerald, the fifth sardonyx, the sixth sardius, the seventh chrysolite, the eighth beryl, the ninth topaz, the tenth chrysoprase, the eleventh jacinth, and the twelfth amethyst.

The twelve gates were twelve pearls: each individual gate was of of one pearl. And the street of the city was pure gold, like transparent glass.

These houses are your houses. If you really believe Jesus Christ as mentioned above, you will be led to heaven by the Holy Spirit. He wants to take all of you to heaven.

Never commit any crimes or sins. If you have any sins, confess them to God. He will forgive any sins you have now. But never commit sins again. I have seen visions of hell many times. I have seen innumerable people thrown into the sulfur fire sea where all kind of metals melt like in a furnace in a steel mill.

Revelation 20: 12-15 And I saw the dead, small and great, standing before God, and books were opened. And another book was opened, which is the Book of Life. And the dead were judged according to their works, by the things which were written in the books. The sea gave up the dead who were in it, and Death and Hades delivered up the dead who were in them. And they were judged, each one according to his works. Then Death and Hades were cast into the lake of fire. This is the second death. And anyone not found written in the Book of Life was cast into the lake of

fire.

They are crying and screaming for help forever, but no one can help them. They want to die, but they cannot kill themselves. They have to live permanently in the fiery sea of hell. They everlastingly lament of their having not believed Jesus in their lifetime. But it is too late for them. They cannot be saved from the fiery sulfur sea of hell. The Holy Spirit never wants you to go there. But if you commit crimes and sins continuously without confessing to God, you have no choice but to be thrown into the fiery sea.

From today, believe Almighty God who created the heavens, the earth, and all the creatures in the universe and believe Jesus, the son of God, who died for you on the cross to pay your sin and to forgive you of your sin. And accept Jesus as your Savior and Lord. Believe and follow the Holy Spirit who will heal all your physical problems and sickness and lead you to heaven.

Believe the Holy Bible 100% as it was written. God will give you a free ticket to heaven where your pure gold house waits, as shown above.

Heaven is so nice that I cannot express everything by mouth. Just believe the heavenly Father, Jesus, and believe all the Bible words as they were written and follow the Holy Spirit's guidance. He will lead you to Heaven.

I love all of you and I am blessing you all.

The Holy Spirit's words were given to Rev. Do Shick Joe, the Chairman of the Whole Race Gospel

& Missionary Service at 12:07 AM, February 25, 1998 in morning prayer.

2. Almighty God gives His great financial blessings to His children who really believe in Jesus Christ.

1) The Holy Spirit raised the price of a $0.50 stock to $136.00

March 14, 2000 The Heavenly Father gives His unlimited blessings to His children who really believe in God.

Deuteronomy 28: 1-14 "Now it shall come to pass, if you diligently obey the voice of the Lord your God, to observe carefully all His commandments which I command you today, that the Lord your God will set you high above all nations of the earth.

And all these blessings shall come upon you and overtake you, because you obey the voice of the Lord your God: "Blessed shall you be in the city, and blessed shall you be in the country.

"Blessed shall be the fruit of your body, the produce of your ground and the increase of your herds, the increase of your cattle and the offspring of your flocks. "Blessed shall be your basket and your kneading bowl. "Blessed shall you be when you come in, and blessed shall you be when you go out.

"The Lord will cause your enemies who rise against you to be

defeated before your face; they shall come out against you one way and flee before you seven ways. "The Lord will command the blessing on you in your storehouses and in all to which you set your hand, and He will bless you in the land which the Lord your God is giving you.

"The Lord will establish you as a holy people to Himself, just as He has sworn to you, if you keep the commandments of the Lord your God and walk in His ways. Then all peoples of the earth shall see that you are called by the name of the Lord, and they shall be afraid of you. And the Lord will grant you plenty of goods, in the fruit of your body, in the increase of your livestock, and in the produce of your ground, in the land of which the Lord swore to your fathers to give you.

The Lord will open to you His good treasure, the heavens, to give the rain to your land in its season, and to bless all the work of your hand. You shall lend to many nations, but you shall not borrow. And the Lord will make you the head and not the tail; you shall be above only, and not be beneath, if you heed the commandments of the Lord your God, which I command you today, and are careful to observe them.

So you shall not turn aside from any of the words which I command you this day, to the right or the left, to go after other gods to serve them.

I have a Christian friend who believes in God with all his heart and follows the Holy Spirit's words I give him without fail.

He used to send us a certain amount of money, every month for several years. We used that money for the Holy Spirit's revival movement through the Whole Race Gospel & Missionary Service. I sent the Holy Spirit's words, written in English, to him to read. Therefore he knew that the Holy Spirit was ministering through me.

Whenever he has any problems, he calls me. As he obeyed the Holy Spirit's words, Almighty God gave him a great blessing. The Holy Spirit said He will give His blessing to him to show to the world how the Holy Spirit performs miracles to glorify the Heavenly Father. Therefore he follows Jesus Christ's words without fail.

He used to work as an important computer engineer receiving a nice annual salary at a big computer software company. When he was working over there, a small computer software company starting a business offered him a job. That offer was for a little less money than the big company but the new company offered stock options. That is, if he worked continuously, the new company would give so many shares per year for 6 years.

The price of the stock was $0.50/share at that time. But if he worked hard for the company, when the price of the stock goes up, all the difference above the original price $0.50/ stock would be his own.

1. Around April 1997, he called me to pray for his question whether he should move or not. When I prayed to Jesus, the Holy Spirit immediately answered his question.

He said, "Move immediately to the new company, saying that God provided the new job for him to give him a great financial blessing." According to God's advice, he moved immediately to the new, small, poor company from the large, worldwide well known company.

2. However after working about 3-4 months at the new company, he called me again, saying that he received a better offer

at another company and he asked me to pray whether he should move to the new company.

However the Holy Spirit immediately said, "No, do not move to another company. You should work at your current company, because the Holy Spirit will perform a financial miracle for him through the current company. Never think about moving to another company." So he followed God's advice not to move.

3. About June 1999, he called me again, saying that he cannot work any more at his current company, because he had to work about 11 to 12 hours a day. And he was sick and tired of the long working hours, and he said, **"I don't care about the money. I want to move to a new job."**

The Holy Spirit answered his question through me, saying, **"No you should not move your job. You should stay at your current company. If you move, you will lose your stock options and you will get nothing. Already through your last two years working, the value of your stocks increased beyond your imagination. Therefore you should stay at your company. Do not worry about anything but keep working at your current company."**

He asked me how long he should stay at that company. The Holy Spirit answered through me that not long after, that company will go public to sell its stock on the stock market. Then you can get your share of money for the stocks you will get through the stock options. After securing all your money for the promised stocks, you may leave the company. He made up his mind again to stay at his same job.

4. After a couple of months, in August 1999, that company went public on the stock market. The stock sold at $12.00/share on the stock market. That is 24 times higher than the original price.

In my morning prayer, the Holy Spirit asked me to tell him, **"Do not sell any of his stocks even one share. His stock price will go up many times higher than the public opening price within several years."**

The Holy Spirit said, **"God will give special blessings to his stocks, therefore the price for the same stocks will go up."**

I delivered the Holy Spirit's words not to sell his stocks but keep them until the Holy Spirit asks him to sell. Because of the Holy Spirit's advice, he received a big financial blessing from God.

He was obedient to God's words all three times, when he had to decide whether to move his job or not. Therefore he could receive the financial blessing. If he did not obey the Holy Spirit's words even one out of three times, he could not receive the blessing. Now he is very happy with God's blessing.

5. Jesus Christ wants to give His financial blessings in this way to His sons and daughters who really believe the Heavenly Father and obey God's words 100%. If you want to receive the special financial blessing of Almighty God, pray and obey the Holy Spirit's words. You will experience how the Holy Spirit performs His ministry to give you financial blessings.

When you make a lot of money through God's blessing, you should donate some part of your profit for God's ministry And He will continuously bless you financially as long as you keep your word with the Holy Spirit.

Genesis 39:1-6 Now Joseph had been taken down to Egypt. And Potiphar, an officer of Pharaoh, captain of the guard, an Egyptian, bought him from the Ishmaelites who had taken him down there. The LORD was with Joseph, and he was a successful man; and he was in the house of his master the Egyptian.

And his master saw that the LORD was with him and that the LORD made all he did to prosper in his hand. So Joseph found favor in his sight, and served him. Then he made him overseer of his house, and all that he had he put under his authority. So it was, from the time that he had made him overseer of his house and all that he had, that the LORD blessed the Egyptian's house for Joseph's sake; and the blessing of the LORD was on all that he had in the house and in the field.

Thus he left all that he had in Joseph's hand, and he did not know what he had except for the bread which he ate. Now Joseph was handsome in form and appearance.

As shown in the Bible passage above, Almighty God gives blessings to the owners, the employees and the belongings of the household in which Christian sons and daughters whom the Lord God loves are living, in order to help God's children and to show that God is with God's children.

The main subject of this testimony is a beloved son of God who believes the Lord God with all his heart and obeys the Holy Spirit's words without fail. Therefore he obeyed only the Holy Spirit's words given through me all three times, he rejected job offers which were better than the one the Holy Spirit recommended but followed only the Holy Spirit's advice. Accordingly he received God's great financial blessing.

The Lord plans to give great financial blessings to His children who believe Jesus Christ with all their heart through the main subject of this testimony.

In addition, God wants to receive some part of the profit given by the Lord's blessing as thanksgiving donations to be used for the Worldwide Holy Spirit Revival Movement through the Whole Race Gospel & Missionary Service. God's children who believe the Lord God with all their heart and obey the Holy Spirit will experience God's abundant blessings all through their life as long as they keep their word with the Holy Spirit.

March 14, 2000 when I write the testimony about the blessings given by the Holy Spirit, the price of the same stock goes up and down between $120.00 and $130.00/share. It is about three years since the main subject of this testimony moved according to the words of the Holy Spirit, the price of his $0.50/ stock went up 240 to 260 times of the original price. Already the words of the Holy Spirit saying that the price of the same stock will go up many times more than the original public price of $12.00/share within several years was realized.

Christians who really believe in God and financially support God's ministry in deed will receive many hundreds or thousands times more than the amount he or she helped God's ministry financially, as rewards from the Holy Spirit. This is the Holy Spirit's miraculous ministry which fed more than 5,000 people with five loaves of bread and the leftover fully filled 12 baskets.

Is it important for you to make more money by working overtime at your occupation? Making money by working overtime is limited and you will be too tired and get sick, if you continuously work without breaks. Please give the time you are using to work overtime at your job to the Almighty Heavenly

Father by praying, supporting God's ministry, and visiting Holy Spirit congregations to meet the Holy Spirit.

Once you meet the Holy Spirit in prayer or in the Holy Spirit's baptism, obey the Holy Spirit's words 100%. Until you are able to hear the Holy Spirit's words spoken in a small voice and until you are able to discern between the Holy Spirit and evil spirits in accordance with the Bible, try to find pastors or Christians who were taught how to discern the spirits directly by the Holy Spirit, and ask them to help you.

If you find the right pastor or Christian filled in the Holy Spirit who is communicating with Holy Spirit 24 hours a day, please obey the Holy Spirit's words given to you through him, then the Holy Spirit will settle all your difficult problems and He will lead you to make many hundreds times more than when you work overtime on your job.

Even if you are suffering from an incurable disease or if you are confronted with impossible problems for you to settle, do not worry. But pray to God, desiring desperately to meet the Holy Spirit and be obedient to the words of the Holy Spirit. If you meet the Holy Spirit in prayer or in Holy Spirit congregations, He will solve all your impossible problems for you and He will heal all your incurable sicknesses also. In addition to that, Jesus Christ will give His unlimited blessings for you and your children for generations.

The Holy Spirit even performs His miracles at your job. Human beings must not try to judge the unlimited power of God who created the universe and who raises even the dead to life, with human knowledge, reason, science and thoughts. We all must fully believe in the power of God and must obey Him and must follow the words of the Holy Spirit in deed. Then the Almighty Heavenly Father will give us His unlimited blessings. Our Lord Jesus who knows the hearts of all the people in the world will bless us and grow and lead us per His ways.

I experience the Holy Spirit's miracles everyday. There are innumerable testimonies of the Holy Spirit which I have experienced, besides the testimonies written in this book. By reading this book you will understand how God performs miraculous ministries. The Holy Spirit cures not only the sickness of patients but also He blesses His children and He changes impossible things to be possible for His children to do.

We must meet the Holy Spirit. This is the only way how we can solve all the problems which are impossible for us to settle. On the contrary, people who do not believe in the Holy Spirit's miraculous ministry and who judge God's ministries by their own reason, common sense, and science, cannot receive the unlimited blessings given by Almighty God.

The Christians who receive the special blessing from the Holy Spirit must thank God for the blessings. They should keep all the promises they made with the Holy Spirit, before the Holy Spirit performed the miracles. If they do not think of the past, or neglect the promises they made to the Holy Spirit, He will tell them several more times to keep those promises, through Christians or pastors filled in the Holy Spirit.

However if the Christian who received special blessings from the Lord does not obey the words of the Holy Spirit given through the men of God filled in the Holy Spirit, He makes all the blessings which were given by the Holy Spirit fly away. I wish all the readers of this testimony to receive the unlimited blessings given by the Almighty. God loves all of us and He wants to give His unlimited blessings to all of us. To receive His unlimited blessings, we have to obey Him faithfully.

In the name of Jesus, I pray for the Almighty Heavenly Father to pour His unlimited blessings to all the readers of this book and for their children for generations.

Almighty God loves you and He blesses you.

The Holy Spirit's words given on March 14, 2000 2000 in early morning prayer

2) The Holy Spirit caught a lot of fish for a fisherman and moves him to bring all the fish to my home for nothing

It was the fall of 2000. When my wife and I were on our way somewhere early in the morning, I said to her, "I want to eat raw fish, sashimi."

That evening when we returned home after finishing all our work, about 30 minutes later one couple whom we know well brought us a large plastic ice container. When I asked him, "What is this?" He said to me, "I went fishing in the sea this morning, and unexpectedly caught lots of fish. The other fisherman who went fishing with me caught nothing, only I caught a lot of fish.

On the way home, I wanted to give all the fish to you. That's why we came to you." When we opened the container, we found the container was full of big black sea bass. It looked like about 40 pounds.

I said to them right away, "These fish were caught by the

Holy Spirit and He sent them to us. This morning on our way going somewhere, I said to my wife, 'I want to eat raw fish, sashimi.' And less than 12 hours since I said that, God sent us the raw fish." We were very pleased to experience the Holy Spirit's miracle so soon.

The next morning when I was praying, the Holy Spirit said to me, "The Holy Spirit arranged for the fisherman to catch fish beyond his expectation, and He moved the fisherman's heart to bring all the fish to you."

John 21: 4-6 But when the morning had now come, Jesus stood on the shore; yet the disciples did not know that it was Jesus. Then Jesus said to them, "Children, have you any food?" They answered Him, "No." And He said to them, "Cast the net on the right side of the boat, and you will find some." So they cast, and now they were not able to draw it in because of the multitude of fish.

As shown in this Bible passage, it is nothing for Jesus to catch a multitude of fish any time He wants to.

Since that time, before we ate all the fish, they would bring more newly caught fish. So our refrigerator freezer always has fish which fisherman caught in the sea. We give some of the fish we received to the pastors in our church and church members. Whenever we eat the fish, we think about the Bible passage in which Jesus caught the multitude of fish for His disciples.

We pray in the name of Jesus for the Almighty Heavenly Father to pour His unlimited blessing on the fisherman who brought a lot of fish to us. And we pray for God to give His blessings to the family and the business of the person who brought us a lot of fish.

The Holy Spirit sends food to His children by moving other people who have special food in the same way He did for us. We always thank the Lord for sending us food or other things which we need badly.

3) The Holy Spirit also sends kimchi to my home

At our home, side dishes such as kimchi, jang a chi (Korean pickles), and others arrive before we eat them all. God always sends us such side dishes. The Holy Spirit moves people who make such dishes to bring them for us. When a large amount comes, we share it with the church members and pastors. This is the Holy Spirit's ministry. God prepares other people or even animals to bring food for His children.

1 Kings 17: 2-7 Then the word of the LORD came to him, saying, "Get away from here and turn eastward, and hide by the Brook Cherith, which flows into the Jordan. And it will be that you shall drink from the brook, and I have commanded the ravens to feed you there." So he went and did according to the word of the LORD, for he went and stayed by the Brook Cherith, which flows into the Jordan.
The ravens brought him bread and meat in the morning, and bread and meat in the evening; and he drank from the brook. And it happened after a while that the brook dried up, because there had been no rain in the land.

As shown in this Bible passage, the Lord commanded the ravens to bring bread and meat for Elijah in the morning and evening everyday. If you obey the words of God and believe really in God, He will move others to bring you the food you need.

In the name of Jesus, we pray always for Almighty God to give His unlimited blessings to the people and to their children for generations who bring us food.

4) The Holy Spirit sends money for all the expenses of a Holy Spirit Meeting

In early morning prayer one day in February 2001, the Holy Spirit asked me to invite Pastor Y. to our church and have Holy Spirit revival meetings in our church.

I answered the Holy Spirit, **"Our church does not have any budget for it and I don't have any money as you know very well."**

The Holy Spirit said to me, **"I will give you all the money needed for the Holy Spirit revival meetings**."

The Holy Spirit asked me to tell to the senior pastor of our church that I would be responsible for all the expenses for the Holy Spirit's meetings.

In obedience to the words of the Holy Spirit, I said to the senior pastor of our church, **"I will be responsible for all the expenses of the Holy Spirit's revival meetings,"** and I asked him to invite Pastor Y. to our church and have the Holy Spirit's revival meetings.

So we decided to have the Holy Spirit's meeting for three days from April 25-27, 2001. We placed large advertisements in newspapers, TV, and on radio. And we successfully finished the Holy Spirit's revival services. The Holy Spirit performed very powerful ministries, so many people received great blessings from Almighty God.

However the donations we collected from the Holy Spirit

meeting were small compared to our expenses. The total donations we received covered about one quarter of our expenses for
the Holy Spirit's meeting. By human calculation, we lost a lot
of money. However I never asked anyone to donate for the
shortage of money for the meeting.

I just reported the results of the financial shortage to the
Spirit in early morning prayer. The Holy Spirit heard my prayer
and moved two people to send checks to me immediately.
When I opened the two envelopes from two different Christians,
I was very surprised to find the amount of the two checks they
sent us covered exactly three-quarters of the total expenses of
the Holy Spirit's revival meetings. After receiving the two
checks, my wife and I were astonished again to find that the
Holy Spirit moved them to send me the exact amount of the
shortage.

We once again thanked to the Holy Spirit who sent us the
exact amount to cover the shortage for the Holy Spirit's revival
meetings.

In the name of Jesus, we prayed for Almighty God to give
His unlimited blessings to the two Christians and their children
for generations who sent us the money needed for the Holy
Spirit's services.

God helps all His children. We believe that the Lord who
helps us helps all of you too. When the Holy Spirit asks you to
do anything, please be obedient to the Holy Spirit whether it is
profitable or not to you or your business.

When the Holy Spirit asks someone to do something for Him,
some pastors and Christians do not obey the Holy Spirit's
words exactly.

But after calculating the results by human reason, if the
works that the Holy Spirit asks are beneficial to them, they fol-

low the Holy Spirit, but if they are a disadvantage to them, they do not do the works which the Holy Spirit asks them to do. If anyone ignores the words of the Holy Spirit in this way, God will give several more times to test him or her, and if he doesn't follow the Holy Spirit's words, He will no longer ask such Christians but unexpected troubles will happen to such a person.

As for the words of the Holy Spirit, whether they are beneficial or disadvantageous to us, we have to follow them exactly as He says. That is the best way for us to act. Sometimes pastors or Christians who deliver the words of the Holy Spirit are libeled, persecuted by the people to whom the words of God are delivered. However the Holy Spirit protects pastors or Christians who boldly deliver the words of God per the instructions of the Holy Spirit, from all kinds of persecution or libel or other intrigues against them.

God sometimes punishes the people who falsely libel, persecute or plot against the pastors or Christians delivering the words of God in order to let them realize what they are doing is against God.

However when the people don't understand the will of the Holy Spirit and keep falsely libeling, persecuting, or plotting against the Christians who deliver the words of the Lord, and obstruct the Holy Spirit's revival movement, the Holy Spirit punishes them fearfully in a way no human beings can solve. And the Holy Spirit gives His unlimited blessings to the Christians who boldly deliver the words of God.

Matthew 5: 10-12 Blessed are those who are persecuted for righteousness' sake, For theirs is the kingdom of heaven. Blessed are you when they revile and persecute you, and say all kinds of evil against you falsely for My sake. Rejoice and be exceedingly glad, for great is your reward in heaven, for so they persecuted the

prophets who were before you.

When you do anything for the ministry of God, please do your best without expecting any rewards for your service for God. When you want to help someone, please help those who are not able to return the help to you. Then the Almighty Heavenly Father will give you more blessings.

Luke 14: 12-14 Then He also said to him who invited Him, "When you give a dinner or a supper, do not ask your friends, your brothers, your relatives, nor rich neighbors, lest they also invite you back, and you be repaid. But when you give a feast, invite the poor, the maimed, the lame, the blind. And you will be blessed, because they cannot repay you; for you shall be repaid at the resurrection of the just."

Please help the poor, homeless people who are wandering and begging for food or money in the streets of cities, orphans, and the dying, sick people who have no one to help them.

Matthew 25: 31-46 "When the Son of Man comes in His glory, and all the holy angels with Him, then He will sit on the throne of His glory. All the nations will be gathered before Him, and He will separate them one from another, as a shepherd divides his sheep from the goats. And He will set the sheep on His right hand, but the goats on the left.
Then the King will say to those on His right hand, 'Come, you blessed of My Father, inherit the kingdom prepared for you from the foundation of the world: for I was hungry and you gave Me food; I was thirsty and you gave Me drink; I was a stranger and you took Me in; I was naked and you clothed Me; I was sick and you visited Me; I was in prison and you came to Me.'

"Then the righteous will answer Him, saying, 'Lord, when did we see You hungry and feed You, or thirsty and give You drink? When did we see You a stranger and take You in, or naked and clothe You? Or when did we see You sick, or in prison, and come to You?'

And the King will answer and say to them, 'Assuredly, I say to you, inasmuch as you did it to one of the least of these My brethren, you did it to Me.'

"Then He will also say to those on the left hand, 'Depart from Me, you cursed, into the everlasting fire prepared for the devil and his angels: for I was hungry and you gave Me no food; I was thirsty and you gave Me no drink; 'I was a stranger and you did not take Me in, naked and you did not clothe Me, sick and in prison and you did not visit Me.'

Then they also answered Him, saying, 'Lord, when did we see you hungry or thirsty or a stranger or naked or sick or in prison, and did not minister to You?'

"Then He will answer them, saying 'Assuredly, I say to you, inasmuch as you did not do it to one of the least of these, you did not do it to Me.' "And these will go away into everlasting punishment, but the righteous into everlasting life."

I believe you can fully understand the meaning of this Bible passage. **Jesus said, "I will send the righteous who help the poor, sick homeless people to eternal life."**

But then He said, "I will send the people who do not help the poor, sick, and dying people into the eternal fire prepared for the devil and his angels."

Jesus Christ told to His disciples to help the poor homeless people wandering and begging for food or money in the streets of the cities where you live. Then Almighty God will be very pleased and He will give you His unlimited blessings, a thousand times more than you helped the poor. This is the will of God and God's love given to you.

The Holy Spirit's words given in early morning prayer on August 16, 2001.

3. Almighty God who gives His unlimited blessing

This is the word of the Holy Spirit which was given in early morning prayer on July 19, 2001.

God loves all of us. God wants to give His blessings to all of us. He wants to give all His blessings, such as health and financial blessings. In addition to that, God wants to take our souls to heaven. This is the love of Almighty God.

Deuteronomy 28: 1-14 "Now it shall come to pass, if you diligently obey the voice of the Lord your God, to observe carefully all His commandments which I command you today, that the Lord your God will set you high above all nations of the earth. And all these blessings shall come upon you and overtake you, because you obey the voice of the Lord your God: "Blessed shall you be in the city, and blessed shall you be in the country.
"Blessed shall be the fruit of your body, the produce of your ground and the increase of your herds, the increase of your cattle

and the offspring of your flocks. "Blessed shall be your basket and your kneading bowl. "Blessed shall you be when you come in, and blessed shall you be when you go out.

"The Lord will cause your enemies who rise against you to be defeated before your face; they shall come out against you one way and flee before you seven ways. "The Lord will command the blessing on you in your storehouses and in all to which you set your hand, and He will bless you in the land which the Lord your God is giving you.

"The Lord will establish you as a holy people to Himself, just as He has sworn to you, if you keep the commandments of the Lord your God and walk in His ways. Then all peoples of the earth shall see that you are called by the name of the Lord, and they shall be afraid of you.

And the Lord will grant you plenty of goods, in the fruit of your body, in the increase of your livestock, and in the produce of your ground, in the land of which the Lord swore to your fathers to give you. The Lord will open to you His good treasure, the heavens, to give the rain to your land in its season, and to bless all the work of your hand.

You shall lend to many nations, but you shall not borrow. And the Lord will make you the head and not the tail; you shall be above only, and not be beneath, if you heed the commandments of the Lord your God, which I command you today, and are careful to observe them.

So you shall not turn aside from any of the words which I command you this day, to the right or the left, to go after other gods to serve them.

The Heavenly Father wants to give these blessings to all of us. In order to receive such great blessings, we have to prepare ourselves to receive them by always praying faithfully, and thanking God for His unlimited blessings.

Innumerable Christians pray to God for His unlimited blessings. However they don't know how to express thanks to God. To receive God's unlimited blessings, we have to pray and thank God at the same time.

We have to thank God from the deepest part of our heart and we have to change our heart to always obey the words of God, whether the words are beneficial or disadvantageous to us, and we have to always pray from our heartfelt mind to God. And then Almighty God who is receiving the prayer will always give His unlimited blessings to His children who pray this way. The Heavenly Father will give you a thousand times more than you are giving to Almighty God.

Malachi 3: 7-12 "Yet from the days of your fathers
You have gone away from My ordinances
And have not kept them.
Return to Me, and I will return to you," Says the Lord of hosts.
But you said, "In what way shall we return?"
"Will a man rob God? Yet you have robbed Me!"
But you say, "In what way have we robbed You?" "In tithes
and offerings. You are cursed with a curse,
For you have robbed Me,
Even this whole nation. Bring all the tithes into the storehouse,
That there may be food in My house,
And try Me now in this," Says the Lord of hosts, "If I will not
open for you the windows of heaven
And pour out for you such blessing
That there will not be room enough to receive it. "And I will
rebuke the devourer for your sakes,
So that he will not destroy the fruit of your ground,
Nor shall the vine fail to bear fruit for you in the field," Says the
Lord of hosts; "

And all nations will call you blessed,
For you will be a delightful land," Says the Lord of hosts.

In this Bible passage, Almighty God said clearly, "Bring the whole tithe into the storehouse, that there may be food in My house. Test Me in this," says the Lord Almighty, "and see if I will not throw open the floodgates of heaven and pour out so much blessing that you will not have room enough for it."

Almighty God said, "I will give My unlimited blessings to My children who give the whole tithe and offerings to the house of God with heartfelt belief. This is God's unlimited blessing given with the love of Jesus. In order to receive the unlimited blessings of God, we have to give our heartfelt tithes and offerings to God. This is the word of the Holy Spirit.

2 Chronicles 1: 1-13 Now Solomon the son of David was strengthened in his kingdom, and the Lord his God was with him and exalted him exceedingly. And Solomon spoke to all Israel, to the captains of thousands and of hundreds, to the judges, and to every leader in all Israel, the heads of the fathers' houses.

Then Solomon, and all the assembly with him, went to the high place that was at Gibeon; for the tabernacle of meeting with God was there, which Moses the servant of the Lord had made in the wilderness.

But David had brought up the ark of God from Kirjath Jearim to the place David had prepared for it, for he had pitched a tent for it at Jerusalem. Now the bronze altar that Bezalel the son of Uri, the son of Hur, had made, he put before the tabernacle of the Lord; Solomon and the assembly sought Him there.

And Solomon went up there to the bronze altar before the Lord, which was at the tabernacle of meeting, and offered a thousand burnt offerings on it.

372 Holy Spirit, Hover Over Me

On that night God appeared to Solomon, and said to him, "Ask! What shall I give you?" And Solomon said to God: "You have shown great mercy to David my father, and have made me king in his place. Now, O Lord God, let Your promise to David my father be established, for You have made me king over a people like the dust of the earth in multitude.

Now give me wisdom and knowledge, that I may go out and come in before this people; for who can judge this great people of Yours?"

Then God said to Solomon: "Because this was in your heart, and you have not asked riches or wealth or honor or the life of your enemies, nor have you asked long life--but have asked wisdom and knowledge for yourself, that you may judge My people over whom I have made you king-- wisdom and knowledge are granted to you; and I will give you riches and wealth and honor, such as none of the kings have had who were before you, nor shall any after you have the like." So Solomon came to Jerusalem from the high place that was at Gibeon, from before the tabernacle of meeting, and reigned over Israel.

In this Bible passage, we find that when King Solomon offered one thousand burnt offerings to Almighty God, God gave His unlimited blessings to Solomon, the king of Israel. King Solomon asked Almighty God only for wisdom and knowledge to judge the people of Israel.

However the Lord told him that He would give him wisdom and knowledge, and in addition to that He would give him riches and wealth and honor. God gave Solomon the greatest blessings given to any king before or after him. God is love. Almighty God wants to give His unlimited blessings to all of us. In order to receive such great blessings, we have to give our offerings from the depths of our heart to God. This is the law of the Lord.

Matthew 25: 31-46 "When the Son of Man comes in His glory, and all the holy angels with Him, then He will sit on the throne of His glory. All the nations will be gathered before Him, and He will separate them one from another, as a shepherd divides his sheep from the goats. And He will set the sheep on His right hand, but the goats on the left.

Then the King will say to those on His right hand, 'Come, you blessed of My Father, inherit the kingdom prepared for you from the foundation of the world: for I was hungry and you gave Me food; I was thirsty and you gave Me drink; I was a stranger and you took Me in; I was naked and you clothed Me; I was sick and you visited Me; I was in prison and you came to Me.'

"Then the righteous will answer Him, saying, 'Lord, when did we see You hungry and feed You, or thirsty and give You drink? When did we see You a stranger and take You in, or naked and clothe You? Or when did we see You sick, or in prison, and come to You?'

And the King will answer and say to them, 'Assuredly, I say to you, inasmuch as you did it to one of the least of these My brethren, you did it to Me.'

"Then He will also say to those on the left hand, 'Depart from Me, you cursed, into the everlasting fire prepared for the devil and his angels: for I was hungry and you gave Me no food; I was thirsty and you gave Me no drink; I was a stranger and you did not take Me in, naked and you did not clothe Me, sick and in prison and you did not visit Me.'

"Then they also will answer Him, saying, 'Lord, when did we see You hungry or thirsty or a stranger or naked or sick or in

prison, and did not minister to You?'

Then He will answer them, saying, 'Assuredly, I say to you, inasmuch as you did not do it to one of the least of these, you did not do it to Me.' And these will go away into everlasting punishment, but the righteous into eternal life."

In the above Bible passage, Jesus clearly says that the people who do not take care of the poor in our neighborhood but are living for their own interests and benefits shall be sent to the eternal fire prepared for the devil and his angels. (Matthew 25:41) But He said to the righteous, "Then the King will say to those on His right hand, 'Come, you blessed of My Father, inherit the kingdom prepared for you from the foundation of the world'"

This is God's love and the word of the Lord. We must all help, with God's love, the poor and the homeless people who are sleeping on the streets and begging for food in our neighborhoods. We must also become Christians who offer donations for thanks to God. And then the Almighty Heavenly Father will give us His unlimited blessings which are many thousand times bigger than what we donate to God's ministry to help the poor and lead them to Jesus.

This is the secret of how to receive God's unlimited blessings for us and our children through the generations.

In the name of Jesus, we pray for God to change all the readers of this book to donate to God's ministry and receive His unlimited blessings which are many thousand times bigger than what they offer to God.

The Holy Spirit said to me, "Deliver the Holy Spirit's message to all the people in the world," in

early morning prayer on July 19, 2001.

4. The Holy Spirit comforted a sick man at the moment of his death and led him to heaven

2 Corinthians 1: 3-4 Blessed be the God and Father of our Lord Jesus Christ, the Father of mercies and God of all comfort, who comforts us in all our tribulation, that we may be able to comfort those who are in any trouble, with the comfort with which we ourselves are comforted by God.

One day in spring 1998 when I was praying early in the morning, an old man named K., who used to go to the same church as me and had been paralyzed for many years, was crying before me without stopping.

He asked me to help him, and the Holy Spirit asked me to visit him and help him. When my wife and I visited the home for the aged where he was staying, he, in a wheel chair, and his wife accepted us with all their heart. The Holy Spirit asked me to tell him about heaven, which I had seen many times before. And I gave him the Holy Spirit's message saying, **"Don't worry about death at all, the Holy Spirit's angels will take you to heaven with them."**

I said to him, **"The Holy Spirit sent me to deliver the Holy Spirit's message to you, and pray for you."** He was very happy to hear what I said to him. I delivered the Holy Spirit's message verbally to him and prayed in the name of Jesus to give him Jesus' love and light, with the Holy Spirit's power and anointing to give him strength.

After I prayed for him, he said to me, "I am very peaceful now in my heart." He thanked me many times for my having visited and delivered the Holy Spirit's message to him, and he was very happy and pleased. He came up to the elevator entrance to see us off. He had a very good sleep that night and the next day he was admitted to a hospital and soon died. He was paralyzed for eight years but the Holy Spirit knew exactly when he would go to heaven, therefore the Holy Spirit sent the Holy Spirit's envoy to comfort him in the last moments of his life.

After he died, when I prayed about him, the Holy Spirit showed me in a vision that Jesus Christ carried him, dressed in a long white gown with a gold crown on his head, in His arms and walked to me in a bright light and asked me to tell all that I had seen to his wife. And Jesus, along with several angels, took him in the very bright light to heaven. His wife was so happy to hear about her husband's having gone to heaven that she cried and held my hands tightly.

In addition to him, there are many people who were taken by Jesus to heaven.
I am the witness who delivered visions showing that people were taken to heaven by Jesus to their family members.

In the meantime, there are many people who were sent to the fiery lake of burning sulfur in hell. The Holy Spirit showed me visions of many people who were sent to the fiery sea of hell. However it is very difficult for me to deliver the Holy Spirit's message telling them that their parents or beloved ones were sent to hell.

Some people try to fight me, saying, "Why was my father sent to hell?" And they become my enemy. **I say to them, "It is the Heavenly Father who decides heaven or hell for him, I am nothing. I am just a messenger who delivers the Holy Spirit's message to people in accordance with the Holy Spirit's instruction."**

Do not blame me but pray to God, and He will show you the truth.

The Holy Spirit loves each of you like this. And He sends His angels to help and protect you. However, most of you cannot communicate with Him and cannot see the angels helping you because of sins not confessed to God. Do not do any deeds which are against God.

When you are alone, you think no one knows about you, but that is a big mistake. The Holy Spirit, your soul, and the angels helping you know about your intentions, before you act. All your deeds are automatically recorded in the record book of your life in heaven and in your heart.

At God's judgment, all your sins will be shown like a video. No one can deny anything that he did. I have seen innumerable people who were thrown into the fiery lake of burning sulfur in hell.

Never think of doing any misdeeds which are against God, even in a dream. We are all people created by the Heavenly Father to shine in the glory of God.

In the meantime, Satan and evil spirits know about your secret misdeeds right away. Satan, demons, and evil spirits take advantage of your misdeeds to lure you into their intrigue which will spiritually destroy you completely.

The Holy Spirit wants to lead each of you all to heaven. Obey the Holy Spirit's message, and He will guide you to heaven without fail. The Holy Spirit loves you and He blesses you.

CHAPTER 10

The Holy Spirit's words and training about angels

1. The angels protect and lead good Christians
2. The Indian burning in the fire: the angels making the impossible possible
3. When I drive a car, angels guide and protect me
4. The Holy Spirit's living water like the sea

1. The Holy Spirit's angels guide Christians who believe in God with their whole heart

Acts 5: 17-20 Then the high priest rose up, and all those who were with him (which is the sect of the Sadducees), and they were filled with indignation, and laid their hands on the apostles and put them in the common prison. But at night an angel of the Lord opened the prison doors and brought them out, and said, "Go, stand in the temple and speak to the people all the words of this life."

24 hours a day, I see angels protecting me and whenever I want, I can talk with them. As soon as I wake up early in the morning, an angel at my bedside asks me to wash my face and hands and go downstairs to worship and pray to God.

All day long whatever I do, angels are at my side, front and back, guiding, protecting and leading me. When I sing hymns by myself early in the morning, angels are singing with me and dancing with me, in rhythm.

When I sing hymns early in the morning, all the creatures in the world are singing and dancing to the rhythm of the song.

The trees are dancing and the clouds high in the sky are dancing to the rhythm, and the wild animals and flowers are dancing to the rhythm of the hymn. All the creatures in the world are singing and dancing to the rhythm of the song.

Therefore, I am always happy and not lonely at all, even if I am singing and praying by myself, because I am singing and dancing with angels surrounding Jesus in the center.

When I drive my car, Jesus is sitting in the center of the back seat, holding a big carp fish in His right hand and shaking it a little bit to show me. And two angels are sitting by Jesus, one on each side. On the floor of the back of my car there are many carps swimming in water about 10 inches deep. Jesus is holding a white lamb in His other arm.

And in front of me, a little girl angel is looking down at me as I drive, with her belly on the roof of my car. She makes me laugh and makes me happy when I drive long or short distances. And a white dove sits on my head or shoulder, sometimes she flies back and forth in my car and sometimes many doves are flying in front of my running car.

I drive my car while talking with Jesus. He talks mainly about how we can raise the Holy Spirit's revival movement all over the world. Only I can hear what Jesus says, or see what He is doing. Sometimes I drive my car with my wife sitting by me, and I can see the angels and talk with Jesus, but my wife cannot see what I see or hear what Jesus says to me.

Spiritually she is blind and deaf. Outside my car several giant angels escort my car, two angels on each side of the car and two angels each, at the back and front of the car, they are running exactly at the same speed of my car. Several angels are also flying above my car at exactly at the same speed of my car, therefore I am not lonely at all.

When I am a little sleepy because of driving for many hours to the Holy Spirit's service, the Holy Spirit knows in advance. He begins to move my belly up and down repeatedly and an angel shakes my shoulders hard. All my sleepiness goes away immediately.

When any big truck passes by my car and comes close to my side
or back, one of the angels comes to me and says, "Do not worry
about the truck, if it comes close to us, we will push it away."
And they are running in between my car and the truck.
If I drive too fast and close to the car in front of me, one of the
angels running in front of the car turns around, and shows me
signs to slow down with his hand like a policeman, while running backwards.
If I drive too fast and rough, the angel running at the side of my
car holds my steering wheel and the angel sitting in the back seat
steps on the brake a little. Even if there is a window, that doesn't
matter, he holds my steering wheel through the window without
opening the window glass, from outside the car.

Sometimes when I feel like exercising my body, the angels ask
me to sit still without moving. Then they give me a full massage
over my whole body by shaking my hands and legs and stretch-
ing the front of my chest or shaking and twisting my shoulders.
They are very powerful, so they move my body softly.
They say that if they move my body with their full power, all my
bones will be crushed. I am always with angels helping and
protecting me in any circumstance, so I am always very happy
and not lonely at all.

When I feel depressed or disappointed with something, the Holy
Spirit comforts me with all kinds of encouragement. When I
meet my old friends who are rich and wealthy, and when I feel
depressed comparing what I am now to what I was before, when
I was doing business, the Holy Spirit shows me immediately the
solid gold houses and furniture decorated with diamonds and
many other things made of precious jewels in heaven and He

tells me that that house belongs to you. And then all my depression disappears immediately from my heart.

The Holy Spirit's angels protect you too.

Acts 10: 1-8 There was a certain man in Caesarea called Cornelius, a centurion of what was called the Italian Regiment, a devout man and one who feared God with all his household, who gave alms generously to the people, and prayed to God always.

About the ninth hour of the day he saw clearly in a vision an angel of God coming in and saying to him, "Cornelius!" And when he observed him, he was afraid, and said, "What is it, lord?"

So he said to him, "Your prayers and your alms have come up for a memorial before God. Now send men to Joppa, and send for Simon whose surname is Peter. He is lodging with Simon, a tanner, whose house is by the sea. He will tell you what you must do."

And when the angel who spoke to him had departed, Cornelius called two of his household servants and a devout soldier from among those who waited on him continually. So when he had explained all these things to them, he sent them to Joppa.

However you are spiritually blind and deaf, because you cannot see and hear the angels who protect and help you. Pray and ask for the Holy Spirit's anointing and power to help you see the secrets in heaven, and the Holy Spirit's angels will help you like Cornelius.

The Holy Spirit wants to help you and protect you anytime, anywhere. You just do not see and hear the angels who are near you. The Holy Spirit wants to lead all the devout Christians who really believe in God to heaven.

2. The Indian burning in the fire: the angels making the impossible possible

At 5:00AM on April 11, 1994 I was taking a walk on the street in Tokyo. Japanese people welcomed me, saying, **"You are a big businessman."**
At that time an Indian driver was driving a taxi without a top. Right at that moment several young Japanese men came to the Indian taxi driver and said to him, **"You are an illegal foreign resident working in Japan. Because of people like you, we are unemployed."**
At the same time several young Japanese men turned over the taxi, to the side of the street by lifting one side of the taxi. The Indian driver was trapped under the taxi and was screaming for help to be rescued.

At that time, a cruel, young Japanese man poured gasoline from a bottle on the taxi and set fire to it. In seconds, the taxi was burning in flame and smoke, and the Indian driver trapped under the taxi was screaming for help with all his power. However all the Japanese people passing by were thinking that it was proper for the Indian driver to be punished like that.
I thought it was very pitiful that an Indian driver was punished so cruelly. I tried to help him but there was nothing that I could do to help him. Already big flames and smoke covered whole area near the taxi, so no one could approach it. I was feeling a strong hostility against the Japanese people and I was wandering here

and there. Meanwhile I woke from my sleep, and I found it was a dream.

That day, I had to go to New York. After the cruel dream, I was hesitating to go. But I went to the Korean Consulate General in New York to get some important business documents certified. It was about 3 PM when I finished all my work at the Korean Consulate General. And I wanted to send the certified papers to Korea by express mail from New York. (Before, I used to send the same documents by express mail from Philadelphia where my home was, after returning home. But that day I felt a strong desire to send them from New York)

I walked about three or four blocks to a post office in New York, by asking the passers by where the post office was located. After mailing the documents to Korea, when I walked out of the post office towards the one-way, four lane street, a taxi was coming towards me and stopped right before me.
When I opened the back door of the taxi, I was very surprised to find that the same Indian taxi driver who was trapped under the burning taxi in Tokyo in my morning dream was driving a real taxi in New York City, which I was about to take. As soon as I sat in the back seat, the Holy Spirit gave me a strong inspiration that the driver did not believe in God. And He told me to tell the driver the gospel to save him and his family.

I asked the driver. "What country are you from?"
He answered, "I am from Bangladesh."
I asked him another question. "Do you believe in God?"
He said, "No, I believe in Hinduism."
I said to him. **"You must believe in God immediately from now on, otherwise you and all your family members believing in Hinduism will be thrown into the fire sea of hell."**

Exodus 20: 3-7 "You shall have no other gods before Me. "You
shall not make for yourself a carved image--any likeness of anything that is in heaven above, or that is in the earth beneath, or
that is in the water under the earth; you shall not bow down to
them nor serve them.

For I, the LORD your God, am a jealous God, visiting the iniquity of the fathers upon the children to the third and fourth generations of those who hate Me, but showing mercy to thousands,
to those who love Me and keep My commandments.

"You shall not take the name of the LORD your God in vain,
for the LORD will not hold him guiltless who takes His name in
vain.

If you read the Bible from the beginning to the end, there are
many passages which say, **"You must believe in the Heavenly
Father, the Almighty God who created the heavens and
earth and all the creatures in the universe and that Jesus, the
Son of God, died on the cross to pay for your sins.
You were forgiven for your sins and you must accept Jesus
Christ as your Savior and Lord and you must believe and
obey the Holy Spirit who controls you and empowers your
daily life and witness and leads you to heaven. That is the
Trinity God."**

Revelation 21: 6-8 And He said to me, "It is done! I am the Al-
Alpha and the Omega, the Beginning and the End. I will give of
the fountain of the water of life freely to him who thirsts. He who
overcomes shall inherit all things, and I will be his God and he
shall be My son. But the cowardly, unbelieving, abominable,
murderers, sexually immoral, sorcerers, idolaters, and all liars
shall have their part in the lake which burns with fire and brimstone, which is the second death."

If you worship other gods, not the one mentioned above, you are committing a big sin against the true Almighty God who created the universe, and will punish you for three to four generations of your family.
He will cast all of your family members into the fire sea in hell. And I told him about the dream I had this morning. In addition to that I told him, **"Do not sin against God any more by believing in Hinduism, but believe in the Almighty God who will save you from all your sins and lead you to heaven."**

I told him about Jesus who is living now and performs miracles through the Holy Spirit all over the world. I told him to go to the prayer houses or the churches where the Holy Spirit powerfully performs miracles, to see how the Holy Spirit performs miracles today. Also I told him about the Holy Spirit's miracle ministries happening at Pastor Benny Hinn's Holy Spirit ministry where you can see with your own eyes the Holy Spirit healing cancer or any other diseases. There are innumerable prayer houses and churches where the Holy Spirit ministers very powerfully all over the world.

John 14: 6 Jesus said to him, "I am the way, the truth, and the life. No one comes to the Father except through Me."

While quoting this Bible passage, I told him that no one can come to heaven except through Jesus Christ.

After hearing all that I said about Jesus, he finally promised me that from the coming Sunday he would go to a Christian church with his two sons and wife. Then I got off the taxi at the Pennsylvania Rail Road Station in New York.

The Holy Spirit used me as a missionary to save the Indian taxi driver for Jesus Christ, because he did not believe in God. The Holy Spirit showed me an Indian taxi driver burning trapped under the taxi in a dream but He reminded me of the truth that the Indian driver burning in the fire in Tokyo was not only related to the Indian taxi driver I really met in New York but also all the uncountable, innumerable people not believing the Almighty God who created the universe, but are worshiping idols and the evil spirits among the billions of people in the world.

That is, anybody not believing in the Almighty God who created the universe, but who worships idols or wrong gods will be thrown into the fire sea in hell instead of being led to heaven. The people who worship idols will face the same kinds of pitiful and miserable fate like the Indian taxi driver who was burning in flames and trapped in a smoke-filled taxi in Tokyo, Japan.

The Holy Spirit said to me, "Deliver Jesus' gospel to such poor and miserable people who know nothing about Jesus, and lead them to Jesus' salvation for them to be saved and be led to heaven."

Mark 16: 15 And He said to them, "Go into all the world and preach the gospel to every creature."

While giving me the Bible passage shown above, the Holy Spirit said to me, **"There are innumerable poor people all over the world who do not believe in God and who will be cast into the fiery lake forever in hell. Do your best to save such miserable souls wherever you go in the world,"**

It is the Heavenly Father's calling for all the Christians to deliver the gospel to all the unbelievers of Jesus Christ, who worship idols and evil spirits all over the world, and to lead the poor, pitiful, miserable souls destined to be thrown into the fire sea in hell to the Heavenly Father who will forgive all their sin, to Jesus Christ, the Son of God who died on the cross to pay for their sins, and to the Holy Spirit who will lead them to heaven.

The Holy Spirit showed me the burning Indian driver in a dream at 5:00 in the morning and I met the real Indian driver at 4:00PM, 11 hours after that dream, in a taxi in New York.

I was wondering how this meeting could be realized. I did not make any appointment with the Indian driver. If he had been delayed a few seconds driving, eating breakfast or lunch, in the bathroom or in busy traffic in New York in the last 11 hours, or if I delayed a few seconds in eating, coming to New York by train, working in the Korean Consulate General Office, walking to the post office or mailing the papers in the post office, I would not ever meet him.

However God showed me the Indian driver at 5:00AM in a dream and I met the real Indian driver at 4:00PM on a busy New York street. If I was one second late or early, we could not meet each other. When I was wondering how we met, I thought that all creatures in the world, whether they are living or dead, believing in God or not believing in God, obey God's order perfectly and on time.

After this incident I purchased many audio tapes recorded with **"Heaven and Hell"** testified by a Christian and I began to give them free to everybody I met in Korea and the U.S.A., in banks, airplanes, buses, restaurants or streets and subways but I paid special attention to handicapped people, senior citizens and taxi drivers. I was very happy whenever I heard that the audio tapes which I gave to someone are being given to their friends to listen.

Someone told me that after he listened to the tape, the Holy
Spirit moved him so that he copied several of them and gave
them to his friends to listen.

After this incident, I was wondering for a long time how the
Holy Spirit arranged the meeting between the Indian taxi driver
and me in the streets of New York at exactly the right time. I
thought about that for years.

**Acts 12: 1-11 Now about that time Herod the king stretched out
his hand to harass some from the church. Then he killed James
the brother of John with the sword. And because he saw that it
pleased the Jews, he proceeded further to seize Peter also.**

**Now it was during the Days of Unleavened Bread. So when he
had arrested him, he put him in prison, and delivered him to four
squads of soldiers to keep him, intending to bring him before the
people after Passover.**

**Peter was therefore kept in prison, but constant prayer was
offered to God for him by the church. And when Herod was about
to bring him out, that night Peter was sleeping, bound with two
chains between two soldiers; and the guards before the door were
keeping the prison.**

**Now behold, an angel of the Lord stood by him, and a light
shone in the prison; and he struck Peter on the side and raised
him up, saying, "Arise quickly!" And his chains fell off his hands.
Then the angel said to him, "Gird yourself and tie on your sandals"; and so he did. And he said to him, "Put on your garment
and follow me." So he went out and followed him, and did not
know that what was done by the angel was real, but thought he
was seeing a vision.**

**When they were past the first and the second guard posts, they
came to the iron gate that leads to the city, which opened to them
of its own accord; and they went out and went down one street,**

and immediately the angel departed from him. And when Peter had come to himself, he said, "Now I know for certain that the Lord has sent His angel, and has delivered me from the hand of Herod and from all the expectation of the Jewish people."

This was impossible for human beings to do. I did not know it at that time. But from 1996 the Holy Spirit opened the spiritual vision for me to see spiritual things. And from that time the Holy Spirit began to show me spiritual visions. From 1997, when I was lost driving, the Holy Spirit showed me green arrows to show me the right way to follow.

Sometimes when I drive for a long time and feel sleepy, an angel shakes my shoulder and moves something powerfully in my stomach to wake me up from sleep. Sometimes they massage my shoulder and back to relieve me from the tired condition caused by the long driving to the prayer houses or churches where the Holy Spirit ministers. The sleepy condition goes away immediately and angels guide me and we continuously sing the gospel song, "The Holy Spirit of our Lord is present with me, I praise the Lord," while driving the long distance.

Sometimes the Holy Spirit tells me how to revive the Holy Spirit movement all over the world. When a big truck comes close to my car, a giant angel running between my car and the truck says to me, "Chairman, do not worry about this truck, if it comes close to us, we will push it away from your car." I have experienced such meetings with angels innumerable times.

After experiencing many meetings with angels, the Holy Spirit said to me, "You had a dream of the Indian taxi driver burning in fire at 5:00AM and you met the same real Indian taxi driver at 4:00PM on the same day in the streets of New York where mil-

lions of cars are running exactly on time. The meeting was prepared by the angels."
And then the Holy Spirit showed me a vision in which two angels were leading me and helping me all day long in New York.
Wherever I went, they went with me all day long. However the
Christians who do not have spiritual vision cannot see the angels
helping them.
Also the Holy Spirit showed me that two other angels were
guiding the Indian taxi driver all day long.
When the Indian taxi driver tries to stop his taxi to receive a
customer, the angels know in advance where the person wants to
go, therefore if someone wants to go a long way from our meeting, the angels obstruct the taxi driver from stopping his taxi.
One angel holds the handle of the steering gear of the taxi and he
drives the taxi, stepping on the gas pump. Then the Indian driver
steps on the brake hard but the taxi goes in the direction where
the angel drives to.

In the streets of New York, there are many places where the
traffic is blocked because of construction or accidents, but the
angels know in advance where the traffic is blocked. Therefore
the angels guide the taxi driver to the road where the traffic is not
congested. Also the Holy Spirit moved even the heart of the
Indian driver who was not believing in God and led him to follow the way the angels guided.
The Holy Spirit showed me the following: when the taxi came to
me, it was close to the rush hour, so many people tried to stop the
taxi. However the angels did not stop the taxi and drove the
empty taxi through many blocks without stopping for other
people who tried to stop the taxi, but stopped the taxi in front of
me, precisely on time. In this way, the angels prepared for me to
really meet the Indian taxi driver who was burning in fire at
5:00AM in my dream, at 4:00PM on the same day without any

appointment.

The angels of the Holy Spirit help Christians who really believe in God in the same way as they did for me, wherever they are in the world. But the Christians who do not have their spiritual vision opened cannot see the angels helping them.
Most of the Christians who believe in God pray really hard for God to help them when they face any problems which are impossible for them to solve. Many such Christians find that the difficult problems for which they were praying are solved by themselves or by some person's help. Or sometimes unexpected blessings come to their family or company.

Some Christians who did not experience the Holy Spirit's miracles say, "It was solved by accident or it was good luck." In reality, they were solved by the angels sent by the Holy Spirit whom you cannot see because your spiritual vision is not opened. The angels of the Holy Spirit always help and protect the Christians with good belief, from dangers they may face.
Sometimes they may be injured in car accidents or by others. All such accidents injuring Christians are caused by demons and evil spirits, the soldiers of Satan. Spirits cannot be seen by normal people.
But many of the Christians who experienced a lot of the Holy Spirit's miracles and received the Holy Spirit's overflowing power and anointing have their spiritual vision opened. The Holy Spirit shows spiritual visions to such Christians, whenever the Holy Spirit wants to.

We should not ignore the ministry by the angels, even if we cannot see them help us while we are trapped in difficult situations. I have seen too many times the angels helping Christians with strong belief in God, and the angels arresting the evil spirits and throwing them into the fiery lake.

If the angels did not help or protect the Christians who really believed in God, they would face traffic accidents, disaster, calamity or incurable sickness in their family every day. However the angels of the Holy Spirit protect you always 24 hours a day and lead you to the way of eternal life, even if you cannot see them. Therefore the evil spirits, demons or the soldiers of Satan cannot harm the good Christians at all.

Under the name of Jesus, we pray for the Almighty Heavenly Father to protect all the readers of this book from any dangers they may face in the world and to give His unlimited blessing to them and their children through generations. Amen

The Holy Spirit's words were given in early morning prayer on July 7, 2000.

3. When I drive a car, angels guide and protect me

I want to testify about the incidents I really experienced with angels. I want to turn all the glory to the Almighty Heavenly Father.

Luke 1: 10-16, 26-38 And the whole multitude of the people was praying outside at the hour of incense. Then an angel of the Lord appeared to him, standing on the right side of the altar of incense.

And when Zacharias saw him, he was troubled, and fear fell upon him.

But the angel said to him, "Do not be afraid, Zacharias, for your prayer is heard; and your wife Elizabeth will bear you a son, and you shall call his name John. And you will have joy and gladness, and many will rejoice at his birth. For he will be great in the sight of the Lord, and shall drink neither wine nor strong drink. He will also be filled with the Holy Spirit, even from his mother's womb. And he will turn many of the children of Israel to the Lord their God.

Now in the sixth month the angel Gabriel was sent by God to a city of Galilee named Nazareth, to a virgin betrothed to a man whose name was Joseph, of the house of David. The virgin's name was Mary.

And having come in, the angel said to her, "Rejoice, highly fa- favored one, the Lord is with you; blessed are you among women!" But when she saw him, she was troubled at his saying, and considered what manner of greeting this was.

Then the angel said to her, "Do not be afraid, Mary, for you have found favor with God. And behold, you will conceive in your womb and bring forth a Son, and shall call His name JESUS. He will be great, and will be called the Son of the Highest; and the Lord God will give Him the throne of His father David. And He will reign over the house of Jacob forever, and of His kingdom there will be no end."

Then Mary said to the angel, "How can this be, since I do not know a man?" And the angel answered and said to her, "The Holy Spirit will come upon you, and the power of the Highest will overshadow you; therefore, also, that Holy One who is to be born will be called the Son of God.

Now indeed, Elizabeth your relative has also conceived a son in her old age; and this is now the sixth month for her who was called

**barren. For with God nothing will be impossible." Then Mary
said, "Behold the maidservant of the Lord! Let it be to me according to your word." And the angel departed from her.**

After I finished reading the bible passages above, the Holy Spirit
said to me, **"Write down everything about how the angels
helped you recently and deliver your testimony to all the
people in the world."**

1) The Holy Spirit's leading and the angels' protect -ion

I did not have many experiences with angels' ministry. I have
read many beautiful stories about angels in the Bible, but I didn't
have many direct experiences. However since April, 1996 I have
seen many times that angels were helping me in prayers and
sometimes they arrested evil spirits and demons and chased
them away from patients for whom I was praying.
Sometimes when the evil spirits and demons, the soldiers of
Satan, tried to attack me, angels appeared immediately and
helped me and they destroyed all the evil spirits with Jesus' lights.
I want to express my greatest thanks to the Almighty God who
sends angels to help me whenever I am in trouble. The angels are
also the servants of the Almighty God, once they receive the
command of God, they obey the words of God with all the power
they have.

It is the angels who fight desperately for God regardless of the
danger, once they receive the words of the Lord. There are innumerable Christians who know the words of the Holy Spirit
given to them are the real word from God, but they think about
the results they may face or about their own interests. Therefore

many of them don't obey the Holy Spirit or they ignore the words of the Holy Spirit, if following the words of the Holy Spirit would be a disadvantage to their own interests.

However the angels know very well about God. If they do not obey the words of the Holy Spirit just once, they know what kind of results will come to them. Therefore upon their receiving the words of the Lord, they work desperately to realize the words of the Holy Spirit.

Since April, 1996 the Holy Spirit began to show me that angels were helping and protecting me from danger whenever I was in trouble. One Friday early in morning prayer, a giant angel whose height was about twice of a normal person appeared suddenly before me. He said very politely to me, **"I am the captain of the angels that will guide you today to the church of Pastor Y. where the Holy Spirit ministers powerfully."**

After saying that, he disappeared. Since then, on the way to the church of Pastor Y. in New Jersey, I have seen angels many times who were guiding me on the side and over the top of my car on the highway.

On November 7, 1997, Friday, I wanted to be absent from going to church because of my having to drive many hours. At about 5:00 PM I left my home for the church in New Jersey to attend the Holy Spirit service starting at 8:30 pm, and left the church at about 12:30AM after finishing the service in the church. On the way back home when I am sleepy, I take one or two hours of sleep in the car, then I arrive at my home at about 5:00AM in the morning. It took about 12 hours for me every Friday when I was going to the church of Pastor Y. in New Jersey for about 10 months in 1997.

Without the help of the angels of the Holy Spirit, it would be very difficult for normal Christians not fully filled with the Holy Spirit to attend that church once every week for 10 months continuously.

Around February 10, 1997, the Holy Spirit introduced me to Pastor Y. who was fully filled in the Holy Spirit. Since that time every Friday when they have the Holy Spirit spiritual service, I have attended without fail for the last 10 months. That is because the Holy Spirit asked me to attend the Holy Spirit Service without fail.

Last Friday also in early morning prayer, the captain of the angels that would guide me said to me, "We are ready to guide you to the Holy Spirit's spiritual service to be held at the church of Pastor Y. tonight." The captain of the angels said to me, "We will guide you safely, do not worry about driving." I said to him, "I cannot go to the church today, because I am tired of driving such long hours" But the angel said to me, "You should go to the church because the Holy Spirit waited for one week for this Holy Spirit's spiritual service."

According to the words of the captain of angels, I left home with my wife for the church at 5:20pm. After driving about 40 minutes, I felt sleepy. But the Holy Spirit said to me, "Do not worry about your being sleepy, I will wake you up," while moving my body powerfully from the bottom of my belly to my chest and shaking my shoulders.

As soon as the Holy Spirit began to move my body from the bottom of my stomach to my chest powerfully and shaking my shoulders, the sleepy feeling in my eyes was gone immediately in the strong Holy Spirit's power.

When I was about halfway to the church on the New Jersey

Turnpike, I saw several angels escorting my car on both sides, above in the air, in front and behind the car. I could see them clearly with spiritual vision, which was open. It was a beautiful scene which I had never seen before in my whole life. When the car behind me was coming too close to my car, two angels appeared at behind my car and said to me, while running, "Chairman, don't worry at all about the cars coming too close. If that car comes too close, we will push it away."

Sometimes when a big truck passed by my car, two angels running between my car and the truck said to me, "Do not worry at all about the truck, if it comes too close, we will push it away from you." Sometimes when I drove too fast, an angel appeared in front of my car running backwards, and makes a signal with his hands to slow the speed like a policeman.

Sometimes when I drive rough, the angel holds the steering wheel with one of his hands through the glass of the car, together with me, to prevent any accidents I may cause. Sometimes when I need to step on the brake, the angel sitting by my seat steps on the brake. When I am sleepy, the Holy Spirit wakes me up by moving my stomach with His power.

My wife sitting next me cannot see the angels who help me to drive the car and wake me from sleep, because she doesn't have open spiritual vision. I told her everything that the angels were doing for me. She wanted to see them like me, but she couldn't see them, so she slept in the car.

I was very pleased to drive while talking with the Holy Spirit and receiving the protection of the angels. Meanwhile we arrived at the church of Pastor Y. It was 8:15 pm. That is, we arrived 15 minutes before the church service. The captain of the angels said to me, "We welcome you to this church. Until you finish your church service, we will wait for you outside the church." There was, in the corner of the parking lot, a small fire in the open air which turned into a large pillar of fire high in the air, shining light all around very far, and angels were flying and circling around the pillar of fire.

Exodus 13: 21-22 And the LORD went before them by day in a pillar of cloud to lead the way, and by night in a pillar of fire to give them light, so as to go by day and night. He did not take away the pillar of cloud by day or the pillar of fire by night from before the people.

Acts 2: 2-4 And suddenly there came a sound from heaven, as of a rushing mighty wind, and it filled the whole house where they were sitting. Then there appeared to them divided tongues, as of fire, and one sat upon each of them. And they were all filled with the Holy Spirit and began to speak with other tongues, as the Spirit gave them utterance.

The angels stand sentry, in turn, on every entrance door, exit door, window and even above my car in the air. I asked why so many angels were standing on sentry? Satan and evil spirits are always trying to attack Reverend Joe,

the Chairman of the Whole Race Gospel & Missionary Service, who is fully filled with the Holy Spirit's anointing, if they have any chance, in order to obstruct the worldwide Holy Spirit movement.

Therefore the angels who were trained to destroy the evil spirits, sent by the Holy Spirit, are guarding Pastor Joe, the Chairman of the Whole Race Gospel & Missionary Service 24 hours a day. He said to me, "Please do not worry about anything."

Hebrews 1: 14 Are they not all ministering spirits sent forth to

minister for those who will inherit salvation?

As soon as I sat down in the church, Jesus, who appeared as a giant, began to write on the wall. After that, the whole scene of the words were immediately changed into a white cloud written high up in the light blue sky in the fall. The Holy Spirit loves you and He explained how to revive the Holy Spirit's Movement all over the world. The Holy Spirit asked me to send messages to people. He also told me what I have to do in detail.

Meanwhile when I fell on the floor under the power of the Holy Spirit, a snow white dove embraced in a bright light was sitting on my forehead and the dove walked slowly on my face, chest and belly. Then the dove wrote some words for me to understand in Korean. When the dove was speaking to me, she wrote words in Korean while moving her beak and head. The dove also explained everything about how to revive the Holy Spirit movement all over the world.

Sometimes when I drive my car, the snow white dove appears and on my head and moves my shoulders and head back and forth, while making the sound, "Kuruk kuruk." The dove sometimes appears when I pray early in the morning too. Sometimes the dove sits on my head while making flying sounds.
Whenever the dove sits on my head, all the worry or uneasiness in my heart immediately goes away and my heart becomes very peaceful. When I drive with my wife, the white dove appears and sits on my wife's head, then moves to me, and moves back and forth. I can see clearly the dove but my wife cannot see the dove. So I tell her that a white dove is sitting on her head and is moving back and forth between me and her.

Matthew 3: 16-17 When He had been baptized, Jesus came up

**immediately from the water; and behold, the heavens were
opened to Him, and He saw the Spirit of God descending like a
dove and alighting upon Him. And suddenly a voice came from
heaven, saying, "This is My beloved Son, in whom I am well
pleased."**

The appearance of the dove means the presence of the Holy
Spirit. The Holy Spirit appears sometimes as Jesus Christ,
sometimes as a small white lamb, sometimes as a dove or
sometimes as crystal clear living water like a sea, river or lake.
All of these show the appearance of the Holy Spirit.

At about 12:30AM the Holy Spirit church service was all over,
and when I began to drive the long way home, I saw the angels
again who were escorting and protecting me all around my car
exactly same as when I was on my way to church. At the same
time, Jesus was sitting in the back seat of my car and began
talking to me. Jesus told me how to revive the Holy Spirit
Movement all over the world. Whenever I felt sleepy, the Holy
Spirit poured the Holy Spirit's power on me and moved my
stomach powerfully with His power. Then the sleepy feeling
immediately went away like when I was on the way to the church.

After driving for about one hour, I took a short sleep at the rest
area by the highway, and I began to drive again. Whenever I felt
sleepy, the Holy Spirit shook my shoulders, then the sleepy
feeling went away immediately. While talking with the Holy
Spirit and watching the angels escorting my car, I drove all the
way, therefore I didn't feel lonesome at all but I felt very pleased.

Jesus said to me, "The angels who escort you now are always
protecting you and all your family members wherever they are in
the world." You receive the messages from the Holy Spirit and

you deliver them to the people whom the Holy Spirit asks you to. Therefore the evil spirits, demons, and the soldiers of Satan always try to attack you, to sever the relationship between you and the Holy Spirit.

In the last 8 years, the evil spirits and demons attempted to kill you more than 100 times, but every time when they tried to kill you, the Holy Spirit and His angels saved you from the Satanic intrigues which plotted to destroy you completely in this world. Satan and his soldiers, evil spirits and demons attempted to kill you so many times as you know.

Therefore the Holy Spirit assigned many angels who were trained especially to destroy evil spirits to protect you from their attacks 24 hours a day. Angels are assigned to all the Christians who really believe in God to protect them from danger 24 hours a day. According to the callings given to each Christian by God, the numbers of angels are assigned.

Pastor Y. is also a target that Satan wants to destroy, therefore the Holy Spirit assigned many angels trained especially to destroy the evil spirits to protect him from any attacks by Satan's soldiers.

I asked the Holy Spirit to show me the angels ministering for Pastor Y. The Holy Spirit showed me a scene in which Pastor Y. was preaching while holding a Bible in his right hand and two angels dressed in snow white long gowns were receiving his preaching words, standing at both sides of Pastor Y.

The scene was as follows. When Pastor Y. preached, crystal, shining, transparent drops of some liquid, like soap drops, rose up from Pastor Y.'s mouth and these drops fell into gold bowls which the angels held beside Pastor Y. The beautiful drops were so shiny and brilliant in the glory of the Almighty God that no one can see clearly with human eyes.

When I asked the Holy Spirit, what are these drops? He said to me, "These are the materials made especially by the power of the Almighty Father to permanently save the words of God. When the bowl was full, the angel covered it with a lid made of solid gold.

Revelation 8: 3-4 Then another angel, having a golden censer, came and stood at the altar. He was given much incense, that he should offer it with the prayers of all the saints upon the golden altar which was before the throne. And the smoke of the incense, with the prayers of the saints, ascended before God from the angel's hand.

At the same time the angel standing at the side received the golden bowl filled with the preaching of Pastor Y. and placed it on the golden tray and placed it on a table. When the preaching was over, the angels moved in turn all the golden bowls laid on the golden tray to a golden table with four wheels and a handle standing on the right side of the throne of the Almighty Heavenly Father.

At that place Jesus Christ explained to the Almighty Father, "This is the preaching of Pastor Y. who offered praising hymns and preaching to glorify the Heavenly Father." At the same time Jesus opened the lids of the golden bowls and showed them to the Heavenly Father. At that time the Heavenly Father received the golden bowls and saw them and Jesus was standing at the right side of the Father.

After the Heavenly Father looked at the beautiful, shining, brilliant drops of special liquid which held Pastor Y.'s preaching in the golden bowls, He gave them to Jesus, who gave them to the angels standing by Him. The angels who received the golden bowls placed the brilliant, shining, beautiful drops into a big golden storage can and covered it with a big golden cover. There were many such golden storage cans on the golden shelves. The angels said to me, "One can belongs to each Christian who really believes in the Trinity God as written in the Bible." And he said to me, "The golden can into which the angel just put the brilliant, shining drops belongs to Pastor Y."

The angels cleaned the golden bowls with clear water in a golden sink and dried them with towels from the kitchen and began to receive the preaching of Pastor Y. And the angel said to me, "Next time also, when Pastor Y. preaches, we will use the golden bowls to receive his preaching."

Revelation 5: 8 Now when He had taken the scroll, the four living creatures and the twenty-four elders fell down before the Lamb, each having a harp, and golden bowls full of incense, which are the prayers of the saints.

At that time, the Almighty Heavenly Father said, "My beloved son, Pastor Y., I love you. Whatever is hard and difficult for you to do for the Worldwide Holy Spirit Revival Movement, do your best with all your power and heart in glorifying the Almighty Heavenly Father. In heaven great rewards are waiting for you."

At the same time the Holy Spirit showed me the outside of the church, where many angels who were specially armed to fight and destroy the evil spirits were standing sentry. In the parking lot of the church, there was an open fire whose fire column rose high up in the air and many angels were flying around the fire column or standing around the open fire.
The light from the fire was so bright that its light shone very far. The Holy Spirit said to me, "This is not normal fire, but it is the fire of the Holy Spirit's power. The angels receive the power of

the Holy Spirit from this fire, therefore many angels were flying or standing around the fire to receive the power of the Holy Spirit.

When the evil spirits or demons see the fire, they run away from it in fear. At the side of the church, there were several grotesque animals that looked like hippopotamuses. These animals tried to attack Pastor Y., however several armed angels appeared and they desperately fought the grotesque animals and finally several big round flying saw blades came from heaven and cut the animals into many pieces and put them into strong steel cages. Angels carried the cages high up in the air above the fire sea and dumped the animals into the fire sea which is burning forever.

When several of the animals were destroyed, all other animals ran away from the scene. After showing the fighting between the angels and demons, Jesus said to me, "You have seen and experienced many spiritual wars and fights in the last 8 years, so you don't have any problem watching such fearful fighting. But it will cause some problems for Pastor Y. to prepare his preaching. therefore I don't show such fearful spiritual fights to Pastor Y. But I want you to tell all the scenes you saw today to Pastor Y. without adding or deducting anything."

And He said, "Many angels are assigned to the church of Pastor Y. to protect many Christians who are members of the church and who really believe in the Almighty God. Angels are assigned even to the pastors through whom the Holy Spirit is not ministering so powerfully. However Satan doesn't need to attack them, because Satan, demons and evil spirits sometimes deceive them and use them for Satanic purposes."

The Holy Spirit said the following to me, "That is, according to the callings of God given to each pastor or saint, the numbers of the angels assigned to them are decided.

Satan, his soldiers, demons and evil spirits always try to attack you because of the callings of God given to you by the Almighty Father, therefore many angels are armed and specially trained to protect you from spiritual war. These angels fight desperately against evil spirits to protect you from the Satanic intrigues to kill you."

The word given by the Holy Spirit was:

Mark 16: 15-16 And He said to them, "Go into all the world and and preach the gospel to every creature. He who believes and is baptized will be saved; but he who does not believe will be condemned."

The Holy Spirit said, **"Now you receive the messages from the Holy Spirit and deliver them to the pastors of big churches whom the Holy Spirit asks you to deliver to, the purpose of your delivering the messages of the Holy Spirit is also to deliver the gospel all over the world."**

He also told me how to revive the Holy Spirit Movement all over the world. The purpose of the Holy Spirit ministering all over the world is to deliver the gospel to all the people in the world and to lead them to Jesus for all Christians to go to the heaven where they can enjoy eternal life, praising the Almighty Heavenly Father.

God loves all His sons and daughters like this. The Almighty Father sends His angels to all His beloved sons and daughters to protect them from the attacks of Satan and his soldiers, and lead them step by step with the Holy Spirit. The Christians who have their spiritual vision opened may see all the works the angels are doing for you now.

The Holy Spirit's words were given in early morning prayer on December 5, 1997.

4. The Holy Spirit's living water like the sea

One night in September 1997, at a Holy Spirit ministering service held at Pastor Y.'s church I fell on the floor for about 30 minutes under the power of the Holy Spirit. When I was going home Jesus was sitting in the back seat of my car and the bottom of the car was full of crystal clear water and many big swimming carps.

I asked Jesus, "What is this?"
He said to me, "This water is the Holy Spirit's living water and these fish are the people whom you will lead to Jesus. When I came home, I found that Jesus had already filled the bathtub with the Holy Spirit's living water which was crystal clear with many big carps swimming in it. The sink tub in the kitchen was also full of water and several fish were in it.
After several minutes, our entire first floor and upstairs were filled with clear water and I found that around my house a clear transparent fence made of plastic was installed. And inside the fence, was full of crystal clear water and many big carps were swimming in the water. Jesus said to me, "The big carps here are the kings, presidents of many countries, and worldwide business

tycoons whom you will lead to Jesus with the Holy Spirit's power. They will financially help and support you in reviving the Holy Spirit movement all over the world."

All our family members were walking here and there in the clear water, and outside of my home several angels were standing on sentry in the water and high in the air. Soon the water flowing from my house completely covered the whole city, field and mountains around my house and it became a big clear sea.

Ezekiel 47: 1-10 Then he brought me back to the door of the temple; and there was water, flowing from under the threshold of the temple toward the east, for the front of the temple faced east; the water was flowing from under the right side of the temple, south of the altar.

He brought me out by way of the north gate, and led me around on the outside to the outer gateway that faces east; and there was water, running out on the right side. And when the man went out to the east with the line in his hand, he measured one thousand cubits, and he brought me through the waters; the water came up to my ankles.

Again he measured one thousand and brought me through the waters; the water came up to my knees. Again he measured one thousand and brought me through; the water came up to my waist. Again he measured one thousand, and it was a river that I could not cross; for the water was too deep, water in which one must swim, a river that could not be crossed.

He said to me, "Son of man, have you seen this?" Then he brought me and returned me to the bank of the river. When I returned, there, along the bank of the river, were very many trees on one side and the other.

Then he said to me: "This water flows toward the eastern region, goes down into the valley, and enters the sea. When it reaches the sea, its waters are healed. And it shall be that every

living thing that moves, wherever the rivers go, will live. There
will be a very great multitude of fish, because these waters go
there; for they will be healed, and everything will live wherever
the river goes.

It shall be that fishermen will stand by it from En Gedi to En
Eglaim; they will be places for spreading their nets. Their fish will
be of the same kinds as the fish of the Great Sea, exceedingly
many.

John 7: 37-38 On the last day, that great day of the feast, Jesus
stood and cried out, saying, "If anyone thirsts, let him come to Me
and drink. He who believes in Me, as the Scripture has said, out of
his heart will flow rivers of living water."

Some parts of the sea were divided into three big blocks with
iron wire nets. In the first block which is like a big fishing
ground, many big carps like whales were swimming but all of
them were hooked to fishing lines. And Jesus Christ was holding
all the fishing lines.
Jesus gave me all the fishing lines and said to me, "These carps
are the kings and presidents of many countries and world-class
giant business tycoons whom you will lead to Jesus with the
Holy Spirit's power. And these fish were pulled without any
resistance in the direction Jesus was leading to. The number of
these fish were so many that no one could count them.

The second block was filled with carps as big as sharks. And all
of them were hooked to fishing lines which were held by Jesus
Christ. Jesus said to me, "These carps are the giant politicians
and big businessmen in the world whom you will lead to Jesus."
The number of the fish was so many that no one could count
them.

In the third block, there were innumerable small fish swimming. Jesus said to me, "These fish also are the ones whom you will lead to Jesus. They are scattered all over the world."

There was a giant raft floating on the sea and on the raft was a giant steel plate on which there was an open fire column rising up high in the air. Some of angels were flying around the fire column and some were on the steel plate around the open fire.
I went to a church I was familiar with, and that church was not filled with the Holy Spirit. Outside of the church water came up to half the wall of the church, but inside the church the water which came in through the cracks of the windows and doors came up to my ankles. But as soon as I walked in the sanctuary, the water followed me and filled the whole church and church members were dancing in water.

The Holy Spirit showed me Pastor Y.'s church where the Holy Spirit's service was being held every week was underwater. Soon all the houses in the city were also covered in water like a sea. On the sea water a giant raft was floating and on top of the raft a giant steel plate covered it and on the steel plate, an open fire was rising high in the air like a column. Several angels were flying around the fire column and some of the angels were standing around the fire on the steel plate.
The Holy Spirit showed me Toronto Airport Christian Fellowship Church which we visited in October, 1997 for 10 days. During our visits to that church the Holy Spirit showed me that church was all covered in water like the sea and a giant steel plate was floating about 3 feet deep from the top of the water and all Christians who visited that church were dancing on the steel plate.
I testified what I saw in a vision at the platform in front of many thousands of the visitors of the church. Today the Holy Spirit

showed me again that the water remains the same as before at that church. On the sea water, a giant raft was floating and on the raft a giant steel plate covered the raft, on which open fire was burning and rising up high in the air, with angels flying around the fire column.

Sometime after Jesus showed me a giant globe (the earth) was floating in the air and the Holy Spirit's living water filled every place. At the same time, Jesus Christ embraced in light holding a Bible in one hand and a lamb in His other hand, He said to me, "As I showed you just now, I will cover this world with the Holy Spirit's living water, and I will baptize all the people with the Holy Spirit power and will revive the Holy Spirit's movement all over the world.
I try to save all the people in the world and lead them to heaven."
I want you to deliver all the messages I give you to the kings and presidents of many countries or world-class business tycoons whomever I ask you to deliver immediately without fail.

Be bold and brave in delivering the Holy Spirit's words to the people whom I ask you to deliver. Do not worry about them, I will be always with you and My angels will protect you from any dangers in the world.

I love you and I am blessing you unlimitedly.

The Holy Spirit's words were given at 4:50AM in morning prayer on November 10, 1997

CHAPTER 11

The Holy Spirit's words given to people who obstruct the Worldwide Holy Spirit Revival Movement

1. The Holy Spirit's words were given to a pastor who was obstructing the Worldwide Holy Spirit Revival Movement

2. The Holy Spirit who uses policemen as angels

3. Even famous, highly respected pastors will be abandoned forever, if they disobey the Holy Spirit to the end.

4. To God's servants who cannot discern the Holy Spirit's words

1. The Holy Spirit's words were given to a pastor who was obstructing the Worldwide Holy Spirit Revival Movement

These Holy Spirit's words were given to the preacher after he finished preaching on Sunday, July 19, 1998. The pastor is a very famous Presbyterian reverend in Christian society in Korea and the USA. He was one of the pastors who opposed the Holy Spirit movement the most strongly in the USA.

He was a pastor who chased out Christians who spoke in heavenly tongues in early morning prayer at his church. When he preached, comparing the miracles of the idols at his church on Sunday July 19, 1998, the Holy Spirit gave this message to him at the same evening.

My beloved son, Pastor!

I love you. I gave you a great mission to deliver the gospel to all the people in the world. However you cannot understand the truth and you are wandering in the darkness.

Your preaching at the 9:00AM Sunday Service today "The life which pleases God."

Hebrews 11: 6 But without faith it is impossible to please Him, for he who comes to God must believe that He is, and that He is a rewarder of those who diligently seek Him.

Hebrews 13: 16 But do not forget to do good and to share, for with such sacrifices God is well pleased.

In your preaching, you distorted several things in the God's truth.

1) Why do you compare God's healing ministry with idols' work?

Why do you compare the holy and divine healing ministry of God with the idolatrous Buddhist monks who are controlled by Satan?
They are people who cannot be saved worshiping idols and are being controlled by Satan. There exists no Buddhist paradise in the universe. Here is something which the Holy Spirit showed to Pastor Joshua D.S. Joe about the idolatrous religions. I want you to refer to them. Wherever you go, you have to believe and testify to the people that you are one of His sons who receive God's unlimited love. You have to act as God's son.

2) The Holy Spirit's words were given after his preaching that Buddhist monks speak in tongue

You said in your Sunday sermon that even the Buddhist monks in the Buddhist temples speak in tongues. They do not speak in the Heavenly Father's tongue but they speak in Satan's tongue. When the monks or sorceress of Buddhism speak in Satan's tongue, if a Christian pastor or believer of God who is fully-filled with the Holy Spirit's power speaks in Heavenly tongues cursing Satan, the monks or sorceress speaking in Satan's tongue shall die on the spot.

Enclosed you find the testimony of Missionary Joshua D.S. Joe
who experienced this at a church in Seoul, Korea.
I want you to read it. From now on you don't have to take example of the things that the idolaters controlled by Satan are
doing. You are one of the well known leaders of Christian society in Korea and the USA.
If you compare the Holy Spirit's holy and divine miracles with
examples of the things that Buddhist monks, idolaters, are doing,
whom will the Christians listening to your preaching in Korea
and the USA follow? Whoever tells you anything, you have to
deliver only the truth of God's words to the Christians listening
to your preaching.

**John 14: 6 Jesus said to him, "I am the way, the truth, and the
life. No one comes to the Father except through Me."**

**John 3: 3 Jesus answered and said to him, "Most assuredly, I
say to you, unless one is born again, he cannot see the kingdom of God."**

**John 3: 5 Jesus answered, "Most assuredly, I say to you,
unless one is born of water and the Spirit, he cannot enter
the kingdom of God."**

"No one can come to the Heavenly Father except through the
Holy Spirit's leading."

**Romans 8: 5-8, 12-14 For those who live according to the flesh
set their minds on the things of the flesh, but those who live according to the Spirit, the things of the Spirit. For to be carnally
minded is death, but to be spiritually minded is life and peace.
Because the carnal mind is enmity against God; for it is not sub-**

ject to the law of God, nor indeed can be.

So then, those who are in the flesh cannot please God. Therefore, brethren, we are debtors--not to the flesh, to live according to the flesh.

For if you live according to the flesh you will die; but if by the Spirit you put to death the deeds of the body, you will live. For as many as are led by the Spirit of God, these are sons of God.

As shown in the Bible passages above, those who live according to the flesh will be dead. It means that the people following the greed of flesh will not be able to go to heaven. But those who live according to the Spirit will live. It means such people will be led to eternal life in heaven. People who are led only by the Spirit of God are the sons of God, and they will be led to heaven.

Galatians 5: 16-26 I say then: Walk in the Spirit, and you shall not fulfill the lust of the flesh. For the flesh lusts against the Spirit, and the Spirit against the flesh; and these are contrary to one another, so that you do not do the things that you wish. But if you are led by the Spirit, you are not under the law.

Now the works of the flesh are evident, which are: adultery, fornication, uncleanness, lewdness, idolatry, sorcery, hatred, contentions, jealousies, outbursts of wrath, selfish ambitions, dissensions, heresies, envy, murders, drunkenness, revelries, and the like; of which I tell you beforehand, just as I also told you in time past, that those who practice such things will not inherit the kingdom of God.

But the fruit of the Spirit is love, joy, peace, longsuffering, kindness, goodness, faithfulness, gentleness, self-control. Against such there is no law. And those who are Christ's have crucified the flesh with its passions and desires. If we live in the Spirit, let us also walk in the Spirit. Let us not become conceited, provoking one another, envying one another.

The Bible passages above clearly say, "In your body the Holy
Spirit and evils are against always each other. You all must follow the Holy Spirit's leading in deeds. Those who follow the
flesh's greed cannot inherit blessings from God. As I warned you
before, such people cannot enter the kingdom of God for the
eternal life.

Those who follow the Holy Spirit will bear the fruit of the Holy
Spirit. There is no law preventing such people from going to
heaven. It means that such people will be led to eternal life in
heaven by the Holy Spirit. Therefore I want all of you follow the
Holy Spirit's guidance, and all of you will be led to heaven where
you will enjoy everlasting life praising the Almighty Heavenly
Father.

**Revelation 2: 7 "He who has an ear, let him hear what the Spirit
says to the churches. To him who overcomes I will give to eat from
the tree of life, which is in the midst of the Paradise of God."**

The word churches here means the Christians who believe in
God.

**1 Corinthians 3: 16-17 Do you not know that you are the temple
of God and that the Spirit of God dwells in you? If anyone defiles
the temple of God, God will destroy him. For the temple of God is
holy, which temple you are.**

The clause "he who has an ear" means all the people in the world.
To him who overcomes I will give to eat from the tree of life,
which is in the midst of the Paradise of God.
It means only the Christians who follow the Holy Spirit's leading
will be led to the Paradise of God in heaven. Whoever he is, if he

doesn't follow the Holy Spirit will be abandoned into the fiery sea. I think you will understand the real meaning of this sentence.

Acts 2: 11 "He who has an ear, let him hear what the Spirit says to the churches. He who overcomes shall not be hurt by the second death."

The above written Bible passage clearly says to you, "He who overcomes shall not be hurt by the second death.
That is, only the people who follow the Holy Spirit's guidance will be led to heaven, but the souls who do not follow the Holy Spirit shall be abandoned into the everlastingly burning fiery lake in hell.

Revelation 20: 13-14 The sea gave up the dead who were in it, and Death and Hades delivered up the dead who were in them. And they were judged, each one according to his works. Then Death and Hades were cast into the lake of fire. This is the second death.

Wherever you go in the world, I want you to deliver the truth of God's words to all the people you meet. It is the mission God gives you, to deliver only the truth of God's words to all the students in your theological seminary and Christians in the churches where you will preach in the world.

3) The Holy Spirit's word about the depth of faith
You preached about the depth of belief.

Mark 16: 17-18 And these signs will follow those who believe: In My name they will cast out demons; they will speak with new

**tongues; they will take up serpents; and if they drink anything
deadly, it will by no means hurt them; they will lay hands on the
sick, and they will recover.**

As said in the Bible passages above, a belief trusting the word of
God as it is written and following it in deed, that is the belief
which can move the Holy Spirit's mercy. Without such a belief it
is difficult to move the Holy Spirit to heal sick patients.

Without believing the Bible completely, and without following
the words of God in deed, Christians or pastors who only believe
in God by mouth cannot move the Holy Spirit to perform miracles. The Holy Spirit uses Christians or pastors who are fully
filled with the Holy Spirit, having a lot of experience of the Holy
Spirit's Ministry and believing the words of God completely as
an instrument to heal sick people.

When you lay your hands on sick people, if the sick do not recover, you have to improve your belief to believe the Bible
100% and follow God's word in deed first.

If you continuously receive the Holy Spirit's powerful baptism
for yourself, the flesh's greed, selfishness, and stubborn heart
will be removed from you by the Holy Spirit's power. Then cast
out in the name of Jesus Christ all the evil spirits, demons, and
devils that were obstructing you from having the close relationship with the Holy Spirit.

After that confess all your sins from your childhood before God,
and then the Holy Spirit will begin to perform miracles through
you. Such believers will be led by the Holy Spirit. Only the Holy
Spirit can perform miracles through your body together with the
word of God.

4) After preaching that the Holy Spirit's healing ministry is not important

As mentioned in the above statement, it is not a regular faith when a Christian or pastor lays his or her hands on the sick and the sick recover. Those who follow the flesh's greed, human reason, selfishness, and the deceit of Satan cannot move the Holy Spirit to heal the sick even if they believed God for many decades.

Only through the believers who believe in God fully and follow the words of God in deed, the Holy Spirit heals the sick in the name of Jesus, through the Holy Spirit's power and the words of the Almighty God. Now you may be able to understand how deep is the belief of Christians through whom the Holy Spirit heals the sick. From now on I want you never to preach about anything which will be a shade against the light of God.

5) Do not distort the truth, now you are obstructing the Holy Spirit's ministry

It is the Holy Spirit's power which is healing the sick and casting the demons, evil spirits and devils from the churches (Christians' flesh) in the name of Jesus Christ. The things that Jesus did the most when He was in the world 2000 years ago were to cure the sick, raise the dead to life, and cast out evil spirits, demons and Satan from sick persons.

The Holy Spirit has performed innumerable miracles through the generations since Jesus went up to heaven, therefore there are countless Christians who truly believe in God all over the world.

It is only the Holy Spirit's power which cast evil spirits, demons and Satan out of sick people in the name of Jesus together with the words of God. No other idols can interfere with the Holy Spirit's ministry. How can the evil spirits, demons and devils

obstruct the Holy Spirit's miracles when Christians or pastors
command them to get out of sick people in the name of Jesus,
with the Holy Spirit's power, and the words of the Almighty
God? It is impossible for evil spirits to oppose the Holy Spirit's
ministry.
Those who libel My servants, the pastors filled in the Holy Spirit
who lead the Holy Spirit Services, as heresy, mysticism or hypnotism are committing great sins against the Holy Spirit. That is,
these actions arouse the wrath of God. As a result of such foolish
deeds, their own spirits are cast into the fiery lake in hell.

**Matthew 12: 31-32 "Therefore I say to you, every sin and blas-
phemy will be forgiven men, but the blasphemy against the Spirit
will not be forgiven men. Anyone who speaks a word against the
Son of Man, it will be forgiven him; but whoever speaks against
the Holy Spirit, it will not be forgiven him, either in this age or in
the age to come."**

The Holy Spirit asks you not to judge according to your own
selfishness, greed of flesh, stubborn mind, human reason and
thoughts, but follow the Holy Spirit's leading and words which
always glorify God and please the Holy Spirit and Jesus. And the
Almighty God will lift you up high above the world.

6) After preaching that the devil asks Christians to do the Worldwide Holy Spirit Revival Movement

Your preaching says that devils and evil spirits lure and charm
Christians to do the Holy Spirit movement all over the world.
This is against the truth of the words of God and you are driving
yourself and all the Christians in your church into the everlasting

426 Holy Spirit, Hover Over Me

sulfur, fiery lake of hell. Satan, the devils, demons and evil spirits are doing their best to obstruct and oppose by any means all over the world the Holy Spirit movement in which Christians and pastors filled in the Holy Spirit command to arrest all the evil spirits, demons, devils and Satan in the name of Jesus and throw them away into the fire sea of hell.

Because good Christians and pastors who have a lot of experience with the Holy Spirit's powerful baptism curse the evil spirits, demons and devils and command to arrest all of them in the name of Jesus and cast them out of the sick people into the fiery lake of hell.

Therefore all the evil spirits and devils oppose and obstruct the Holy Spirit movement desperately with deceits and by all means. Because the evil spirits which were dwelling in the Christians who were not filled with the Holy Spirit and without any Holy Spirit power for many decades know that they will be bound by the Christians filled with the Holy Spirit power and will be commanded to come out of the Christians not filled with the Holy Spirit and will be thrown into the fire sea of hell. So the evil spirits fear most the Christians and pastors filled with the Holy Spirit.

Therefore your preaching which says that the evil spirits, demons and Satan decoy and lure the Christians and pastors who do the Holy Spirit movement all over the world is an absurd remark.

It distorts the truth of God's word, and does not match with human reason and common sense. You are now wandering in the darkness because of the deceit of Satan, while preaching the perversive remarks to the Christians in your church. Your foolish deeds of preaching, distorting the truth of God's words arouse the wrath of God and you are driving yourself and the Christians listening to your preaching in your church into the fiery lake of hell.

You know that it is the Holy Spirit who does the Holy Spirit
movement all over the world. But how are you who should deliver the truth of God's word distorting the truth and luring the
Christians in your church into the fiery lake?

**Matthew 15: 14 Let them alone. They are blind leaders of the
blind. And if the blind leads the blind, both will fall into a ditch.**

Because of your selfishness, stubborn mind, the greed of the
flesh and the obstruction of Satan, as the above written Bible
passage, you are a blind teacher who leads the blind into a ditch.
How can Satan and evil spirits ask the Christians and pastors to
do the Holy Spirit's movement which curses Satan's soldiers,
devils and demons and commands to arrest Satan and evil spirits
in the name of Jesus and throw them away into the fire sea of
hell? It is the devils, demons, religious spirits, evil spirits and
Satan that are opposing the Holy Spirit's movement all over the
world desperately by any means. It is the evil spirits dwelling in
your soul and flesh that prevent you from doing the Holt Spirit's
movement all over the world.
Therefore the Holy Spirit wants to pour the Holy Spirit's powerful anointing not only on the Christians in your church but also
all the Christians in the world in order to arrest all the evil spirits,
demons and devils in all the Christians in the name of Jesus and
cast them out of all the Christians in the world. It is God's intention that only the Holy Spirit should dwell in your body to
protect you from the evil spirits and lead you to heaven through
the Holy Spirit's leading.

This is spiritual war and without it you cannot be led by the Holy
Spirit to heaven. By doing so, the Holy Spirit will save you from
Satan's chains and drive away all the evil spirits which deceive
you from your flesh and He will lead you to heaven for your

eternal life. The worldwide Holy Spirit movement is a plan made by God's intention, therefore no one can change or move what was prepared according to God's plan. No one can challenge the Holy Spirit movement. Your foolish deeds of preaching, while distorting the truth of the God's intention, are driving not only yourself but the innocent Christians listening to your perversive preaching into the everlasting fiery lake of hell.

7) After preaching that miracles of the Holy Spirit are fearful and dangerous

You are preaching to the Christians in your church not to have a deep faith in God by saying that the Holy Spirit's ministry performing miracles and wonders is fearful and dangerous if something goes wrong. As explained in the above mentioned passages, those who truly believe in God and follow the Bible in deed and if they are baptized powerfully by the Holy Spirit and confess all their sins, the Holy Spirit performs miracles and wonders through such saints. The saint with the belief without the Holy Spirit's miracles and wonders is not fully grown. Jesus Christ said clearly as following:

Mark 16: 17-18 And these signs will follow those who believe: In My name they will cast out demons; they will speak with new tongues; they will take up serpents; and if they drink anything deadly, it will by no means hurt them; they will lay hands on the sick, and they will recover.

John 14: 12-14 "Most assuredly, I say to you, he who believes in Me, the works that I do he will do also; and greater works than these he will do, because I go to My Father. And whatever you ask in My name, that I will do, that the Father may be glorified in the

Son. If you ask anything in My name, I will do it."

Jesus said for you to measure the belief of Christians. In addition
to pastors and elders, anyone believing in God really can experience the Holy Spirit's miracles everyday. God gave His
unlimited Holy Spirit's power to arrest devils, demons and cast
them away from people who are suffering from evil spirits, to
His children, Christians who really believe in God.

Christianity is not a religion in which believers go to the church
once a week to worship and praise God. The Christians who
really believe in God and follow God's words in deed today also
experience the Holy Spirit's miracles every day, exactly as Jesus'
disciples did in the first century. The angels guide them on the
road and protect Christians and wake them when they are sleepy
while driving. And the angels sing psalms together with saints.
Sometimes the Holy Spirit gives His messages to His children to
deliver to someone the Holy Spirit wants.
The Christians who really believe God everyday experience all
kinds of miracles which modern scientists cannot prove or understand. The Holy Spirit gives His anointing to anyone who
really believes in God. How pitiful and miserable you are! You
know nothing about such things but deliver foolish preaching,
distorting the truth of God's words. It is the worldwide Holy
Spirit movement through which Jesus baptizes Christians with
the powerful Holy Spirit's anointing and leads them to heaven.

Read the following Bible passages. **Romans 8: 5-9, 11-14,
Galatians 5: 16-26 and Revelation 2: 7, 11, 17.**

   **Romans 8: 13 For if you live according to the flesh you will die;
but if by the Spirit you put to death the deeds of the body, you will
live.**

As in the Bible passages above, those who follow the Holy Spirit will be saved and led to eternal life by the Holy Spirit but those who follow the flesh will be dead. That is, they cannot be led to heaven but will be abandoned into the fire sea of hell.

Even if you believed Jesus all your life, if you cannot be led to heaven, what will you do? In order to solve all such problems, the Holy Spirit asks all His children, Christians all over the world, to participate in the worldwide Holy Spirit movement which will settle such spiritual problems.

You don't need to be fearful of evil spirits, Satan and demons. The Almighty Heavenly Father already gave the Holy Spirit's power and authority to arrest such evil spirits in the name of Jesus and throw them away into the fiery lake. You don't practice the Holy Spirit's power to arrest the evil spirits, therefore you don't know whether you received it or not. If you want, the Holy Spirit is pleased to give you the power to arrest the evil spirits.

How to discern between the Holy Spirit and evil spirits

The Holy Spirit gives the Holy Spirit anointing to discern the spirits to His children who really believe in God. How to discern the spirits on the basis of the Bible is recorded in this book in detail. The Holy Spirit gives His messages together with the Bible passages so you can easily discern the evil spirits. You don't need to worry about such things because the Holy Spirit will teach you in detail one by one.

In addition to that, you have the Bible with which you are able to compare the messages you receive from the Holy Spirit or the evil spirits. You may ask such questions to the pastors who have experienced a lot of the Holy Spirit's ministries. Or you may bring the spiritual problems to Missionary Joshua D.S. Joe, the author of this book.

Pastor Joe has been spiritually trained by the Holy Spirit for the last 13 years and he will teach you how to arrest evil spirits, demons and cast them out of your flesh, to discern between the Holy Spirit and evil spirits, how to pray for the sick, or any other spiritual problems you may have.

If there is anything that he didn't experience, he will ask the Holy Spirit, who will answer him immediately on the spot. I want you to abandon the fear of the Holy Spirit's miracles and wonders, but be a good pastor who is able to preach the truth of the Bible, God's word, to all the Christians in your church and theological seminary, like the disciples of Jesus Christ of the first century who were all martyred for the sake of Jesus.

Right at this moment the Holy Spirit performs miracles all over the world, exactly as in the first century when Jesus was living in the world. I want you to lead all the saints in your church and all the students in your theological seminary to participate in the worldwide Holy Spirit's movement where they can experience the Holy Spirit's miracles. I want you to be a faithful pastor who will preach the truth of God's words without distorting them even if you are at moment of being martyred like the disciples of Jesus.

Meanwhile I request you to have the belief like Shadrach, Me-shach, and Abed-Nego who kept their faith and didn't move even if the King, Nebuchandnezzar, said to them, "If you do not worship, you shall be cast immediately into the midst of the burning fiery furnace."

I love you. I want to give the powerful Holy Spirit anointing to you. Go to Pastor Y. or Missionary Joe, who will pray for the Holy Spirit to pour His powerful anointing for you. And confess all your sins before God and forgive all the persons who did anything wrong against you in the past. And believe God's words fully while following them in deed.

Do not try to judge the Holy Spirit's miracles by human reason, knowledge, common sense, or theology anymore. The Holy Spirit doesn't perform any miracles through such persons. Therefore the Holy Spirit doesn't perform any miracles through such pastors and elders who are serving only through their mouth, even if they believed Jesus for many decades.
If you follow the Holy Spirit's words which I gave you now, the Holy Spirit will pour His powerful anointing in your church and theological seminary. In addition to that, He will bless you and your family forever.

The Holy Spirit's words were given on the night of July 19, 1990 during prayer.

2. The Holy Spirit who uses policemen as angels

In April 1999, in a college auditorium in a large US city, there was a Holy Spirit congregation led by a well known Holy Spirit-filled pastor from Korea. At that time several Korean churches desperately opposed the Holy Spirit congregation being held in that city. However the meeting proceeded as planned. But the

churches which opposed the meeting libeled this pastor with
groundless false reports to the college. The libel was reported to
the college as follows.

The pastor who will lead the Holy Spirit meeting this time belongs to the church of the same sect whose 913 members committed suicide in Johnstown, South America many years ago.
And this time the pastor will lead the entire congregation to
commit group suicide in your school.
This groundless false report was secretly given to the college
administration office managing the auditorium. The Holy Spirit
meeting was scheduled to be held for three nights. However the
school administration office which received the groundless false
report was surprised, and canceled the third night's meeting
without any advance notice. The school administration office
didn't listen to anyone who told the truth.
No one could persuade the school at that time, and the third
meeting was canceled unconditionally by the school. The pastor
who prepared this meeting announced that he received the above
mentioned cancellation notice from the school suddenly, therefore he informed the congregation that the next meeting would
be held at a different place.

However the advertisements in the newspapers carried only the
college address. Therefore many Christians who wanted to come
to the meeting were not able to attend the congregation because
of the location change. All the Christians who heard the cancellation announcement were praying to Almighty God. The Holy
Spirit who knew, in advance, the groundless false libeling plot of
the churches opposing the Holy Spirit meeting, prepared His
miracles through the author of this book to prevent the cancellation of the Holy Spirit meeting.
The Holy Spirit did as follows. About three weeks before the

Holy Spirit meeting was scheduled to be held, the pastor who prepared the congregation asked me to arrange a police patrol in the meeting area. I prayed for a reply from the Holy Spirit, who told me to help the meeting by calling the police to arrange police security for the meeting. So the author of this book wrote a letter asking for police security for the Holy Spirit service. I received a response from the police saying that they would send three policemen for the security of the Holy Spirit meeting.

On the day of the Holy Spirit meeting, I called the pastor who requested that the police come to the meeting about 30 minutes ahead of time. However the pastor's wife told me that they didn't need police, so please cancel the police security.

However the Holy Spirit told me that we needed police security. When I called the police, they said that the policemen were already sent. When I arrived, three policemen were at the main entrance. The Holy Spirit asked me to take three sets of earphones and give one set to each policeman, so I gave one set to each policeman and told them that the preaching would be translated into English and to listen to the preaching. They were very happy to hear that the preaching would be translated into English.

The Holy Spirit's meeting was very successful and the policemen were very pleased with the preaching and they said, "We received great grace and were moved greatly by the Holy Spirit's ministry." And they thanked me many times for giving them the ear phones. When the school canceled the Holy Spirit meeting, the Holy Spirit gave me and my wife the following message.

"Ask the policemen who listened to the preaching in English last night to witness to the school that your church does not belong to the sect whose members committed suicide in Johnstown, South America. Ask them to testify that the preacher was not a pastor who would drive all the members

**to commit suicide, but he was a Holy Spirit-filled pastor who
moves the Holy Spirit to be present with the congregation."**

The Holy Spirit repeated the same message to me many times,
until I called the pastor who prepared the Holy Spirit's meeting.
Early in the morning I called him and gave him the phone number of the police and delivered the same message the Holy Spirit
gave me.
When the pastor called the police and asked the policeman to be
a witness of what they heard in English, the policeman was very
pleased to call the school administration and told them that the
pastor was a Holy Spirit-filled pastor through whom Jesus performs the Holy Spirit's miracles and they also received the great
grace.

The school administration officers who listened to the police
testimony understood that they were deceived by the people who
made groundless statements against the Holy Spirit's meeting.
And the school apologized for having canceled the meeting.
They asked the pastor who prepared the Holy Spirit's meeting to
resume, as scheduled. The meeting went on as planned, and
Satan's plot to oppose the Holy Spirit's meeting was completely
demolished.
All these were established with the help of the Holy Spirit. If the
Holy Spirit didn't help the meeting, the meeting might have been
completely canceled, and the pastor who prepared the meeting
might have been placed in a difficult position. However the Holy
Spirit, the Spirit of Almighty God who knew in advance everything about the devil's plot to cancel the meeting, asked the author of this book to arrange the police security. As a result of that,
the Holy Spirit used the policemen to help resume the Holy
Spirit's meeting as scheduled.
Satan and evil spirits spread groundless rumors against Holy

Spirit-filled pastors and Christians by any means. This intrigue was plotted by several persons opposing the Holy Spirit movement but this was controlled by the deceitful lies of Satan, demons and evil spirits.

Satan, devils, evil spirits and demons fear most the churches and prayer houses where the Holy Spirit performs miracles. Because the Holy Spirit-filled pastors or saints arrest Satan, demons, and evil spirits in the name of Jesus Christ, and cast them away from the sick. When the Holy Spirit comes into the heart of someone who was possessed by demons, devils, or evil spirits, all these dirty spirits must go out of the same person because of the Holy Spirit's power.

You will be able to fully understand the above statement if you read carefully,

"Why is the Worldwide Holy Spirit Revival Movement necessary?" and **"How to discern between the Holy Spirit and evil spirits,"** in this book.

Therefore the evil spirits living in the Christian who oppose the Holy Spirit movement tell all kinds of lies to the persons in whom the evil spirits are living, to obstruct the Holy Spirit's meetings by any means. Such persons do not understand that they are being deceived by Satan's groundless lies and they are doing things against Almighty God for the sake of evil spirits.

This is same as in the first century when Jesus' apostles like Peter or Paul were filled with the Holy Spirit and delivered Jesus' gospel all over the world. The Israelite religious leaders were jealous of the Holy Spirit's miracles performed through the apostles. They arrested them and put them into jail and sometimes killed them.

These kinds of deeds are great sins against Almighty God. The Holy Spirit showed me a scene of the fiery lake in hell where the

Israelite religious leaders and their followers who committed
greats sins against God by persecuting and killing the apostles of
Jesus, 2000 years ago, were crying and wailing forever. The
Holy Spirit said to me, "These people are the ones who crucified
Jesus on the cross and killed the Jesus' apostles and innumerable
Christians in the first century." They were all crying, wailing,
and weeping forever with loud screams and yelling in the ever
burning fire sea of hell.

**Matthew 12: 31-32 "Therefore I say to you, every sin and blas-
phemy will be forgiven men, but the blasphemy against the Spirit
will not be forgiven men. Anyone who speaks a word against the
Son of Man, it will be forgiven him; but whoever speaks against
the Holy Spirit, it will not be forgiven him, either in this age or in
the age to come."**

While explaining this Bible passage to me, the Holy Spirit said
clearly and powerfully, **"The deeds which oppose and obstruct the Holy Spirit's meeting are same blaspheming
against the Holy Spirit."**

**The Holy Spirit said to me, "Spread the fact to all over the
world that foolish human beings who are opposing and obstructing the Holy Spirit movement according to their own
greed, selfishness, for their own interests should not commit
such sins which will throw them away into the ever burning
fire in hell. They should understand that their deeds which
oppose the Holy Spirit movement are great sins blaspheming
the Holy Spirit."**

**Mark 3: 28-29, "Assuredly, I say to you, all sins will be forgiven
the sons of men, and whatever blasphemies they may utter; but he
who blasphemes against the Holy Spirit never has forgiveness, but**

is subject to eternal condemnation"

I tell you this as a servant who delivers the messages of the Holy Spirit to the people whom the Holy Spirit instructs. Innumerable persons who opposed and obstructed the Holy Spirit movement fell down permanently, and did not understand it themselves. I sincerely ask you never do such foolish deeds again. No one is allowed to do anything against Almighty God.

Such acts are same as the persons who try to demolish a rock which is bigger than the earth, with an egg. Your own deeds will only kill yourself. No one should do anything against the Holy Spirit's ministry. If you did blaspheme against the Holy Spirit's movement in the past, I want to ask you to confess your sins immediately, kneeling down before God, and praying for God to forgive your sins from your deep heart with tears in your eyes. God is love.

We should never obstruct the Holy Spirit's movement or ministry. I want you to read "How to discern between the Holy Spirit and evil spirits, which the Holy Spirit taught me on the basis of the Bible" in this book. Then you will clearly understand how to discern the spirits and the deeds which please God and the acts which displease Almighty God but please Satan or evil spirits. We all must do only the things which will please the Holy Spirit.

Psalm 100: 2-4 Serve the Lord with gladness; Come before His presence with singing. Know that the Lord, He is God; It is He who has made us, and not we ourselves; We are His people and the sheep of His pasture. Enter into His gates with thanksgiving, And into His courts with praise. Be thankful to Him, and bless His name.

In the first century a young man named Saul believed that any-

thing that the religious leaders of Israelites were doing was right,
for the sake of God. Therefore when the Israelites stoned
Stephen, who was full of the Holy Spirit, Saul consented to his
death. And Saul made havoc of the church, entering every house
and dragging out men and women who followed Jesus, committing them to prison.

In addition to that, he went to other countries and arrested
Christians and tried to bring them to Jerusalem to put them in jail.
But on the way to Damascus he met Jesus, embraced with the
light, which blinded him.

He regained his sight by the Holy Spirit's healing power through
the prayer of Ananias, who was one of the apostles of Jesus.
After that he came to understand that he was doing (dragging
men and women following Jesus from every house and putting
them in jail and persecuting and killing them) was not right for
God. All that he was doing according to the instructions of Jewish religious leaders was against Almighty God.

**Acts 9: 1-9, 17-19, Then Saul, still breathing threats and mur-
der against the disciples of the Lord, went to the high priest and
asked letters from him to the synagogues of Damascus, so that if
he found any who were of the Way, whether men or women, he
might bring them bound to Jerusalem.**

**As he journeyed he came near Damascus, and suddenly a light
shone around him from heaven. Then he fell to the ground, and
heard a voice saying to him, "Saul, Saul, why are you persecuting
Me?" And he said, "Who are You, Lord?"**

**Then the Lord said, "I am Jesus, whom you are persecuting. It
is hard for you to kick against the goads." So he, trembling and
astonished, said, "Lord, what do You want me to do?" Then the
Lord said to him, "Arise and go into the city, and you will be told
what you must do."**

And the men who journeyed with him stood speechless, hearing

a voice but seeing no one. Then Saul arose from the ground, and when his eyes were opened he saw no one. But they led him by the hand and brought him into Damascus. And he was three days without sight, and neither ate nor drank.

And Ananias went his way and entered the house; and laying his hands on him he said, "Brother Saul, the Lord Jesus, who appeared to you on the road as you came, has sent me that you may receive your sight and be filled with the Holy Spirit." Immediately there fell from his eyes something like scales, and he received his sight at once; and he arose and was baptized. So when he had received food, he was strengthened. Then Saul spent some days with the disciples at Damascus.

After his meeting with Jesus, embraced by the light, he understood that all he did: arresting, persecuting the disciples and men and women following Jesus according to the religious leaders of the Israelites, was against the will of God. So he confessed all his sins to God. From that time wherever he went, he testified that Jesus was the Son of God and he witnessed to all the people all over the world wherever he went, evangelizing the gospel of Jesus until he was martyred because of his faith in Jesus Christ.

His name was also changed to Paul, whom all Christians regard as the greatest missionary of Jesus' gospel since the first century. This young man named Saul was lucky to meet Jesus, and the Apostle Paul was led to heaven by the Holy Spirit. However, all the Israelites such as the religious leaders of Israel, high priests, priests, elders, and scribes who arrested the disciples and the followers of Jesus, put them into jail and killed them, were all sent to the ever burning fire sea of hell. The Holy Spirit showed me the fire sea where the religious leaders of Israelites who crucified Jesus were crying and weeping forever, since the first century.

How to discern the spirits is very important. If you follow Satan's leading like the Israelites who crucified Jesus on the cross,
you have no choice but your spirit will be cast into the fiery lake.
However if you follow the apostles' way, like the Apostle Paul,
you will be sent to heaven.
We should all follow the way the Holy Spirit leads. The Holy
Spirit wants all of us to participate in the worldwide Holy Spirit
movement without fail and help the Holy Spirit movement. The
deeds which oppose and obstruct the Holy Spirit movement are
acts against God.
Almighty God loves all of us and He wants to lead all of us to
heaven.

The Holy Spirit's words were given in early morning prayer on July 18, 2001.

The Holy Spirit's Reply No. 1

3. Even famous, highly respected pastors will be abandoned forever, if they disobey the Holy Spirit to the end.

Pastor L. asked me the following question. "Whoever does not
follow the Holy Spirit's orders, however big a servant he is, will

he be cast into the fiery sea? Where are such words in the Bible?"

The Holy Spirit answered as follows:

Ezekiel 3: 20-21, "Again, when a righteous man turns from his righteousness and commits iniquity, and I lay a stumbling block before him, he shall die; because you did not give him warning, he shall die in his sin, and his righteousness which he has done shall not be remembered; but his blood I will require at your hand. Nevertheless if you warn the righteous man that the righteous should not sin, and he does not sin, he shall surely live because he took warning; also you will have delivered your soul."

As shown in the above Bible passages, when the righteous men commits iniquity, his righteousness which he has done shall not be remembered. It means that even the big servants who did great righteousness for God, when they do not obey the Holy Spirit's words, they become sinners again.

Revelation 2: 11 "He who has an ear, let him hear what the Spirit says to the churches. He who overcomes shall not be hurt by the second death."

It means that he who does not obey the Holy Spirit to the end shall be abandoned to the second death, that is to throw him into the fiery lake in hell.

Revelation 21: 8 "But the cowardly, unbelieving, abominable, murderers, sexually immoral, sorcerers, idolaters, and all liars shall have their part in the lake which burns with fire and brimstone, which is the second death."

Mankind was created by God. Read Genesis 1: 26 to the end of

Genesis chapter 3, and you will understand how human beings
were created, and how Adam committed sin. Therefore the Lord
God sent him from the Garden of Eden to work the ground from
which he had been taken. That is, God created human beings.
And God has forgiven all the sins, which have accumulated
since Adam for all mankind, by crucifying His only son, Jesus,
on the cross.
God saved all human beings again from the sins committed
against God by washing sin with the blood of His only son on the
cross. Therefore, human beings' flesh was created by God and all
human beings' sins were forgiven by His only son having been
crucified on the cross. The door leading to heaven, where God
lives, is open again for human beings to enter.
Read Matthew chapter 27, from the beginning to the end, and
you will understand how cruelly Jesus was killed by having been
crucified on the cross, to save human beings from sin.

**Psalm 100: 3 Know that the LORD, He is God; It is He who has
made us, and not we ourselves; We are His people and the sheep
of His pasture.**

Therefore all human beings, whether they are in heaven or in hell,
all belong to God. So whoever does not obey God's words, he or
she becomes a sinner again. Adam was born whole without any
sins and the Lord God did say to Adam and Eve, "You must not
eat the fruit from the tree that is in the middle of the garden, and
you must not touch it, or you will die."
But Eve, Adam's wife, took some of the fruit from the tree that is
in the middle of the garden and gave some to her husband, who
was with her, and he ate it. That is, Adam and Eve did not obey
God's words and sinned against God. Therefore God banished
Adam, and all his descendants became sinners who lost all God's
blessings. Adam became a sinner by not obeying God's words.

However big a servant of God one is, if he does not obey the Holy Spirit's order, he is committing a big sin against God and he becomes a sinner again.

Therefore, however big and righteous works for God he did, if he does not obey God's order and does not do the works ordered by the Holy Spirit to the end, it is God's truth that whoever he is, he should be thrown into the fiery sea in hell. God does not want to throw His beloved servant into the fiery sea. But if he refuses to obey God's words to the last moment, God has no other choice but must throw him into the fiery sea. This is God's universal truth.

The Holy Spirit's words were given at 4:30 PM prayer on September 9, 1997.

The Holy Spirit's Reply No. 2

4. To God's servants who cannot discern the Holy Spirit's words

Question: Pastor L. asked me the following question. Among the pastors who received the Holy Spirit's message, Pastor L. does not know whether the message was from the Holy Spirit or not, so he cannot decide what to do. I prayed about this, and the Holy Spirit answered as follows.

The Holy Spirit's Reply:

You have to learn how to discern between the Holy Spirit and evil spirits. The Holy Spirit clearly explained this to me according to the Bible, and that is in a separate chapter in this book. The Holy Spirit taught Pastor Joshua Doshick Joe, the author of this book, in detail how to discern between the Holy Spirit and evil spirits in accordance with the Bible. I want you to learn how to discern the spirits in this book. I will simply explain to you the following.

1) Check if the messages you received from other Christians were written in accordance with the Bible. The Holy Spirit always speaks according to the Bible.

2) Check whether the Holy Spirit's messages you received from others will glorify Almighty God? Or does it cloud the glory of the Almighty Heavenly Father? The Holy Spirit ministers only works which will glorify the Heavenly Father. The Holy Spirit never ministers anything that will shade the glory of the Most High.

3) Decide according to the spiritual fruit of the Christians who deliver the message.

Galatians 5: 22-23, But the fruit of the Spirit is love, joy, peace, longsuffering, kindness, goodness, faithfulness, gentleness, self-control. Against such there is no law.

Was the Christian who delivered the Holy Spirit's message changed as in the above shown Bible passages? Do the messages he delivered bear fruit? Or do they not bear any fruit? Does the

Holy Spirit minister the Holy Spirit miracles through the one who delivered the messages to you? This is to know whether he received only the grace of prophecy or other graces of the Holy Spirit, too.

God's servants who received the grace of prophecy generally received other graces too. In addition to that, the Holy Spirit performs many different kinds of miracles through such servants. By examining the results above, you can decide whether the messages you received are from the Holy Spirit or evil spirits. If the messages you received are proven to be from the Holy Spirit, you have to follow the messages in deed.

There are many good pastors with wisdom who understand their callings by God and the Holy Spirit's words immediately, and follow them in action.

On the contrary there are many uncountable stubborn servants who cannot understand the Holy Spirit's words due to their personal greed and Satan's false plots to obstruct them in the world, even if the Holy Spirit persuades them to follow the His words. Therefore many Holy Spirit revival congregations are open all over the world, but such stubborn shepherds not only refuse to attend such congregations but many of the shepherds who have experienced the Holy Spirit's ministry think that it is nothing after some time passes, because of Satan's deception. Such shepherds translate and analyze the Bible in the way which is the most beneficial for their own interests and follow their own way. There are many shepherds like this in the world.

That is, the Holy Spirit is showing much Holy Spirit ministry through the shepherds filled with the Holy Spirit. But there are still uncountable shepherds who are convicting, slandering and criticizing the servants filled with the Holy Spirit and leading Holy Spirit congregations, calling them mystics, caught by evil demons, or hypnotized. Such servants are the same as the people who do not believe in Jesus Christ, who was resurrected from death through the Holy Spirit's ministry.

They are the same people as the religious leaders of the Jewish people who killed Jesus Christ by crucifying Him on the cross 2,000 years ago. Many prophets prophesied that our Savior (Jesus) would come. And Jesus came and performed many miracles. That is, He healed Lazarus who had been dead for four days, smelling of a bad odor, cleansed lepers clean, made blind people see, and cured uncountable patients with incurable diseases. However the religious leaders of the Jewish people killed Him who had come to save mankind from sin and death, by crucifying Him on the cross.

In addition to that not only Jesus' disciples but many Christian believers following Jesus Christ were martyred by the religious leaders of the Jewish people. These Christian believers also performed many miracles, healing incurable diseases, showing many miracles and making impossible works possible.

However they were executed by the religious leaders who were so-called believers of God. Do you think that the religious leaders who killed Jesus and His disciples and followers are now in heaven? They are now crying forever in the eternal fiery sea in hell. If they had understood wisely the callings by the Holy Spirit and followed the Holy Spirit's words in acts, they might have entered into Heaven.

However they were too stubborn, and thinking of everything beneficial for their own interests and for their own minds, for such foolish acts, they have to spend eternal life crying with screams, and lamenting for having killed Jesus and His followers. The Holy Spirit at that time also performed many incredible miracles and told them the Holy Spirit's words to save them.

However they ignored the Holy Spirit's words and revelations and acted per their own stubborn thoughts. For their having not obeyed the Holy Spirit's words, they have to spend the eternity in the fiery sulfur sea of hell. What is incredible is that many of God's servants ignore the Holy Spirit's words today and do not obey the Holy Spirit, as in the past.

The Holy Spirit's Envoy will send the Holy Spirit's message or words to His servants who receive God's callings, presidents or kings of countries and business tycoons, in accordance with the Holy Spirit's instructions. And the Holy Spirit will let them understand that that is from the Holy Spirit.

However the people who ignore and do not obey the Holy Spirit's message due to Satan's obstruction and each individual person's stubborn mind, will be thrown into the fiery sea of hell.

However the ones who confess their sins, repent their wrongdoings before God, understand wisely their own calling by God, and act faithfully, will receive eternal life and will be led to Heaven. In the meantime I want to tell you that if any person could not perform God's calling, God's calling are transfered to the children of the person who received God's calling or to the next person who will be assigned to the position, in lieu of the first person who received God's calling.

In the Bible you may read of certain kings who obeyed and faithfully worshiped God and received great blessings from God.

In 2 Chronicles, from chapter one to chapter nine, you will understand that how great blessings King Solomon, who had obeyed and faithfully worshiped God, received from God.

On the other hand, certain kings who had been stupid, stubborn, ignored God's messages or words, and acted per his own mind, lost his own country, all his family members were killed, and finally he was also killed. He understood finally his wrongdoings when he was thrown into the fiery sea at God's angry judgment.

Read 1 Chronicles 10: 1-14, and you will understand how King
Saul, who did not obey God, and did everything according to his
own stupid and stubborn thoughts, was killed. All his sons were
also killed.

God's stubborn servants who do not obey God's message are
same as King Saul in the Bible.

You do not need to think. Just send the Holy Spirit messages to
the people who receive God's calling in accordance with the
Holy Spirit's instructions. The Holy Spirit will decide and deal
with the balance of the work per God's timing.

**The Holy Spirit's words were given at 2: 20 PM on
September 10, 1997.**

CHAPTER 12

The punishment given to Christians who disobey God's word

1. The Holy Spirit changed an elder who really didn't believe in God

Isaiah 1: 18-20, "Come now, and let us reason together," Says the Lord, "Though your sins are like scarlet, They shall be as white as snow; Though they are red like crimson, They shall be as wool. If you are willing and obedient, You shall eat the good of the land; But if you refuse and rebel, You shall be devoured by the sword"; For the mouth of the Lord has spoken.

One day in October 1996 when I was praying early in the morning, the Elder named J. appeared before me and was crying without end. The Holy Spirit asked me to visit him.
When I visited his office, he was sitting helplessly on a sofa, because he was suffering from liver cancer. At the same time the Holy Spirit began to speak to him through me.

"You are an elder but you serve the church without your full heart worshiping God. You are only following for business and money per your greedy mind given by Satan. If you live continuously in this way, you will be abandoned to the fiery sea of hell. That's why the Holy Spirit's angels hit you with an incurable disease, to change you and save you for eternal life in heaven. In order to save your eternal life, I sent the Holy Spirit's envoy to you today. I want you to follow all the Holy Spirit's messages spoken through his mouth."
Elder J. was very obedient to the Holy Spirit's message. I spoke

everything that the Holy Spirit asked me to tell him. He carefully listened to the Holy Spirit's words spoken by my mouth.

In addition to that, the Holy Spirit showed me a vision where Elder J. and his wife were drowning in a river of blood, red like scarlet. Jesus with several angels appeared and were saving them with a life saving rope. After saving their lives from the river of blood, Jesus cleaned and clothed him with a new white long gown and a gold crown and carried him in His arms to the light. I told the vision which the Holy Spirit showed me to Elder J. and his wife.

And I told him everything the Holy Spirit asked me to, such as how to confess all his sins, and to forgive all the people who did anything wrong to him or hurt him. When I prayed for him with my hand placed on his chest, suddenly God's language, the Holy Spirit's tongue began to come from my mouth. I could not control it and whole my body and hands were shaking very hard for some time. Elder J. told me that before my prayer, he was very uneasy and impatient, but after my praying for him, his heart was very peaceful and calm.

The Holy Spirit told him to read and memorize the Disciples' Creed continuously, whenever he feels lonesome or afraid of anything. For several months he seemed to be very healthy and strong, but after about one year he was taken to heaven.

About one month before he died, the Holy Spirit asked me to visit him and tell him about heaven, which I had seen innumerable times.

"Do not worry about death, all human-beings, regardless of who they are, are to die some day. The problem is not death but whether he will be sent to heaven or hell. The Holy Spirit promises to lead you to heaven."

I delivered the above message to him. He was very happy to hear the Holy Spirit's message. After he died, when I was praying, the Holy Spirit showed me that Jesus carried Elder J., dressed in a long white dress and wearing a gold crown on his head, in His arms and went to heaven in the light.

Jesus asked me to tell what I had seen to his wife. So I told her what I had seen. He died in his early fifties but he is now in heaven.
The Holy Spirit tells you, "Even if you die in your forties or fifties, but if the Holy Spirit sends you to heaven, you are very blessed.

Even if you live longer than 100 years, if you are sent to hell, what good is it?" The problem is whether you can enter the kingdom of God or not. The Holy Spirit wants to lead all of you to heaven.

2. God's blessing of an elder who confessed his sins and obeyed the Holy Spirit

One day in November 1996 when I was praying early in the morning, Elder L. was crying in front of me. The Holy Spirit asked me to chase the demons from him.

Mark 5: 1-13, Then they came to the other side of the sea, to the country of the Gadarenes. And when He had come out of the boat,

immediately there met Him out of the tombs a man with an unclean spirit, who had his dwelling among the tombs; and no one could bind him, not even with chains, because he had often been bound with shackles and chains.

And the chains had been pulled apart by him, and the shackles broken in pieces; neither could anyone tame him. And always, night and day, he was in the mountains and in the tombs, crying out and cutting himself with stones.

When he saw Jesus from afar, he ran and worshiped Him. And he cried out with a loud voice and said, "What have I to do with You, Jesus, Son of the Most High God? I implore You by God that You do not torment me." For He said to him, "Come out of the man, unclean spirit!" Then He asked him, "What is your name?" And he answered, saying, "My name is Legion; for we are many."

Also he begged Him earnestly that He would not send them out of the country. Now a large herd of swine was feeding there near the mountains. So all the demons begged Him, saying, "Send us to the swine, that we may enter them." And at once Jesus gave them permission. Then the unclean spirits went out and entered the swine (there were about two thousand); and the herd ran violently down the steep place into the sea, and drowned in the sea.

When I began to pray for him at his home, the Holy Spirit began to speak to him through me, "You are an Elder who should serve your church with all your heart, worshiping God. But you go to Atlantic City to gamble, drink, smoke cigarettes, and do all kinds of bad things which Satan gives to you."

Elder L. agreed 100% with what the Holy Spirit told him through me. And he said to me, "I will never do the same things but do my best to serve God."

When I prayed again, my whole body began to shake, and from my mouth God's tongue began to come for some time. In the mean time, the Holy Spirit showed me a vision showing Elder L. covered in all black clothes and his skin color also seemed to be black. He was gambling with several black people like Elder L. When I continuously prayed and arrested the demons with the name of Jesus, Almighty God's words, and the Holy Spirit's power, and threw them away from Elder L.'s body, he said to me, "I feel very peaceful and calm now."

For some time he stopped smoking, drinking and gambling, and he did his best in serving God. However demons eventually got him again, and Satan decoyed him back into his old habits.
Several weeks ago, I visited him again and arrested all the evil spirits luring him into Satanic intrigue, and threw them away from him.
He is now doing his best to serve God. He quit all his bad habits with the help of the Holy Spirit's power. The Holy Spirit wants to help you too, if you have any problems like Elder L.

3. The Holy Spirit changed a prodigal missionary

There was a missionary named C. who was leading the church choir in a church in Seoul, Korea. He was handsome, tall, and in his early forties. The Holy Spirit asked me to deliver a warning message to him, when I was praying in the morning.

Revelation 21: 8 But the cowardly, unbelieving, abominable, murderers, sexually immoral, sorcerers, idolaters, and all liars shall have their part in the lake which burns with fire and brim-

stone, which is the second death.

It was some time in June 1996 when Missionary C. tried to lure any beautiful unmarried woman coming to his church. And he had immoral sexual relations with three different women in the church where he served as choir leader.

The Holy Spirit asked me to tell the truth to him and give him a warning. I said to the Holy Spirit, "How can I tell him without any witnesses? He asked me to tell what the Holy Spirit told me to Pastor L. serving in the same church. So I told the story which the Holy Spirit told me in prayer, to Pastor L. He was very surprised to hear that the Holy Spirit told me in morning prayer and he said that all the Holy Spirit told me was true.

The next Sunday, I went to the church very early and sat in the fourth row from the front at the 11 o'clock service. I was very astonished to see that Missionary C. was leading the choir and was tied all around his body from his feet to his neck, except for his head, by a giant green and red snake, about 20 cm in diameter and about 8 meters in length. In the mean time, the big snake mouth tried to bite the Missionary's head, moving his tongue in and out. I was so scared, I could not move my body at all.

But at the same time, fall's light blue sky opened my eyes. The sky was so high and clear that I could not find anything in the sky. But soon a giant cross on which Jesus Christ was crucified appeared high in the clear sky. Right under the cross, Jesus, in long white robe began to write with a white cloud, saying,

"My beloved son, Joshua Doshick Joe, do not worry about the vision you saw just now. Be bold and deliver the Holy Spirit's message you have. I am always with you."

Soon the scene of the cross in the sky disappeared. As soon as

the church service was over, I took Missionary C. with me to an
empty room, and there I told him everything that the Holy Spirit
showed me during the service, that is, about the giant snake and
the cross in the sky.

I told him about the story which the Holy Spirit told me, that he
had immoral sexual relations with three different women in the
church.

After that, I delivered the Holy Spirit's message, "If you lure any
more innocent Christian women in this church, and if you have
any more immoral sexual relations with them, the Holy Spirit's
angels are going to take you with them immediately and throw
you into the fiery lake of hell for your eternal life."

The Holy Spirit asked me to deliver the above message to you.
When I told him the message, he immediately began to cry and
said to me, "I am a sinner. I will never commit the same sins
again. Please forgive me."

In addition to that, he told me the following, "Even if I pray for a
long time, I cannot have any peace in my heart. Please pray for
me." So I prayed for him.

After this incident, he said, "I am planning to go to China to
deliver Jesus' gospel." After that, I never heard about him. The
Holy Spirit finds the people who commit sins against God in
church. He wants to change them by giving them the Holy
Spirit's messages and saving them for eternal life in heaven. If
you have any secret sins with you, do not hesitate to confess
them to God. He will gladly clean all your sins and will forgive
you. He loves all of you and He wants to lead all of you to
heaven.

4. The Holy Spirit changed a Christian who committed adultery

Matthew 5: 27-30, "You have heard that it was said to those of old, 'You shall not commit adultery.' But I say to you that whoever looks at a woman to lust for her has already committed adultery with her in his heart.

If your right eye causes you to sin, pluck it out and cast it from you; for it is more profitable for you that one of your members perish, than for your whole body to be cast into hell. And if your right hand causes you to sin, cut it off and cast it from you; for it is more profitable for you that one of your members perish, than for your whole body to be cast into hell."

There was a male deacon named K. and a female missionary named L. in a church in Seoul, Korea. This incident happened some time through summer and fall of 1996. These two people were not a married couple. However it seemed that they had had immoral sexual relations between them.

The Holy Spirit asked me to give them the Holy Spirit's warning message. The Holy Spirit showed me a vision and asked me to tell the vision to the male Deacon K. The vision showed a big, clear river turned red with blood. And He said to me, "That is the sin committed between men and women."

Human beings commit big sins unknowingly. I delivered the Holy Spirit's message to Mr. K. and said to him, "Man should not have any sexual relations with any woman except his wife arranged by God." They repented for what they had done before God, but soon after they committed the sin again.

The Holy Spirit showed another vision where the female mis-

sionary L. gave birth to a son who was mentally handicapped in
a very poor, small country village home. Her son later grew up
and was very pessimistic about his fate, and he killed both his
mother and father with a knife. The Holy Spirit asked me to
deliver the vision He showed me to both Deacon K. and Missionary L.

I delivered the same vision which the Holy Spirit showed me to
Deacon K. and said to him, "You must stop your immoral sexual
relations with Missionary L. immediately. If you continue your
immoral sexual relations, you will have the same mentally
handicapped child, and later he will kill both of you like the
vision which I tell you now. That is the Holy Spirit's message to
both of you. This is the price for the sins you commit with Missionary L."

I delivered the Holy Spirit's message as it was, and they promised me that they would never commit these sins again. And they
repented for their sins before God.

**1 Corinthians 3: 16-17, Do you not know that you are the tem-
ple of God and that the Spirit of God dwells in you? If anyone
defiles the temple of God, God will destroy him. For the temple of
God is holy, which temple you are.**

However, about one month later, the Holy Spirit showed me
another vision about them. It was very fearful, and in the vision
Deacon K.'s real wife was very young and beautiful but Missionary L. was a very old lady with gray hair and a bent back.

At the same time they were sleeping secretly in a room, but two
of the Holy Spirit's giant angels came into the room and cut
Deacon K. and Missionary L. into pieces with a big sword and
threw all of the pieces into the fiery sea of hell. After that, the
Holy Spirit asked me to deliver the Holy Spirit's message to both

of them.

So I met both of them and told them the vision which the Holy Spirit showed me, and I told them, "This is the Holy Spirit's message to deliver to you both." As soon as they heard the Holy Spirit's message, they began to cry with tears continuously dropping from their eyes, they repented for their sins before God, and I prayed for them and they swore to God that they would separate from each other.

After that, Deacon K. returned to his home where his original wife and children were living and he had happy family relations again with his real wife, and Missionary L. met a nice, devout Christian man and they got married and they began a happy family home.

Dear Readers!

The Holy Spirit never allows immoral sexual relations between men and women. At the same time the Holy Spirit asked me to announce all the Holy Spirit's messages I delivered to all the people in the world. Innumerable people including Christians and even pastors commit sins of immoral sexual relations.

Uncountable pastors and elders were thrown away into the fiery sea of hell from the gate to heaven, because of women and money. Especially pastors and elders of big churches commit more sins than the small ones. Do not try to enjoy your life temporarily, while following your flesh's greed. But control your greed for the flesh's desire, and the Holy Spirit will lead you to heaven.

Romans 8: 5-8, 13-14, For those who live according to the flesh set their minds on the things of the flesh, but those who live according to the Spirit, the things of the Spirit.

**For to be carnally minded is death, but to be spiritually minded
is life and peace. Because the carnal mind is enmity against God;
for it is not subject to the law of God, nor indeed can be. So then,
those who are in the flesh cannot please God.**

**For if you live according to the flesh you will die; but if by the
Spirit you put to death the deeds of the body, you will live. For as
many as are led by the Spirit of God, these are sons of God.**

The above mentioned Bible passages say clearly, "If you live
according to sinful nature, you will die." It means that you cannot go to heaven, but you will be thrown into hell.
But the mind controlled by the Spirit is life and peace. And those
who are led by the Spirit of God are sons of God. It means that,
"If you control your mind by the Spirit, you will get eternal life
and peace in heaven. And you are sons of God."

**1 John 1: 8-10, If we say that we have no sin, we deceive our-
selves, and the truth is not in us. If we confess our sins, He is
faithful and just to forgive us our sins and to cleanse us from all
unrighteousness. If we say that we have not sinned, we make Him
a liar, and His word is not in us.**

If you have already committed sins which are not confessed yet,
confess all your sins before God. He will gladly forgive all your
sins. However, never try to commit sins again. You have to
control your mind by the Holy Spirit. That is the Heavenly Father's truth.
We are all sinners before God. However, if you confess all your
sins with all your heart before God, He will clean all your sins in
the book of life. The Holy Spirit loves you all and He wants to
lead you to heaven.

5. The spirits crying and lamenting in the fiery sulfur lake of hell

July 18, 1997 at 5:30AM when I was praying, Jesus Christ, dressed in a long white gown, carrying a little lamb in His arms appeared before me. While turning His back, He pointed with His right finger to the fiery sulfur sea in which all metals were melting like a furnace in a steel mill.

The fire sea was so big that I could not see the edge of it. Three people burning in the fire were screaming with all their power, lamenting of their past having not believed in Jesus Christ when they were living. They were at a loss of what to do in the burning fire sea. When they were coming closer to me, I was very surprised to find who they were.

The person crying for help in the center of the three was the late chairman of a giant worldwide business group. At his right the late President of a country, who established the economic foundation of that country was screaming for help, and at his left the person crying for help was the late President of a country who was the most powerful man in that country.

All three people were thrown into the fiery sulfur sea, and they were burning, crying, screaming for help and lamenting for their past. No human beings could see the miserable and deplorable scene without tears in their eyes. The same scene appeared to me for about 35 minutes whether I closed or opened my eyes.

After that, Jesus brought them before Him and I was near Jesus in prayer. Fire was burning continuously on them. They were crying and rolling on the ground to extinguish the fire but nothing could stop the burning fire.

After that, Jesus commanded the fire to stop burning. Immediately the fire stopped burning. The three people did not have any marks showing fire burns. But all their bodies were black like black people. All three people immediately knelt down before Jesus sitting on a chair with a lamb in His arms. They were continually begging, and crying with tears in their eyes to Jesus for their lives to be saved from the fiery sea.

The scene of begging for help was so miserable and deplorable that no human being could see it without tears. Soon several giant angels appeared and tied the three people with ropes one by one separately and took them to the fiery sulfur sea and threw them one by one into the fiery sea again. The three people began to scream and cry with a loud voice for help in the ever-burning fiery sea, but no one came to save them.

Revelation 20: 12-15, And I saw the dead, small and great, standing before God, and books were opened. And another book was opened, which is the Book of Life. And the dead were judged according to their works, by the things which were written in the books.

The sea gave up the dead who were in it, and Death and Hades delivered up the dead who were in them. And they were judged, each one according to his works. Then Death and Hades were cast into the lake of fire. This is the second death. And anyone not found written in the Book of Life was cast into the lake of fire.

Jesus told me to deliver exactly what I saw today, without any addition or deduction, to the children of the three people and the people whose names were written on the list He gave me.

In addition to that, He told me to give them the book *The Holy*

Spirit's Words and Ministry one by one. Tell them to believe that Jesus is the Son of God and that He died on the cross to pay for their sin. And if they believe in Jesus, they can be forgiven of their sin and go to heaven. And tell them to be pioneers for "The Worldwide Holy Spirit Revival Movement" and do their best to deliver these truthful words all over the world to save all the human beings in the world.

If any children of the three people or the people whose names were written in the list do not believe that Jesus died on the cross to pay for their sin, do not believe the Holy Spirit's words or do not obey in action, not only the children of the three and the people whose names were written but also all their family members and their offspring will be thrown into the same fiery sulfur sea which you see and where the late chairman of a world -class business group and the two late Presidents are eternally crying for help.
Jesus gave me the list. (The names will be informed individually only, one by one.) Jesus told me that He would give me a separate message for each person later.

6. God's fearful punishment given to idolaters

At 2: 21 AM on December 20, 1997 in morning prayer, suddenly it became as bright as day, and a sulfur burning fire sea appeared in front of me, in which all kinds of metals were melting, as in

the furnace of a steel mill. High in the air above the fiery sea,
there sat Jesus Christ whose figure was a giant, and Jesus was so
great that a large part of the sky was covered by Him.

Right by the fiery sea there sat millions of Buddhist statues in a
big group.

Right at that time, Jesus, rising from His seat, said, **"You liars,
Buddhist statues! The paradise you are talking about is
here."**

Jesus, holding a giant sickle in both hands, turned around and
swung the sickle. At the same time all the Buddhist statues were
cut in half by Jesus' sickle. And all the Buddhist statues were
thrown into the sulfur burning fire sea. All the Buddhist statues
burning in the fiery sea were crying, weeping and begging Jesus
for their life.

**Revelation 14: 14 Then I looked, and behold, a white cloud,
and on the cloud sat One like the Son of Man, having on His
head a golden crown, and in His hand a sharp sickle.**

Next, millions of Buddhist monks dressed in long gray gowns
appeared at the same place where the Buddhist statues had been.
Jesus, holding a giant sickle high, turned His whole body to the
right and made a full swing like He was playing golf. Then all
the Buddhist monks were cut in half by Jesus' sickle and all of
the cut bodies flew into the fiery burning lake of sulfur.

**Jesus said to them, "Here is the paradise you are talking
about. Do not lure innocent people with your groundless
deceit. There is no paradise in the universe. This is the punishment for your sins."**

It was so fearful, miserable and poor to see millions of Buddhist
statues and Buddhist monks crying, weeping and lamenting for

what they did wrong in the past. No one can look at the scene of the sulfur burning fiery lake in hell without tears in their eyes.

Next, millions of Buddhist believers dressed in Korean traditional clothing, wearing white paper hats on their heads, dancing and playing the drums, appeared at the same place where the Buddhist statues and monks had been. Jesus Christ, holding a giant sickle in both His hands, turned to to right, and made a big and powerful swing in front of Him. At the same time all the Buddhist believers who were dancing and playing drums were cut in half and all the bodies were thrown into the ever burning fire sea.

Jesus said to them, "This is the paradise about which the Buddhist statues and monks whom you were worshiping were talking. You should spend all your eternal life in this sulfur burning fire sea."

And He said to me, "Wherever you go in the world, tell what you have seen today to everyone you will meet, without adding or removing even a little bit. Except for the Christians believing in the Trinity God: Heavenly Father, His Son Jesus Christ and the Holy Spirit, all the other people believing in heretic gods or religions made by Satan will be punished exactly in the same way you have seen today."

Malachi 4: 1-3, "For behold, the day is coming, Burning like an oven, And all the proud, yes, all who do wickedly will be stubble. And the day which is coming shall burn them up," Says the Lord of hosts, "That will leave them neither root nor branch. But to you who fear My name The Sun of Righteousness shall arise With healing in His wings; And you shall go out And grow fat like stall-fed calves. You shall trample the wicked, For they shall be ashes

under the soles of your feet On the day that I do this," Says the Lord of hosts.

Revelation 20: 12-15, And I saw the dead, small and great, standing before God, and books were opened. And another book was opened, which is the Book of Life.

And the dead were judged according to their works, by the things which were written in the books. The sea gave up the dead who were in it, and Death and Hades delivered up the dead who were in them.

And they were judged, each one according to his works. Then Death and Hades were cast into the lake of fire. This is the second death. And anyone not found written in the Book of Life was cast into the lake of fire.

Revelation 21: 8 But the cowardly, unbelieving, abominable, murderers, sexually immoral, sorcerers, idolaters, and all liars shall have their part in the lake which burns with fire and brimstone, which is the second death.

Exodus 20: 3-7 "You shall have no other gods before Me. "You shall not make for yourself a carved image--any likeness of anything that is in heaven above, or that is in the earth beneath, or that is in the water under the earth; you shall not bow down to them nor serve them.

For I, the Lord your God, am a jealous God, visiting the iniquity of the fathers upon the children to the third and fourth generations of those who hate Me, but showing mercy to thousands, to those who love Me and keep My commandments.

"You shall not take the name of the Lord your God in vain, for the Lord will not hold him guiltless who takes His name in vain."

To the unbelievers who do not believe in God!

The Almighty Heavenly Father loves all the people in the world. God created all human beings. Therefore we, Christians, call Him our Father and we pray to Him. God created you too. God loves human beings so much. In order to save you from your sins and death, Almighty God gave His only Son to be crucified on the cross.

However there are innumerable people who do not believe in God, instead they believe in and worship idols, because they are deceived by Satan. But the Almighty Heavenly Father still loves them and waits for them to come into the arms of the God who created them.

The Heavenly Father never wants to punish anyone in the way mentioned above. If anyone abandons their idols and comes to the Heavenly Father, believes in God, confesses all their sins, and repents for what he has done wrong against Almighty God, He will forgive all your sins. And He will accept you as one of the most beloved sons and daughters of God.

We pray for you who do not believe in God yet to come to Jesus' love immediately and receive all God's unlimited blessings waiting for you.

Isaiah 1: 18-20, "Come now, and let us reason together," Says the Lord, "Though your sins are like scarlet, They shall be as white as snow; Though they are red like crimson, They shall be as wool. If you are willing and obedient, You shall eat the good of the land; But if you refuse and rebel, You shall be devoured by the sword"; For the mouth of the Lord has spoken.

I think you can easily understand the meaning of these Bible passages. God loves you so much. Therefore if you abandon the idols, and come to the Almighty Heavenly Father, He will forgive all your sins, will give you His unlimited blessings and will lead you to heaven for your eternal life.

The meaning of the Bible passages shown above are as follows: If you ignore the words of Almighty God, disobey God, and continuously believe in and worship idols created by Satan, Almighty God will punish you in the way shown above.

I pray for you to come to Jesus' love immediately and receive all the blessings and love God will give you. According to the words of the Holy Spirit, I testified to all that I have seen and experienced without adding or deducting anything to the power of the Holy Spirit's anointing. This is to save you from the fiery sea of hell. I sincerely pray for you come to Jesus as soon as possible.

John 1: 12 But as many as received Him, to them He gave the right to become children of God, to those who believe in His name

The Holy Spirit's words were given at 2:39 AM in prayer on December 20, 1997.

7. The Holy Spirit asks Christians to solve all their problems with Jesus' love

The Holy Spirit does not allow pastors or preachers to curse or speak wrong of in prayer, the Christians who have had bad relations with them, or who left their church.
He says, "Solve all your problems with Jesus' love."

James 3: 8 But no man can tame the tongue. It is an unruly evil, full of deadly poison.

In Seoul, Korea there was a couple whom I have known for many years and both of them are pastors of a church. This married couple has served a small church having 40 to 50 Christians every Sunday. These pastors fearfully cursed the Christians who left their church. This was caught by the Holy Spirit. I know them very well and they are my friends. One day in December 1996 the Holy Spirit showed me a very special vision, all day long.
It was as follows: The two pastors including all their brothers and sisters and family members were individually tied up with ropes all around their bodies, and their noses were hooked on individual hooks, one by one. And they were tied across a 30 meter long iron pipe with about 30 other people.
That is, one person per meter was tied to the iron pipe, and several angels were pulling them wherever I went from morning until night. I saw this vision all day long whether I closed or opened my eyes.
The Holy Spirit asked me to deliver the vision I saw, along with the Holy Spirit's message, to the same two pastors. The Holy Spirit's message was as follows:
Both you pastors tied many Christians, by cursing them when

they left your church. All the Christians you cursed were tied up
per your cursing, and both you pastors were tied up 10 times
more than they were. In addition to that, the Holy Spirit's angels
tied all the family members of the pastors plus the pastors'
brothers and sisters and their children.

In the meantime the Holy Spirit showed me five or six pipes,
with about 30 people tied to one pipe, that means 30 x 6 = 180
people were tied to 6 pipes. And both ends of the pipes were tied
to one big rope about 3 meters apart. That is, all six different
pipes were tied to two big ropes at each end of the pipes 3 meters
apart. The people tied to the pipes were Christians, both pastors'
family members, their brothers, sisters, and their children.

The two pastors were tied by so much rope that they couldn't be
tied to the pipes to which the other people were tied, but each
was individually tied. And the ropes which were used to tie the
female pastor were carried by a specially made 50-ton truck, and
the male pastor was carried by a 25-ton truck.

Showing me this vision, the Holy Spirit asked me, "Draw a picture of the vision and show it to the two pastors and tell them.
This is how you tied the innocent Christians who left your
church by cursing them, since you started your church many
years ago. As you tied the innocent Christians who left your
church, you had to be tied 10 times more, plus all your family
members and your brothers and sisters and their children were
tied too.

**Matthew 12: 36-37, But I say to you that for every idle word
men may speak, they will give account of it in the day of judgment.
For by your words you will be justified, and by your words you
will be condemned.**

When I delivered this message together with the picture showing the people tied to both pastors, the couple was astonished, very depressed, and they were at a loss of what to do. The Holy Spirit said to them, "You know all the people you tied one-by-one, untie all of them one-by-one by praying to God. And pray to bless them one-by-one.

If they left your church, call them one-by-one by phone or visit them one-by-one and confess to them individually for your sins. And ask them individually to forgive your sins. After that, confess all your sins before God. Otherwise, you will be thrown eternally into the fiery sea of hell.

And from now on never do such stupid and foolish misdeeds any more but try to solve everything by Jesus' love." Later the Holy Spirit said to me that they confessed all their sins before God and they followed the Holy Spirit's message and were forgiven for their sins by the Heavenly Father. Now they solve all their problems with Jesus' love.

The Holy Spirit knows all of your secrets in detail. Before you think about secrets and realize them in action, the Holy Spirit knows all about them in your mind.

Never curse or condemn others, or you will receive 10 times more. If you have sins for having condemned or cursed others, confess all your sins before God and follow the Holy Spirit's message which was given to the two pastors mentioned above. And then the Holy Spirit will forgive all your sins gladly.

That is the only way for your sins to be cleaned. The Holy Spirit loves you. Do not think that only the above mentioned two pastors committed so much sin by cursing and condemning others. Confess all your sins you committed before God, since you were young. Your sins will cause your eternal life to be destroyed.

The Holy Spirit loves you all. He wants to save you from your sins. We are all sinners before God. He understands whatever sins you have. Just confess all your sins before Him, and the Heavenly Father will forgive you of your sins.

The Holy Spirit loves you and He is blessing you.

The Holy Spirit's words were given at early morning prayer on February 26, 1999.

8. The Holy Spirit changed a missionary who was luring Christians to other churches

This happened in a small church in Seoul, Korea in August 1996. About 40 Christians were serving in that church, and that church was not growing in number. When the church was first established, the missionary invested a large amount of money but the relationship between the missionary and the pastor in the church was not good. Therefore the missionary was secretly taking new Christians coming to the church to another church. This was found by the Holy Spirit.

Acts 5: 1-11, But a certain man named Ananias, with Sapphira his wife, sold a possession. And he kept back part of the proceeds, his wife also being aware of it, and brought a certain part and laid it at the apostles' feet.

But Peter said, "Ananias, why has Satan filled your heart to lie to the Holy Spirit and keep back part of the price of the land for yourself? While it remained, was it not your own? And after it was sold, was it not in your own control? Why have you conceived this thing in your heart? You have not lied to men but to God."

Then Ananias, hearing these words, fell down and breathed his last. So great fear came upon all those who heard these things. And the young men arose and wrapped him up, carried him out, and buried him.

Now it was about three hours later when his wife came in, not knowing what had happened. And Peter answered her, "Tell me whether you sold the land for so much?" She said, "Yes, for so much." Then Peter said to her, "How is it that you have agreed together to test the Spirit of the Lord? Look, the feet of those who have buried your husband are at the door, and they will carry you out."

Then immediately she fell down at his feet and breathed her last. last. And the young men came in and found her dead, and carrying her out, buried her by her husband. So great fear came upon all the church and upon all who heard these things.

The Holy Spirit asked me to deliver the Holy Spirit's warning message about the missionary's plan to take new Christians to another church. So I asked the Holy Spirit, "How can I do this without any witnesses?" He asked me to tell what the Holy Spirit told me to the woman missionary named L.

When I told woman missionary L., she was very surprised to hear that the Holy Spirit knows everything done secretly by Missionary K. And she told me that all that I heard from the Holy Spirit was true. After the Sunday service was over, I took Missionary K. with me to an empty room, and I delivered the Holy Spirit's message verbally.

That is, "You are now being deceived by Satan and you are obstructing and destroying God's church. Confess immediately the wrong you did against your God. Immediately stop destroying the church with your deeds. The Holy Spirit knows everything that you are doing.

Do not try to tell a lie before the Holy Spirit. If you continue to
destroy the church, you will be abandoned by the Holy Spirit's
angels into the fiery lake of hell immediately. And I want you to
serve Pastor L. in your church, as you serve God."

As soon as I said the Holy Spirit's message, he said, "I am a
sinner. I committed sins against God. Please forgive me. I will
never do it again." He told me that he would confess to God and
pray before Him. And he asked me to pray for him. So I prayed
for him. Since that incident, that church has started to grow in
number.

Like this, the Holy Spirit informs sinners of their sin through His
servants and He changes him or her and lets them confess what
they did wrong against God to lead them to the right way. This is
the love of God.

9. The Holy Spirit's words given at closing of the book

My Dear Readers!

The Holy Spirit loves all of us. The Holy Spirit knows all your
deeds in detail. Your spiritual eyes are not open, and your spiritual ears are deaf, therefore you cannot see what the Holy Spirit
and His angels are doing and you cannot hear what the Holy
Spirit and His angels say to you. Therefore you commit sins
against God per your flesh's mind. Never think of anything that
is against God. The Holy Spirit knows your heart before you

think about it.

All the incidents and testimonies shown in this book are stories which I really experienced through the Holy Spirit's power or the words given to me in prayer by the Holy Spirit. I believe that when you read this book, you have experienced the Holy Spirit's miracles and God's blessings.

While reading this book, if you did not experience the Holy Spirit's miraculous power, I want you to open your heart fully. Please do not think of anything else but the contents of this book and read the book again slowly and carefully. I believe the Holy Spirit will perform His miracles through you and will give you God's unlimited blessings.

In addition to the testimonies which I witness in this book, there are innumerable cases which I did not even mention. Such as the Holy Spirit's warm advice to the pastors who are wandering in the darkness. Or The Holy Spirit's messages to the pastors who translate, analyze, and understand the Bible per their own interests and selfishness. The Holy Spirit wants to teach the truth to all of us to go to the Heaven, the kingdom of God.

There are stubborn pastors who continuously do not obey the Holy Spirit's messages, while following their own thoughts, knowledge learned in theological seminaries, their own selfishness, and the greed which Satan gives them. Such pastors are being punished very severely by the Holy Spirit's angels. The pastors themselves, their family members, their assistant pastors, the elders helping the pastors, or even Christians coming to the churches led by such pastors are sometimes punished by the Holy Spirit's angels.

I can testify any time, anywhere in the world, about what I had experienced through the Holy Spirit, if you want me to do.

The Holy Spirit in your heart knows everything about you and all your secrets in detail. Never try to deceive anyone or tell lies, or try to do anything that the Holy Spirit does not permit you to do, while thinking that no one knows about you. You cannot see the Holy Spirit and you cannot hear Him because you are completely surrounded by sins which are not confessed to God. Because of these sins you cannot communicate with Him. The cloud in the sky cannot move the sun. The cloud can temporarily block the sun's light, but the sun stays high in the sky.

The Holy Spirit wants to save all of us. He does not want to punish any of His sons and daughters like us. He loves all of us, therefore the Heavenly Father sent His only Son, Jesus Christ, to be crucified on the cross to clean our sins with His precious blood, and to save us for our eternal life in heaven.

The Holy Spirit sometimes saves even non-Christians by giving them incurable diseases, and leading them to accept Jesus as their Savior, leading them to confess all their sins before God, and taking them with Him to Heaven.

I am a living witness who delivers His messages to any person He chooses. Human beings only follow small interests or profits which they can see right in front of them. However the Holy Spirit examines everything from the view point of whether it can glorify the Heavenly Father, Almighty God, who created the universe and His Only Son, Jesus Christ, who sacrificed His own life by being crucified on the cross to save us from hell, for eternal life in heaven. The Holy Spirit thinks of our eternal life in heaven rather than our current life which sometimes only follows our greed given by Satan.

Therefore the way which is led by the Holy Spirit to heaven is very difficult and hard, like running on steep rocky mountains covered with many hazardous obstructions. But we have to follow the way the Holy Spirit leads. That is the only way to heaven. All of us will die someday, without fail. After we die, there is God's judgment, and after that there is heaven or hell. If we do not believe in God, it is not that heaven, hell and God's judgment will be moved away from us. We are only blind, not able to see with spiritual vision and we are deaf, not able to hear what the Holy Spirit says to us.

It is too late to save our souls after they are thrown into the fiery sea of hell. However hard we cry, lament and weep, that will not be able to save our souls once they are thrown into the fiery sea of hell. Your flesh will die when you live all your life given by God, but your spirit will live forever, so even if you try to kill your spirit, you can do nothing against it. That is God's truth.

Who lives longer and who dies earlier is not the problem. The real problem is who goes to heaven and who is sent to hell. Whether you will be able to go to heaven or not is the real problem you have to solve.

Even if some one dies earlier at a young age because of an incurable disease, if he or she is accepted in heaven, they are the most blessed, lucky people. Do not feel sad because your beloved ones go to heaven earlier. The problem is who goes to heaven and who goes to hell.

I have seen innumerable heavenly secrets: heaven, hell, God's judgment, angels, our life record book, and many others. You cannot live forever, your life is very limited. You can live 100 to 120 years maximum, but you are not guaranteed to live that long. If the Heavenly Father calls you, you must go immediately, without delaying even one day.

Some people must go while sleeping, some people must go while eating, some people must go while working, some people go while driving. If you are sent to hell, you can do nothing to save your eternal life. You have to do it while you are living in the world.

Even though the way to heaven by the Holy Spirit's guidance may be difficult for you to follow, you must follow the way He leads. Otherwise you will be cast into the ever burning sulfur fire sea of hell.

The most pitiful and miserable people in the world are not the poor and sick blind people begging on the street, but the wealthy people with lots of money who don't know that the Holy Spirit and His angels are watching them, who commit all kinds of sins against God. The rich people who try to make more money by telling all kinds of lies are the most pitiful and miserable people in the world, because they do not know that they will be cast into the fiery lake of burning sulfur in hell.

They do not believe in Jesus Christ, who was crucified on the cross for them. I have seen too many spirits of wealthy people crying forever in hell.

Innumerable people in the world commit adultery with other women or men, even if they were married. In human society, committing adultery doesn't seem like a big sin. But we should know that committing adultery is a big sin against the Almighty Heavenly Father.

I have seen too many rich and wealthy people who were very famous and well-known for their wealth when they were living, who are crying forever in the fiery lake of burning sulfur in hell.

I am the Holy Spirit's servant, a living witness who receives the Holy Spirit's messages directly from the Holy Spirit and delivers His messages to the sons and daughters of wealthy people who died earlier and are crying in the fiery lake.

The Holy Spirit's messages to them are to inform the children of the wealthy and rich people that their foolish, wealthy, and rich fathers who knew nothing about God but tried to make more money by deceiving the poor and following the greed given by Satan are now crying in the fiery sea of hell. The Holy Spirit tells them not to follow the same track of their foolish fathers leading to hell, but to follow the way the Holy Spirit leads to heaven.

Never even think of doing anything wrong against God, even if you are alone by yourself. The Holy Spirit knows our thoughts before we commit the sins against God. All our sins committed in our hearts, all our sins committed by our mouths, and our sins committed by our deeds are recorded in our life record book in heaven and in our hearts. The Holy Spirit asks us to confess all our sins before God by ourselves. He will gladly forgive all your sins, if you follow the Holy Spirit's messages delivered to you. His purpose is to save you from hell. He loves you and He wants to lead you to heaven.

Holy Spirit, Hover Over Me, showing the testimonies of the Holy Spirit's miracles which I experienced and the words of the Holy Spirit given to me in prayer will be published continuously in the future. We published only some of the testimonies which I experienced in the last 13 years.
I believe by reading this book you understood how the Holy Spirit ministers miracles to save all the human beings from hell and what kinds of words He gave to us to save us from Satan's plot to destroy all human beings in the fiery sea of hell. This is the truth of God. However hard it is we have to do all our best not to be deceived by Satan's lure to decoy us to destruction, and we must only follow the way the Holy Spirit leads to heaven.

In the name of Jesus we pray for God to give His unlimited blessings and grace to you and your children for generations, and for the Holy Spirit to lead you and all your family members and your children through generations to eternal life in heaven

God loves you and He blesses you unlimitedly.
Holy Spirit, Hover over all of us. Amen.

On December 31, 2002 written in the Holy Spirit's anointing.

At closing the correction of the book

Who could believe what we delivered?
Our difficult and stormy life for the last 13 years.
God's miracle is ready to spread all over the world.

The Holy Spirit selected a man who could not even write nice letters and He led him to write a book.

God placed us, who were going up all the time, into the deepest depth of the earth.

Now we can understand a little of Your will which makes men with wisdom shamed by the newly born.

You used a beginner who was the target of fears and doubts as your instrument.

We thought You were planning to give us a stormy tempest.

But our Lord, Jesus Christ, You gave us Your peace, freedom and love. I was weeping on and off while correcting the manuscript of the book.

Oh, Almighty Heavenly Father,

I was communicating with the Holy Spirit, who gave me powers and anointing to continue the correction.

You are my power. Oh my Lord, Jesus, I love You with all my heart.

The Holy Spirit led us through His miracles everyday for many years.

Now we understand a little of Your miraculous powers which

you poured on us through the last 13 years.

Now we are spiritually changed, like a baby in front of You.

We are ready to deliver Your gospel all over the world.

Holding Your hands tightly, we will deliver all the messages You give to all the people in the world.

With Your unlimited love, with Your miraculous powers and with the authority to be Your son and daughter,

We thank You, our Lord Jesus Christ for Your miraculous book, Holy Spirit, Hover Over Me.

We call Your name, Jesus Christ, with all our heart and power for all the people in the world to hear our cry.

Our Lord Jesus, You gave us our beloved children and many brothers and sisters.

We all will be united in glorifying the Almighty Heavenly Father. We are all Yours, whether we are alive or dead.

Oh our Lord, Jesus Christ, You were crucified on the cross for all of us. You are our eternal king, we praise Your name high.

We are all doing our best to glorify our Almighty Heavenly Father.

We thank You, the great Holy Spirit who spiritually trained a beginner and used him to write the miracles You performed through him again.

Under the name of Jesus, we pray God's unlimited love and blessing to remain forever on all the readers of the book, Holy Spirit, Hover Over Me.

Amen
By Sun H. Joe (Mrs. Joshua Doshick Joe) on May 22, 2003

486 Holy Spirit, Hover Over Me

picture

Rev. Joe is raising one of his hands to tens of thousands of church members at the Ju An Presbyterian Church, one of the ten largest churches in the world. The newly built two-story sanctuary was fully packed. At the same time, in the old sanctuary, they received this preaching through specially designed TV screens.

The front of the two-story sanctuary in the Ju An Presbyterian Church

Rev. Na Gyum Il, Dr. Belk, Rev. Joe and Rev. Paul Kim in a meeting for worldwide missions.

Author as President of the Federation of Korean Associations in the USA, meeting with the President of the USA, Mr. Ronald Reagan, at the White House

Author as President of the Federation of Korean Associations in the USA, meeting with the President of the USA, Mr. George Bush

Author as President of the Federation of Korean Associations in the USA, meeting with the President of Korea, Mr. Du Hwan Jun

Author as President of the Federation of Korean Associations in the USA, meeting with the President of Korea, Mr. Tae Woo Roh

Author as President of the Federation of Korean Associations in the USA, representing all 2.5 million Korean-Americans in the US, addresses Korean Prime Minister, Mr. Jung Yul Kim, at his office.

Author as President of the Federation of Korean Associations in the USA, meeting with Korean Foreign Minister, Mr. Kwang Soo Choi, at his office

Author as President of the Federation of Korean Associations in the USA, meeting with the Speaker of the Korean National Assembly, Mr. Jae Hyung Lee

Author as Chairman of the World Conference of Leaders of Koreans Living Overseas, meeting with Japanese Prime Minister Kawasaki

Author delivers a speech as Chairman of the World Conference of Leaders of Koreans Living Overseas, representing all seven million Koreans living overseas, at the welcome reception in Tokyo, Japan in 1987.

Author as President of the Federation of Korean Associations in the USA, extends a welcome speech to the leaders of Korean residents' associations in Japan.

Author as President of the Federation of Korean Associations in the USA, gives a speech to the leaders of Korean Associations representing local cities and states in the USA.

Author as President of the Federation of Korean Associations in the USA, delivers a welcome speech to the 1984 L.A. Olympic champions from Korea

From left: Mr. Yong Kun Lim, State Senator of Oregon, Rev. Joe and Mr. Duk Soo Kim, the Chairman of Jung Ang TV in Philadelphia

Author as Chairman of World Conference of Leaders of Koreans Living Overseas, greeting Mr. Byung Hun Park, President of Korean Residents Association in Japan (Mindan) in Tokyo, 1987

The author, as President of the Federation of Korean Associations in the USA, is giving a plaque to the Korean Consulate General in Washington, D. C., Mr. Kie Mun Ban. He is now the Foreign Minister of Korea.

Author with Mr. Oh Young Lee, former President of the Federation of Korean Associations in the USA, at the Inaugural Ball for the President of the USA, Mr. George W. Bush, January 2005

Dr. & Mrs. Belk and Rev. & Mrs. Joe at the commencement ceremony for Henderson Christian University Theology Seminary.

Author and his wife meeting with Pennsylvania Governor, Mr. & Mrs. Dick
Thornburgh

Rev. & Mrs. Joshua Doshick Joe at the inaugural Ball for the President of the
USA, Mr. George W. Bush, January2005